LONDON
BOROUGH
OF ENFIELD

REFERENCE
SERVICE

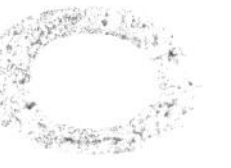

HEAD-DRESS BADGES OF THE BRITISH ARMY

HEAD-DRESS BADGES OF THE BRITISH ARMY

VOLUME TWO

FROM THE END OF THE GREAT WAR TO THE PRESENT DAY

ARTHUR L. KIPLING

and

HUGH L. KING

FREDERICK MULLER LIMITED
LONDON

First published in Great Britain in 1979 by
Frederick Muller Ltd., Victoria Works, Edgware Road, London, NW2 6LE

British Library Cataloguing in Publication Data

Kipling, Arthur Lawrence
Head-dress badges of the British Army.
Vol. 2: From the end of the Great War to the present day
1. Great Britain. Army – Medals, badges, decorations, etc.
2. Badges
I. Title II. King, Hugh Lionel
355.1′4 UC535.G7

ISBN 0–584–10949–0

Book designed and edited by Laurence V. Archer

Printed in Great Britain by Butler & Tanner Ltd, Frome and London

TO

VIOLET AND PAMELA

FOR

THEIR PATIENCE AND UNDERSTANDING

Contents

Chapter		*page*
Introduction		ix
Acknowledgements		xi
1	The Cavalry	1
2	The Royal Artillery, Royal Engineers and Royal Corps of Signals	20
3	The Guards Division	23
4	Infantry of the Line: Officers	28
5	Infantry of the Line: Other-ranks	47
6	Airborne Forces	72
7	Special Service Forces: Second World War	74
8	The Brigade of Gurkhas	75
9	The Royal Marines	83
10	Department and Corps	88
11	Schools and Miscellaneous	98
12	Women's Services	104
13	The Plastic Badges of the Second World War	107
14	The Yeomanry	120
15	Territorial Army Infantry: 1920 to 1947	148
16	Territorial Army Infantry from 1947, and the Territorial Army Volunteer Reserve	161
17	The London Regiments	169
18	The Home Guard	177
19	The Officers Training Corps	180
20	Further Notes for Collectors	222
21	Glossary of Terms Used	228
22	Regimental Titles	230
	Index	235

Introduction

Army Order 509 of November 1920 stated 'His Majesty has been graciously pleased to approve of changes in titles and designations of cavalry and infantry regiments of the Regular Army with effect from 1st January 1921', and these titles are used in the present volume.

Only minor changes occurred in these designations until after the conclusion of the Second World War. The withdrawal of troops from India, following the granting of Independence, caused all regiments to be reduced to one battalion each but, even so, the number of regiments was deemed excessive for our Defence requirements and many were amalgamated.

The Infantry was grouped first into regional brigades and subsequently into five administrative divisions. A further step was taken with the formation of 'Large' regiments whereby, what previously had been individual regiments, now became battalions of one regiment with a common title for all and this entailed changes in the badges worn.

Although full-dress was not resumed after the Great War the *Dress Regulations* published in 1934 gave details of the badges which would be worn on the helmet, and lance-cap plates of the cavalry regiments amalgamated in 1922. Specimens are seen occasionally and, with the permission of the Controller, Her Majesty's Stationery Office, descriptions of these are included.

The Territorial Force, now re-named The Territorial Army, was re-constituted in 1920 but no great change took place until after the Second World War when the Territorial Army was re-formed again. Mostly regiments resumed the titles they had borne previously, or had adopted during the war, but this did not last very long. Amalgamations followed in rapid succession until the identity of units almost disappeared but, eventually, some stabilisation was achieved with the establishment of The Territorial Army Volunteer Reserve. These amalgamations naturally affected the cap-badges worn and these too are shown.

By virtue of a tripartite agreement between Britain, India and Nepal four regiments of Gurkhas were transferred to the British Establishment in 1947 and became The Brigade of Gurkhas. Subsequently Engineer, Signal and other supporting Arms were added. The badges they have worn since 1948 are included and we are indebted to Brigadier J. L. Chapple M.B.E. for information on these and the type of head-dress on which they are worn.

There is an enormous number of badges worn by the contingents of The Officers Training Corps and many of these do not indicate the unit but bear only the school arms. To assist in identification a chapter on both the Senior and Junior Divisions has been included.

Wherever the information was available, the date a particular badge was sealed is given and, usually, the new design was taken into wear soon afterwards. However, this was not always the case. In some instances existing stocks of the previous pattern were used-up first and some revised badges never were worn although a sealed-pattern exists. Sometimes, a badge was sealed in a different metal from that in which it was manufactured and, when known, this fact is noted. It will be observed that a large number of Territorial badges were sealed in 1916: apparently, although worn since 1908, they were not sealed officially until that year.

Although the badges of so many units have changed over the last fifty years there are some that have remained unchanged. These appeared in the first volume of this work and, for the sake of completeness, they are repeated here. However, to avoid any confusion, their original figure-numbers have been retained so that no two illustrations throughout the two volumes bear the same number. It is hoped that this will be of assistance to collectors when referring to badges.

Finally, we are very grateful to the numerous purchasers of the first volume whose demand for a second, to bring the record up to date, encouraged us to produce this.

August 1979

Arthur L. Kipling
Hugh L. King

Acknowledgements

We would like to record our appreciation of the help given in the preparation of this volume by:

Brigadier T. R. Birkett O.B.E.
Brigadier J. L. Chapple M.B.E.
J. W. F. Gaylor Esq.
Brigadier D. M. Pontifex C.B.E.
D. A. Rutter Esq.
Colonel K. G. Style, Incorporated Photographer
Lieutenant-Colonel I. G. Thomas

and others whose assistance has been acknowledged in the first volume of this work.

To the editor, Laurie Archer, go special thanks for his invaluable guidance particularly in respect of Chapter 20, the greater part of which he contributed.

August 1979

Arthur L. Kipling
Hugh L. King

CHAPTER 1

The Cavalry

THE HOUSEHOLD CAVALRY

A few months before the close of the Great War, the Household Battalion was disbanded and its personnel dispersed amongst the regiments of The Household Cavalry and the Foot Guards.

In 1919 the forage-cap was introduced into the regiments of The Household Cavalry and, with it, the new-pattern badge which was to be common to all three regiments: the Royal Cypher surrounded by the Garter and surmounted by the Imperial Crown.

Under Army Order 133 of 1922 the two regiments of Life Guards were amalgamated with the new title The Life Guards (1st and 2nd) (Army Order 186 of 1922). They retained that title until 1928 when it became simply The Life Guards (Army Order 110 of 1928).

The accession of King Edward VIII, King George VI and Queen Elizabeth II caused a change in the Royal Cypher, and in the latter case the crown as well, otherwise the design has remained unaltered.

On the 23rd March 1969 the Royal Horse Guards (The Blues) and The Royal Dragoons (1st Dragoons) were amalgamated to form The Blues and Royals (Royal Horse Guards and 1st Dragoons).

Details of the badges follow: those which appeared in Volume 1 carry their original figure-numbers and those which appear now, for the first time, have new figure-numbers.

The Service-dress Cap

1st Life Guards
The Royal Cypher of King George V pierced, within a circlet inscribed *First Life Guards* and surmounted by an Imperial crown. In brass (Fig. 727). Also in bronze for officers.

2nd Life Guards
The Royal Cypher of King George V pierced, within a circlet inscribed *Second Life Guards* and surmounted by an Imperial crown. In brass (Fig. 728). Also in bronze for officers.

The Life Guards
(1) The Royal Cypher of King George V pierced, within a circlet inscribed *Life Guards 1st and 2nd* and surmounted by an Imperial crown. In bronze (Fig. 729).

(2) The Royal Cypher of King George V pierced, within a circlet inscribed *The Life Guards* and surmounted by an Imperial crown. In bronze (Fig. 730).

(3) The Royal Cypher of King Edward VIII pierced, within a circlet inscribed *The Life Guards* and surmounted by an Imperial crown. In brass (Fig. 1874).
Note: It is doubtful if this pattern, although made, was ever worn.
(4) The Royal Cypher of King George VI pierced, within a circlet inscribed *The Life Guards* and surmounted by an Imperial crown. Sealed 15th February 1937. In bronze (Fig. 1875).
(5) The Royal Cypher of Queen Elizabeth II pierced, within a circlet inscribed *The Life Guards* and surmounted by St. Edward's crown. In gilding-metal (Fig. 1876). Also anodised: sealed 16th October 1958.

Royal Horse Guards (The Blues)
(1) The Royal Cypher of King George V pierced, within a circlet inscribed *Royal Horse Guards* and surmounted by an Imperial crown. In brass (Fig. 731). Also in bronze for officers.
(2) The Royal Cypher of King George VI pierced, within a circlet inscribed *Royal Horse Guards* and surmounted by an Imperial crown. Sealed 15th February 1937. In bronze (Fig. 1877).
(3) The Royal Cypher of Queen Elizabeth II pierced, within a circlet inscribed *Royal Horse Guards* and surmounted by St. Edward's crown. In gilding-metal (Fig. 1878) and in bronze. Sealed 30th March 1953. Also anodised.

The Blues and Royals
The Royal Cypher of Queen Elizabeth II pierced, within a circlet inscribed *The Blues and Royals* and surmounted by St. Edward's crown. In bronze (Fig. 1879).

The Forage-cap
The Household Cavalry
(1) The Royal Cypher of King George V pierced, within the Garter and surmounted by an Imperial crown. In brass (Fig. 732).
(2) The Royal Cypher of King George VI pierced, within the Garter and surmounted by an Imperial crown. Sealed 15th February 1937. In gilding-metal (Fig. 1880).
(3) The Royal Cypher of Queen Elizabeth II pierced, within the Garter and surmounted by St. Edward's crown. In gilding-metal (Fig. 1881). Also anodised, sealed 22nd August 1962.
(4) The Royal Cypher of King George V pierced, in gilt on a red-enamel ground, within a pierced gilt Garter on a blue-enamel ground and surmounted by a gilt Imperial crown. For officers (Fig. 1882).
(5) The Royal Cypher of King George VI pierced, in gilt on a red-enamel ground, within a pierced gilt Garter on a blue-enamel ground and surmounted by a gilt Imperial crown. For officers (Fig. 1883). Sealed 15th February 1937.
(6) The Royal Cypher of Queen Elizabeth II pierced, in gilt on a red-enamel ground, within a pierced gilt Garter on a blue-enamel ground and surmounted by a gilt St. Edward's crown. For officers (Fig. 1884). Sealed 29th September 1953.

Full-dress helmet
The Life Guards
(1) Officers: within a wreath of oak-leaves and laurel, on a frosted gilt centre surmounted by a crown, the Star of the Order of the Garter. Round the centre, the Collar of

706

the Order with the George upon the lower ends of the stems of the wreath. The colours of the Garter, Cross and field are in enamel. The Star in silver, the remainder gilt (Fig. 706).

(2) Other-ranks: same design as for officers but all in gilding-metal, except the Star which is in white-metal (Fig. 707).

Royal Horse Guards
Officers: same design as for the Life Guards except that the field of the Cross is in silver.

The Blues and Royals
Same as for Royal Horse Guards.

White Foreign Service Helmet
The Life Guards
The Star of the Order of the Garter, a crown above. In gilt metal.

707

The Beret
The Life Guards
Officers: as forage-cap but in gold embroidery.

The Blues and Royals
Officers: as Service-dress cap but in gilt.

CAVALRY OF THE LINE AND ROYAL ARMOURED CORPS

At the conclusion of the Great War, apart from the Household Cavalry, there were twenty-eight horsed regiments and Army Order 520 of 1920 brought some slight changes of title. These are used in the descriptions of the badges which follow.

Under Army Order 319 of 1921 a general reduction in the number of cavalry regiments was ordered and the four junior regiments were to be disbanded, viz.

5th Royal Irish Lancers
19th Royal Hussars (Queen Alexandra's Own)
20th Hussars
21st Lancers (Empress of India's).

Owing to the considerable opposition to this course it was decided to achieve the same object by reducing some of the remaining regiments to two squadrons each, re-constituting the disbanded regiments on a one-squadron basis and subsequently amalgamating them.

The following changes took place under Army Order 133 of 1922:

3rd Dragoon Guards (Prince of Wales's) and The Carabiniers (6th Dragoon Guards) amalgamated to form 3rd/6th Dragoon Guards.

4th Royal Irish Dragoon Guards and 7th Dragoon Guards (Princess Royal's) amalgamated to form 4th/7th Dragoon Guards.
5th Dragoon Guards (Princess Charlotte of Wales's) and The Inniskillings (6th Dragoons) amalgamated to form 5th/6th Dragoons.
13th Hussars and 18th Royal Hussars (Queen Mary's Own) amalgamated to form 13th/18th Hussars.
5th Royal Irish Lancers reconstituted and amalgamated with 16th The Queen's Lancers to form 16th/5th Lancers.
19th Royal Hussars (Queen Alexandra's Own) reconstituted and amalgamated with 15th The King's Hussars to form 15th/19th Hussars.
20th Hussars reconstituted and amalgamated with 14th King's Hussars to form 14th/20th Hussars.
21st Lancers (Empress of India's) reconstituted and amalgamated with 17th Lancers (Duke of Cambridge's Own) to form 17th/21st Lancers.

In the period up to the formation of the Royal Armoured Corps in 1939 there were various changes in nomenclature; during the Second World War additional regiments were raised; and since the end of the war many more amalgamations have taken place. All these are recorded below:

1927 Change of title of 5th/6th Dragoons to 5th Inniskilling Dragoon Guards (A.O. 179/1927).
1928 Change of title of 3rd/6th Dragoon Guards to 3rd Carabiniers (Prince of Wales's Dragoon Guards) (A.O. 238/1928).
1931 The Prussian Eagle badge restored to the 14th/20th Hussars.
1932/3 Change of title of 15th/19th Hussars to 15th The King's Royal Hussars (A.O. 177/1932) and a further change to 15th/19th The King's Royal Hussars (A.O. 207/1933).
1935 Change of title of 5th Inniskilling Dragoon Guards to 5th Royal Inniskilling Dragoon Guards (A.O. 110/1935).
Change of title of 13th/18th Hussars to 13th/18th Royal Hussars (Queen Mary's Own) (A.O. 240/1935).
1936 Change of title of 4th/7th Dragoon Guards to 4th/7th Royal Dragoon Guards (A.O. 182/1936).
Change of title of 14th/20th Hussars to 14th/20th King's Hussars (A.O. 233/1936).
1937 The Austrian Eagle badge restored to The King's Dragoon Guards.
1939 The Royal Armoured Corps formed and the Royal Tank Corps became part of it, changing its title to Royal Tank Regiment (A.O. 581/1939).
1940 (10th December). The following new regiments formed:

22nd Dragoons
23rd Hussars
24th Lancers.

1941 (30th January). The following new regiments formed:

25th Dragoons
26th Hussars
27th Lancers.

1943 The Reconnaissance Corps, which had been formed on 14th January 1941, was transferred to The Royal Armoured Corps as from 1st January 1944 (A.O. 227/1943).
1946 (1st August). The Reconnaissance Corps disbanded (A.O. 146/1946).

1948 (June). The six new regiments raised in 1940–1941 were disbanded, i.e. 22nd Dragoons, 23rd Hussars, 24th Lancers, 25th Dragoons, 26th Hussars and 27th Lancers.

1954 Change of title of 16th/5th Lancers to 16th/5th The Queen's Royal Lancers.

1958 (24th October). 4th Queen's Own Hussars and 8th King's Royal Irish Hussars amalgamated to form The Queen's Royal Irish Hussars.

1958 (3rd November). 3rd The King's Own Hussars and 7th Queen's Own Hussars amalgamated to form The Queen's Own Hussars.

1959 (1st January). 1st King's Dragoon Guards and The Queen's Bays (2nd Dragoon Guards) amalgamated to form 1st The Queen's Dragoon Guards.

1960 (11th September). 9th Queen's Royal Lancers and 12th Royal Lancers (Prince of Wales's) amalgamated to form 9th/12th Royal Lancers (Prince of Wales's).

1961 (15th May). 1st The Royal Dragoons redesignated The Royal Dragoons (1st Dragoons).

1969 (25th October). 10th Royal Hussars (Prince of Wales's Own) and 11th Hussars (Prince Albert's Own) amalgamated to form The Royal Hussars (Prince of Wales's Own).

1971 (2nd July). 3rd Carabiniers (Prince of Wales's Dragoon Guards) and The Royal Scots Greys (2nd Dragoons) amalgamated to form The Royal Scots Dragoon Guards (Carabiniers and Greys).

Details of the badges follow: those which appeared in Volume 1 carry their original figure-numbers and those which appear now, for the first time, have new figure-numbers.

In a number of instances the date the pattern was sealed is known now and this information has been added.

1st King's Dragoon Guards

(1) An eight-pointed star, the topmost point displaced by an Imperial crown. On the star, the letter *K* above the letters *DG* within the Garter. The star and crown in white-metal, remainder in gilding-metal (Fig. 735).

(2) The double-headed Eagle of the late Emperor of Austria. In gilding-metal: sealed 28th January 1938 (Fig. 1885). Also in white-metal: sealed 7th October 1949.

The Queen's Bays (2nd Dragoon Guards)

(1) The word *Bays* in old-English lettering within a laurel-wreath surmounted by an Imperial crown. In brass: sealed 8th September 1911 (Fig. 737).

(2) As above but with St. Edward's crown. In gilding-metal: sealed 17th December 1954 (Fig. 1886). Also anodised: sealed 14th April 1959.

1st The Queen's Dragoon Guards

The double-headed Eagle of the late Emperor of Austria. In white-metal (Fig. 1887). Also anodised; also chromed finish. Sealed 15th September 1965.

3rd Dragoon Guards (Prince of Wales's)

The Prince of Wales's plumes, coronet and motto above a scroll inscribed *3rd Dragoon Guards*. The coronet and scroll in gilding-metal, remainder in white-metal (Fig. 739).

The Carabiniers (6th Dragoon Guards)

On crossed carbines the Garter surmounted by an Imperial crown. In the centre the Roman numerals *VI* over the letters *DG*. Below the Garter a scroll inscribed *Carabiniers*. The centre and scroll in white-metal, remainder in gilding-metal (Fig. 747).

727

728

729

730

1874

1875

1876

731

1877

1878

1879

732

1880

1881

1882

1883

1884

3rd Carabiniers (Prince of Wales's Dragoon Guards)
On crossed carbines the Prince of Wales's plumes, coronet and motto. Across the butts of the carbines a scroll inscribed *3rd Carabiniers*. The coronet and scroll in gilding-metal, remainder in white-metal. Sealed 5th July 1929 (Fig. 1888). Also anodised, sealed 7th October 1963.

The Royal Scots Greys (2nd Dragoons)
(1) An Eagle with a wreath of laurels on its breast upon a plinth inscribed *Waterloo*. Below, a scroll inscribed *Royal Scots Greys*. The Eagle in white-metal, scroll in gilding-metal. Sealed 14th December 1903 (Fig. 752). Also anodised, sealed 28th June 1963.
(2) A fired grenade. Worn by bandsmen. In gilding-metal (Fig. 1889).
There is another version with slightly different flames.

The Royal Scots Dragoon Guards
An Eagle with a wreath of laurels on its breast upon a plinth inscribed *Waterloo* superimposed upon a pair of carbines crossed with a scroll across the butts inscribed *Royal Scots Dragoon Guards*. Carbines and scroll in gilding-metal, remainder in white-metal (Fig. 1890). Also anodised.

4th Royal Irish Dragoon Guards
The Star of the Order of St. Patrick. Below, a scroll inscribed *4th Royal Irish D. Guards*. The Star in white-metal, remainder in gilding-metal (Fig. 740).

7th Dragoon Guards (Princess Royal's)
The Crest of Earl Ligonier: a demi-lion issuant from a coronet. Below, a scroll inscribed with the Earl's motto *Quo fata vocant*. In brass (Fig. 749).

4th/7th Royal Dragoon Guards
An eight-pointed star, thereon a circlet inscribed *Quis Separabit MCMXXII*. Within the circlet St. George's Cross with the coronet of the Princess Royal superimposed thereon. In white-metal: sealed 30th January 1930 (Fig. 742). Also anodised, sealed 24th February 1964.

5th Dragoon Guards (Princess Charlotte of Wales's)
A circlet inscribed *Vestigia nulla retrorsum* surmounted by an Imperial crown. In the centre the White Horse of Hanover with the Roman numeral *V* above and the letters *DG* below. The centre in white-metal, remainder in gilding-metal (Fig. 744).

The Inniskillings (6th Dragoons)
The Castle of Inniskilling with St. George's flag flying from the central turret. Below, a scroll inscribed *Inniskilling*. The Castle in white-metal, scroll in gilding-metal (Fig. 758).

5th Royal Inniskilling Dragoon Guards
(1) The monogram *VDG* surmounted by an Imperial crown. In white-metal: sealed 30th January 1929 (Fig. 745).
(2) As above but with St. Edward's crown: sealed 7th January 1955 (Fig. 1891). Also anodised, sealed 30th October 1936.

735 1885 737 1886

1887 739 747 1888

752 1889 1890 740

749 742 744 758

745 1891 751 1892

The Royal Dragoons (1st Dragoons)

(1) The Royal Crest with Imperial crown above a scroll inscribed *The Royal Dragoons.* The Royal Crest in gilding-metal, scroll in white-metal (Fig. 751).

(2) An Eagle with a wreath of laurel on its breast upon a plinth inscribed *105.* In gilding-metal (Fig. 1892).

(3) As (2) but larger and with the laurel-wreath and plinth in white-metal, remainder in gilding-metal, sealed 15th March 1949 (Fig. 1893). Also anodised, sealed 30th December 1963.

3rd The King's Own Hussars

(1) The White Horse of Hanover on ground. Below, a scroll inscribed *3rd King's Own Hussars.* The Horse and ground in white-metal, scroll in gilding-metal (Fig. 753).

(2) As above but scroll inscribed *3rd The King's Own Hussars.* Sealed 4th September 1930 (Fig. 1894).

7th Queen's Own Hussars

(1) A circlet inscribed *7th Queen's Own Hussars* surmounted by an Imperial crown. Within the circlet the letters *QO* reversed and intertwined. The monogram in white-metal, remainder in gilding-metal: sealed 12th November 1901 (Fig. 760).

(2) As above but with St. Edward's crown: sealed 7th January 1955 (Fig. 1895). Also anodised.

The Queen's Own Hussars

The White Horse of Hanover on ground. Below, a scroll inscribed *The Queen's Own Hussars.* Horse and ground in silver, scroll in gold-anodised: sealed 15th September 1958 (Fig. 1896).

4th Queen's Own Hussars

(1) A circlet inscribed *Queen's Own Hussars* with a spray of laurel in the bottom centre of the circlet. In the centre the Roman numerals *IV* in ornamental characters. The whole ensigned with an Imperial crown. Below the circlet a scroll inscribed *Mente et Manu.* The numerals and scroll in white-metal, remainder in gilding-metal. Sealed 16th October 1907 (Fig. 756).

(2) As above but with St. Edward's crown (Fig. 1897). Sealed 23rd September 1954.

8th King's Royal Irish Hussars

The Irish Harp surmounted by an Imperial crown. Below, a scroll inscribed *8th King's Royal Irish Hussars.* The Harp in white-metal, remainder in gilding-metal. Sealed 30th November 1904 (Fig. 762).

The Queen's Royal Irish Hussars

(1) The Irish Harp within a circlet inscribed *Queen's Royal Irish Hussars* ensigned with the Royal Crest. A scroll below inscribed *Mente et Manu.* Harp and scroll in silver-anodised, remainder in gold-anodised (Fig. 1898).

(2) An improved anodised design of the above (Fig. 1899).

9th Queen's Royal Lancers

(1) On crossed lances the numeral *9* surmounted by an Imperial crown. Across the butts of the lances a scroll inscribed *Lancers.* In white-metal. Sealed 30th July 1903 (Fig. 764).

1893 753 1894 760

1895 1896 756 1897

762 1898 1899 764

1900 768 1901 1902

765 766 1903 771

(2) As above but with St. Edward's crown. Sealed 9th July 1954. Also anodised. (Fig. 1900).

12th Royal Lancers (Prince of Wales's)

(1) On crossed lances the Prince of Wales's plumes, coronet and motto. Above these the Imperial crown. Below, the Roman numerals *XII.* The plumes, motto and lower portion of the lance-pennons in white-metal, remainder in gilding-metal. Sealed 5th November 1930 (Fig. 768).

(2) As above but with St. Edward's crown. Sealed 1st December 1954 (Fig. 1901). Also anodised.

9th/12th Royal Lancers (Prince of Wales's)

On crossed lances the Prince of Wales's plumes, coronet and motto. Above these St. Edward's crown. Across the butts of the lances a scroll inscribed *IX–XII.* The plumes, motto and lower portion of the lance-pennons in silver-anodised, remainder in gold-anodised (Fig. 1902).

10th Royal Hussars (Prince of Wales's Own)

The Prince of Wales's plumes, coronet and motto resting on a scroll inscribed *10th Royal Hussars.* The coronet and scroll in gilding-metal, remainder in white-metal. Sealed 17th May 1898 (Fig. 765). Also anodised.

11th Hussars (Prince Albert's Own)

The Crest of the late Prince Consort, Prince Albert of Saxe-Coburg-Gotha, with a scroll below bearing his motto *Treu und Fest.* In gilding-metal. Sealed 21st June 1898 (Fig. 766). Also anodised, sealed 6th November 1964.

The Royal Hussars (Prince of Wales's Own)

The Prince of Wales's plumes, coronet and motto resting on a scroll inscribed *The Royal Hussars.* The coronet and scroll in gold-, remainder silver-anodised (Fig. 1903).

13th Hussars

On the numerals *13* a Z-shaped scroll inscribed *Hussars* and surmounted by an Imperial crown. In gilding-metal (Fig. 771).

18th Royal Hussars (Queen Mary's Own)

A circlet inscribed *Queen Mary's Own* surmounted by an Imperial crown. Below the circlet two sprigs of laurel. In the centre the Roman numeral *XVIII.* In white-metal (Fig. 788).

13th/18th Royal Hussars (Queen Mary's Own)

(1) On the centre of the letter *H* the monogram *QMO.* In the top half of the letter the Roman numerals *XIII* and in the bottom half, *XVIII.* The whole ensigned with an Imperial crown. The monogram in white-metal, remainder in gilding-metal (Fig. 1904).

(2) The monogram *QMO* superimposed upon which is a scroll in the shape of the letter Z. The top arm of the scroll rests on the top of the monogram and is inscribed with the numerals *XIII.* The lower arm of the scroll supports the bottom of the monogram and is inscribed with the numerals *XVIII.* The diagonal of the scroll joins the right

end of the top arm with the left end of the bottom arm and is inscribed *Royal Hussars*. The whole ensigned with an Imperial crown. In gilding-metal (Fig. 1905).

(3) As (2) but with St. Edward's crown. Sealed 15th February 1955 (Fig. 1906). Also anodised, sealed 7th May 1962.

14th King's Hussars

Within the Garter the Royal Crest. Below the Garter a scroll inscribed *14th King's Hussars*. In gilding-metal (Fig. 774).

20th Hussars

The letter *H* surmounted by an Imperial crown with the Roman numeral *X* on either side. In gilding-metal (Fig. 793).

14th/20th King's Hussars

(1) Within the Garter the Royal Crest. Below the Garter a scroll inscribed *14th/20th Hussars*. In gilding-metal (Fig. 775).

(2) The Prussian Eagle in gilding-metal. Sealed 7th March 1932 (Fig. 1907). Also anodised.

(3) As (2) but black-painted anodised. Sealed 28th July 1961 (Fig. 1908).

15th The King's Hussars

The Royal Crest within the Garter. Below the Garter *XVKH* resting on a scroll inscribed *Merebimur*. The Royal Crest in white-metal, remainder in gilding-metal (Fig. 777).

19th Royal Hussars (Queen Alexandra's Own)

The letter *A* cypher of the late Queen Alexandra ensigned with a coronet. Interwoven with the cypher is the Danebrog and in the centre of this the date *1885*. In white-metal (Fig. 791).

15th/19th The King's Royal Hussars

(1) The Royal Crest within the Garter. Below the Garter *XV.XIX* resting on a scroll inscribed *Merebimur*. The Royal Crest in white-metal, remainder in gilding-metal. Sealed 10th September 1929 (Fig. 778).

(2) As above but with St. Edward's crown in the Royal Crest (Fig. 1909). Also anodised, sealed 8th September 1959.

16th The Queen's Lancers

(1) On crossed lances the numeral *16* surmounted by an Imperial crown. Below, a scroll inscribed *The Queen's Lancers*. The lower portion of the lance-pennons, the numerals and the scroll in white-metal, remainder in gilding-metal. Sealed 5th July 1905 (Fig. 781).

(2) As (1) but smaller, of the same size as the collar-badge, and worn by Warrant Officers only. Officers wore the same badge in silver-and-gilt on the forage-cap but both the beret-, and the side-cap, badge were embroidered versions.

5th Royal Irish Lancers

On crossed lances a circlet inscribed *Quis Separabit* with a spray of laurel in the bottom-centre of the circlet. In the centre the numeral *5*. The numeral and lower portion of the lance-pennons in white-metal, remainder in gilding-metal (Fig. 757).

16th/5th Queen's Royal Lancers

(1) On crossed lances the numeral *16* surmounted by St. Edward's crown. Below, a scroll inscribed *The Queen's Lancers*. The lower portion of the lance-pennons, the numerals and the scroll in white-metal, remainder in gilding-metal (Fig. 1911). Also anodised, sealed 25th October 1956, which is the pattern worn officially on all head-dress by all other-ranks.

(2) As (1) but smaller and for Warrant Officers only (Fig. 1910). Officers wore a silver-and-gilt version of this small pattern on the forage-cap and embroidered versions, on other head-dress. All of these badges had to be purchased: they were not on general issue.

17th Lancers (Duke of Cambridge's Own)

A pair of thigh-bones with a skull superimposed thereon. A scroll across the lower portion of the bones inscribed *Or Glory*. In white-metal. Sealed 30th July 1927 (Fig. 782).

21st Lancers (Empress of India's)

On crossed lances the cypher of Queen Victoria as Empress of India surmounted by an Imperial crown. Below, the Roman numerals *XXI*. The lower portion of the lance-pennons in white-metal, remainder in gilding-metal (Fig. 797).

17th/21st Lancers

As 17th Lancers. In white-metal; also anodised, sealed 14th July 1961.

22nd Dragoons

The capital letter *D*. surmounted by an Imperial crown. Within it the Roman numerals *XXII* and below it a scroll inscribed *Dragoons*. In white-metal (Fig. 1912). An all gilding-metal version struck for sealed pattern only, sealed 1st May 1941.

23rd Hussars

The capital letter *H* surmounted by an Imperial crown. Below, a scroll inscribed *23rd Hussars*. The *H* in white-metal, remainder in gilding-metal. Sealed 1st May 1941 (Fig. 1913).

24th Lancers

A circlet inscribed on the lower portion *Lancers*; within the circlet and extending to its outer rim a pair of crossed lances with pennons flying outwards. Across the centre of the circlet, and in front of the cross of the lances, the Roman numerals *XXIV*. In white-metal (Fig. 1914). An all gilding-metal version struck for sealed pattern only, sealed 1st May 1941.

25th Dragoons

A pair of crossed swords points uppermost. On the cross of the swords the Roman numerals *XXV*. Above the numerals and in the upper part of the swords the Imperial crown. Below the numerals a scroll inscribed *25th Dragoons*. The swords in white-metal, remainder in gilding-metal. Sealed 9th August 1941 (Fig. 1915).

26th Hussars

The Prussian Eagle with a scroll below inscribed *XXVI Hussars*. In gilding-metal. Sealed 9th August 1941 (Fig. 1916).

788
1904
1905
1906
774
793
775
1907
HONI SOIT QUI MAL Y PENSE
MEREBIMUR
1908
777
791
778
781
THE QUEENS LANCERS
QUIS SEPARABIT
757
1909
1910
OR GLORY
1911
782
797
1912

27th Lancers
A pair of crossed lances with pennons flying outwards. On the cross an elephant's head. Above, and within the upper portion of the lances, an Imperial crown. Below the elephant's head the figures *27*. Elephant's head in white-metal, remainder in gilding-metal. Sealed 1st May 1941 (Fig. 1917).

Royal Armoured Corps
(1) Within a laurel-wreath the letters *RAC* in script characters. The whole ensigned with an Imperial crown. In gilding-metal (Fig. 1918).
(2) A mailed gauntlet for the right hand, fist clenched, palm to the front, with a billet on the wrist inscribed *RAC*. Issuing from the wrist upwards two concentric circles barbed. The whole ensigned with an Imperial crown. In white-metal. Sealed 3rd January 1942 (Fig. 1919). For a plastic version of this badge see Fig. 2199 p. 109.
(3) As (2) but with St. Edward's crown (Fig. 1920). Sealed 28th October 1954. Also anodised: sealed 20th June 1958.

Royal Tank Regiment
(1) A laurel-wreath surmounted by an Imperial crown. Across the top of the wreath a scroll inscribed *Tank* and across the bottom of the wreath a scroll inscribed *Corps*. Within the wreath an early-pattern Tank. In gilding-metal (Fig. 1156).
(2) A Tank within a laurel-wreath ensigned with an Imperial crown. Across the bottom of the wreath a scroll inscribed *Fear Naught*. In gilding metal. Sealed 22nd October 1924 (Fig. 1921).
(3) As (2) but different details in the Tank. In white-metal (Fig. 1922).
(4) As (2) but different details in the Tank which now faces left. In white-metal (Fig. 1923).
For plastic version of this badge see Fig. 2200 p. 109.
(5) As (4) but with St. Edward's crown. In white-metal (Fig. 1924). Also anodised.

Reconnaissance Corps
(1) A vertical spear with point uppermost: on each side forked-lightning. On the bottom of the spear and lightning a scroll inscribed *Reconnaissance Corps*. In white-metal, also in gilding-metal. Sealed 7th August 1942 (Fig. 1925).
(2) As above but with the White Rose of York superimposed on the centre of the spear. In white-metal (Fig. 1926).

OFFICERS' BADGES

Although full-dress for the cavalry was not resumed after the end of the Great War, a new edition of *Dress Regulations for the Army*, published in 1934, gave details of the badges to be worn on such dress and included those authorised for the regiments which had been amalgamated. The majority of the badges worn on the white foreign-service helmet and the forage-cap were of the same design as those for the men but made of superior material. Service-dress cap-badges were the same as for the forage-cap but finished in bronze.

In 1969, publication commenced of a series of pamphlets entitled *Dress Regulations for Officers of the Army* and Pamphlet No. 3, for the Royal Armoured Corps, was issued on the 24th January 1972 covering all the amalgamations which had taken place since the end of the Second World War.

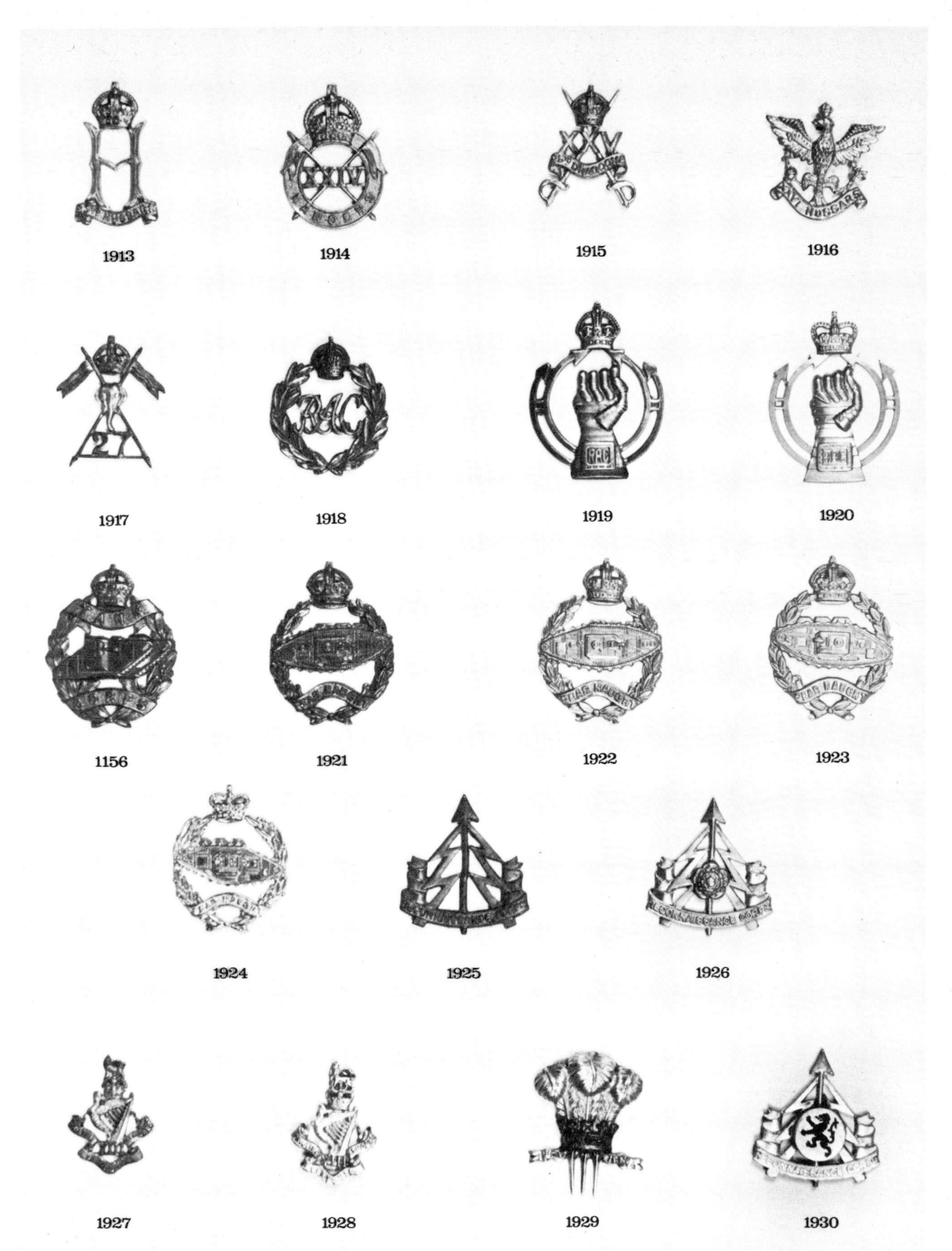

1913 1914 1915 1916

1917 1918 1919 1920

1156 1921 1922 1923

1924 1925 1926

1927 1928 1929 1930

With the kind permission of the Controller of Her Majesty's Stationery Office we are able to reproduce official descriptions from both of these publications but details are given only of those badges which differed in design from those of the men as previously described.

3rd Carabiniers (Prince of Wales's Dragoon Guards)
Full-dress Head-dress (1934)
On the Garter Star in silver the Garter with motto in gilt or gilding-metal, pierced on a ground of blue-enamel. Within the Garter in silver on crossed carbines, the Prince of Wales's plumes and coronet on a scarlet-enamel ground.

4th/7th Royal Dragoon Guards
Full-dress Head-dress (1934)
On the silver Garter Star an oval in gilt pierced with *Quis Separabit* and *MCMXXII* on a ground of Royal-blue-enamel. In the centre, on a white-enamel ground, the Cross of St. George in gold and red-enamel. Superimposed on the Cross the Princess Royal's coronet in gilt and red-enamel.

Beret
As forage-cap in silver embroidery.

5th Royal Inniskilling Dragoon Guards
Full-dress Head-dress (1934)
In gilt or gilding-metal the Garter Star with an elliptical ring inscribed *Inniskilling Dragoon Guards*. Within the ring *5* in silver.

Beret
As forage-cap in gold embroidery.

The Queen's Own Hussars
Forage-cap
Embroidered badge: in the centre *QO* reversed and interlaced. Above, the White Horse in silver on red cloth, surrounded by a blue Garter with motto in gold wire surmounted by St. Edward's crown in gold, silver and crimson embroidery.

8th King's Royal Irish Hussars
Forage-cap
(1) The Irish Harp surmounted by the Royal Crest. Below the Harp the Roman numerals *VIII*. Below all a scroll inscribed *Pristinae virtutis memores*. The Harp in silver-plate, remainder gilt (Fig. 1927).
(2) As above but with St. Edward's crown in the Royal Crest (Fig. 1928).

10th Royal Hussars (Prince of Wales's Own)
Beret and Tent-cap
The Prince of Wales's plumes, coronet and motto. The coronet gilt, remainder silver-plate (Fig. 1929).

14th/20th King's Hussars
Forage-cap and Service-dress cap
The Prussian Eagle in black-japanned metal (Fig. 1907).

Beret
As above but gold embroidered.

16th/5th The Queen's Royal Lancers
Full-dress Head-dress (1934)
The universal plate in gilt or gilding-metal. On the plate in silver the Royal Arms and scroll *Sixteenth-Fifth Lancers.* No battle honours.

17th/21st Lancers
Full-dress Head-dress (1934)
On a gilt or gilding-metal plate, in silver, the Royal Arms with the death's head and scroll inscribed *Or Glory.* No battle honours.

Reconnaissance Corps
(1) As other-ranks (Fig. 1925) but in bronze; hall-marked silver; in silver-plate with the spear in gilt; and with the spear and scroll in gilt and the lightning in silver-plate.
(2) As above but with a small circular red-enamel plate bearing the Scottish Lion rampant superimposed on the centre of the spear. Chromed (Fig. 1930). Worn by officers of Scottish units.
(3) As above but with the White Rose of York superimposed on the centre of the spear. In silver-plate (as Fig. 1926). Worn by officers of Yorkshire units.

CHAPTER 2

The Royal Artillery, Royal Engineers and Royal Corps of Signals

---

ROYAL HORSE ARTILLERY

(1) The Royal Cypher of King George v within the Garter surmounted by an Imperial crown. A scroll below inscribed *Royal Horse Artillery*. Worn in puggaree abroad; issued for Silver Jubilee parades. In white-metal (Fig. 1931).
(2) As above, but with centre voided and with the Royal Cypher of King Edward VIII. In gilding-metal (Fig. 1932). Also in gilt.
(3) As (2) but with the Royal Cypher of King George VI. In gilding-metal. Sealed 25th August 1948 (Fig. 1933). Also in gilt and in white-metal.
(4) As (3) but with the Royal Cypher of Queen Elizabeth II and with St. Edward's crown. In gilding-metal. Sealed 28th November 1956 (Fig. 1934). Also in white-metal, gilt, and anodised. Sealed 22nd March 1966.
These later patterns were authorised for wear on the beret only.

THE ROYAL REGIMENT OF ARTILLERY

(1) A gun with scroll above inscribed *Ubique* surmounted by an Imperial crown. A scroll below inscribed *Quo fas et gloria ducunt.* In gilding-metal (Fig. 808). Also in gilt and bronze and with the wheel of the gun mounted separately.
(2) A grenade of seven flames with, below, a scroll inscribed *Ubique*. Worn on the F.S. Cap in the Second World War. In gilding-metal (Fig. 1935).
(3) As (1) but smaller size for wear on the beret. In gilding-metal. Sealed 16th October 1947. (Fig. 1936).
(4) As (1) but with St. Edward's crown. In gilding-metal. Sealed 6th December 1954 (Fig. 1937). Also anodised, sealed 3rd February 1960. Officers: gold-embroidered on forage-cap and in bronze on service-dress cap.
(5) As (3) but with St. Edward's crown. In gilding-metal. Sealed 20th January 1954 (Fig. 1938). Also anodised, sealed 23rd June 1954. Gilt for officers.

THE CORPS OF ROYAL ENGINEERS

(1) Within a wreath of laurel the Garter surmounted by an Imperial crown. In the centre the Royal Cypher of King George v. Across the base of the wreath a scroll inscribed *Royal Engineers* (Fig. 853). In gilding-metal. Gilt for officers.

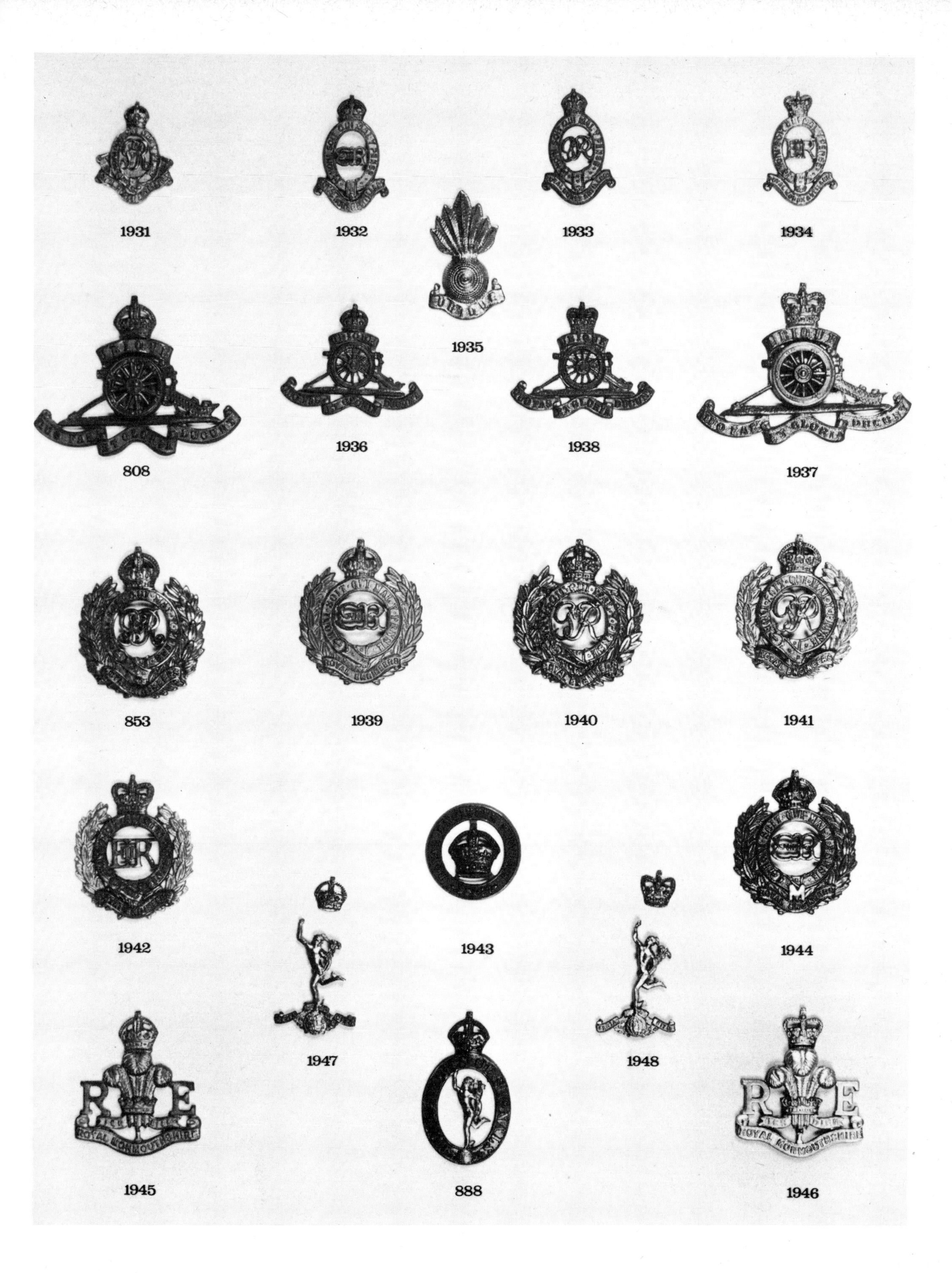
1931
1932
1933
1934
1935
808
1936
1938
1937
853
1939
1940
1941
1942
1943
1944
1947
1948
R E
ROYAL MONMOUTHSHIRE
R E
ROYAL MONMOUTHSHIRE
1945
888
1946

(2) As above but with the cypher of King Edward VIII. In gilding-metal (Fig. 1939).
(3) As above but with the cypher of King George VI. In gilding-metal (Fig. 1940).
(4) As (3) but with the wreath in white-metal and the remainder raised above the laurel-wreath and in gilding-metal. Sealed 17th January 1949 (Fig. 1941). Officers: in silver-plate and gilt.
(5) As (4) but with the cypher of Queen Elizabeth II and with St. Edward's crown (Fig. 1942). In same metals. Officers: in bronze for service dress.

Royal Engineer Services
A circlet inscribed *Royal Engineer Services* with a sprig of laurel at the base. In a voided centre an Imperial crown. In bronze (Fig. 1943). Worn by officers only. Also found non-voided and in gilt and silver for full-dress.

Royal Engineers Militia
Within a wreath of laurel the Garter surmounted by an Imperial crown. In the centre the Royal Cypher of King Edward VIII. Across the base of the wreath a scroll inscribed *Royal Engineers*. Above this the letter *M*. All in gilding-metal except the letter *M* which is in white-metal (Fig. 1944). This pattern is found in all types up to King George VI and was worn latterly by the Fortress Company, Malta.

Royal Monmouthshire Royal Engineers (Militia)
(1) The Prince of Wales's coronet, plumes and motto surmounted by an Imperial crown. On either side of the plume the letters *R* and *E*. Below, a scroll inscribed *Royal Monmouthshire*. The plumes and motto in white-metal, remainder in gilding-metal (Fig. 1945).
(2) As above but with St. Edward's crown. In gold- and silver-anodised (Fig. 1946).

ROYAL CORPS OF SIGNALS

(1) An oval inscribed *Royal Corps of Signals* with, in the bottom centre, the Globe with a sprig of laurel either side. The oval surmounted by an Imperial crown. In the centre the figure of Mercury, holding a caduceus in his left hand and his right hand held aloft, poised on the Globe with his left foot. Oval and crown in gilding-metal, remainder in white-metal. Officers' in gilt-and-silver-plate, also in bronze. Worn 1920–1946 (Fig. 888).
(2) The figure of Mercury holding a caduceus in his left hand, his right hand held aloft, poised on the Globe superimposed on a scroll inscribed *Certo Cito*, the whole ensigned with an Imperial crown which is detached from the remainder of the badge. Mercury and the Globe in white-metal, remainder in gilding-metal. Sealed 18th September 1946 (Fig. 1947).
(3) As (2) but with St. Edward's crown (Fig. 1948). Also anodised, sealed 31st March 1955.

CHAPTER 3

The Guards Division

No change has been made in the head-dress badges of the Foot Guards except, where appropriate to the Royal Cypher worn as a distinctive device on the fused-grenade by officers and N.C.O.s of the Grenadiers.

As from the 1st July 1968 The Brigade of Guards was re-titled the Guards Division.

GRENADIER GUARDS

1911–1936

(1) Officers: a fused grenade with the cypher of King George v interlaced and reversed and surmounted by an Imperial crown mounted on the ball. All gilt.
(2) Staff: as above but with cypher and crown in silver mounted on the ball (Fig. 1949).
(3) Sergeants and Musicians: as (1) but the cypher and crown struck on the ball (Fig. 893).
(4) Other-ranks: a fused grenade with a plain ball. All brass (Fig. 891). This was worn also in bronze by officers in service-dress.

1937–1954

(1) Officers: a fused grenade with the cypher of King George vi interlaced and reversed and surmounted by an Imperial crown mounted on the ball. All gilt.
(2) Commissioned Quartermasters: as above but with cypher and crown in silver mounted on the ball.
(3) Warrant Officers: as above but in gilding-metal with the cypher and crown in silver (Fig. 1950). Sealed 23rd March 1941.
(4) Sergeants and Musicians: as (1) but in gilding-metal and the cypher and crown struck on the ball (Fig. 1951). Sealed 23rd March 1941.

1954–

(1) Officers: a fused grenade with the cypher of Queen Elizabeth ii interlaced and reversed and surmounted by St. Edward's crown mounted on the ball. All gilt.
(2) Commissioned Quartermasters: as above but with cypher and crown in silver mounted on the ball.
(3) Warrant Officers: as above but in gilding-metal with the cypher and crown in silver (Fig. 1952).
(4) Sergeants and Musicians: as (1) but in gilding-metal and the cypher and crown struck on the ball (Fig. 1953). Sealed in metal 19th September 1956 and in anodised 20th September 1963.
(5) Other-ranks: a fused grenade with a plain ball, sealed in anodised 19th March 1962.

Puggaree badges
Officers: a pierced Garter with blue-enamel backing surmounted by an Imperial crown. In the centre the cypher of King George v interlaced and reversed with red-enamel backing (Fig. 894).
Other-ranks: as officers' but all brass (Fig. 1954).

Small-type other-ranks' puggaree badges
(These formed part of the shoulder-titles)
(1) The Garter surmounted by an Imperial crown. In a voided centre the cypher of King George v interlaced and reversed. In gilding-metal (Fig. 896).
(2) As above but with the cypher of King George vi. Sealed in brass 20th May 1936.

COLDSTREAM GUARDS

Officers' Field cap
The Garter Star in silver with blue-enamel backing to the Garter and red-enamel backing to St. George's Cross (Fig. 897).

Officers' Service-dress cap
As above but smaller (Fig. 898). Also in bronze.

Warrant Officers' and Staff Sergeants' Forage-cap
The Garter Star in white-metal with blue-enamel backing to the Garter and red-enamel backing to St. George's Cross (Fig. 899).

Other-ranks' Forage-cap
The Garter Star in gilding-metal (Fig. 901). Also anodised, sealed 20th May 1958.

Puggaree badges
Officers: the Garter Star in silver with blue-enamel backing to the Garter and red-enamel backing to St. George's Cross (Fig. 902).
Warrant Officers and Staff Sergeants: as above but in white-metal (Fig. 903).
Other-ranks: as above but all in gilding-metal (Fig. 904).

SCOTS GUARDS

Forage-cap and Puggaree
Officers: the Star of the Order of the Thistle in silver. The circlet inscribed with the motto and the thistle with two leaves in the centre in gilt. Green-enamel background to the centre (Fig. 905).
Warrant Officers, Regimental and Battalion Staff: similar to officers' but the Star is of a slightly different shape (Fig. 906).
Colour-Sergeants, Sergeants and Musicians: similar to above but Star in white-metal, motto-circlet and thistle centre in gilding-metal (Fig. 907). Sealed in anodised 26th June 1964.
Lance-Sergeants and below: similar to above but all in gilding-metal (Fig. 908). Sealed in anodised, 20th May 1958.

893
891
1951
1949
1950
846
1952
1953
894
1954
898
899
901
897
903
904
902

Officers' Service-dress cap
The Star of the Order of the Thistle in silver. The centre and circlet in gilt. Green-enamel ground to centre (Fig. 910).

Pipers' badge
Within a strap inscribed *Scots Guards* the Star of the Order of the Thistle (Fig. 911).
(Sergeant-Pipers wear a Sergeant's star, and Pipe-Majors a Warrant Officers' star, within the strap.)

IRISH GUARDS

Forage-cap
Officers: the Star of the Order of St. Patrick. The Star in silver, the pierced circlet with the motto of the Order *Quis separabit* and the Roman numerals *MDCCLXXXIII* (the date of the foundation of the Order) in gilt with light-blue-enamel backing. In a voided centre, St. Patrick's Cross in red-enamel; superimposed on this a gilt and green-enamel shamrock-leaf with three gilt crowns on the leaf (Fig. 912).
Warrant Officers and Staff Sergeants: similar to officers' but the centre portion is not raised so high (Fig. 913).
Other-ranks: similar to above but in gilding-metal only (Fig. 914). Sealed in anodised, 20th May 1953.

Officers' Service-dress cap
As the forage-cap but smaller (Fig. 915).

Puggaree badge
Officers: the Star of the Order of St. Patrick in gilt with silver centre (Fig. 916).
Other-ranks: as above but all in bronze (Fig. 917).

Pipe-Major's caubeen badge
The Star of the Order of St. Patrick in silver. A gilt circlet with motto voided on a light-blue-enamel ground. In the centre a red-enamel edged gold St. Patrick's Cross on a white-enamel ground. On this a green shamrock-leaf with three red crowns on the leaf (Fig. 918).

Pipers' caubeen badge
As above but all in white-metal (Fig. 919).

WELSH GUARDS

Forage-cap
A Leek. In gilding-metal (Fig. 920). Also anodised. Officers: in gilt and in bronze.

Puggaree badge
A circlet inscribed *Cymru am byth* surmounted by an Imperial crown. In a voided centre a leek. In gilding-metal with red-cloth backing to the badge (Fig. 921).

The Guards Parachute Company wore the Parachute Regiment's badge with Imperial crown in white-metal with a backing of diagonal alternate red and blue stripes, cut in the outline of the badge and slightly larger.

905
910
906
SCOTS GUARDS
907
911
908
915
918
914
919
916
912
913
917
920
921
CYMRU AM BYTH

CHAPTER 4

Infantry of the Line: Officers

Although full-dress was not resumed by Infantry of the Line after the Great War, the new *Dress Regulations for the Army* of 1934 still gave full details of the badges to be worn by officers on the standard helmet-plate, the white foreign-service helmet, the forage-cap and the service-dress cap; with suitable equivalents for the special head-dress worn by the Fusilier, Rifle, and Scottish Regiments.

In most cases there was little change from the information published in the previous edition but, because it constitutes the last record of badges to be worn on full-dress uniforms before they became obsolete, it is repeated here with the kind permission of the Controller, Her Majesty's Stationery Office.

With few exceptions, officers' forage-cap badges were similar to those worn by the men, as described in Chapter 5, but made in finer metals, e.g. silver, and gilt, sometimes embellished with enamels. The same patterns of badges were worn in service-dress caps but in bronze and, to avoid continuous repetition, officers' badges are illustrated only when the format differs materially from that worn by the men.

In 1946 the 'Royal' title was awarded to The Lincolnshire Regiment, The Leicestershire Regiment and The Hampshire Regiment for their services in the Second World War, and consequently new badges were struck for these three regiments incorporating the new designations.

Pamphlet No. 5 of the new *Dress Regulations for Officers of the Army* dealt with the Infantry and, fortunately, it was not published until 23rd May 1973.

By that date, the re-organisation of the Infantry into Divisions, the abolition of Regional Brigades with their distinctive badges, and the final amalgamations of Infantry regiments had been completed, so the detail published below, with the permission of Her Majesty's Stationery Office, constitutes a complete list of the authorised head-dress badges for all the modern regiments as they stand today.

The Royal Scots (The Royal Regiment)
Bonnet, White F.S. Helmet, Glengarry cap and Tam o' Shanter bonnet
In silver, the Star of the Order of the Thistle; in gilt or gilding-metal on the Star a raised circlet inscribed *Nemo me impune lacessit.* Within the circlet, on a ground of green-enamel, the Thistle in gilt or gilding-metal (Fig. 1955).

The Queen's Royal Regiment (West Surrey)
Helmet-plate
On a scarlet-velvet ground, the Paschal Lamb in silver. On the universal scroll *The Royal West Surrey Regiment.* Above the Garter a silver scroll inscribed *The Queen's.*

White F.S. Helmet and Forage-cap
The Paschal Lamb in frosted gilt or gilding-metal.

The Buffs (East Kent Regiment)
Helmet-plate
On a black-velvet ground the Dragon in silver. On the universal scroll *The East Kent Regiment.* Above the Garter a silver scroll inscribed *The Buffs.*

White F.S. Helmet and Forage-cap
The Dragon in silver. On a scroll beneath *The Buffs.*

The King's Own Royal Regiment (Lancaster)
Helmet-plate
In silver, on a crimson-velvet ground, the Lion of England. On the universal scroll *Royal Lancaster Regiment.* Above the Garter a silver scroll inscribed *The King's Own.*

White F.S. Helmet and Forage-cap
The Lion in silver. Below the Lion *The King's Own.*

The Northumberland Fusiliers
Full-dress Head-dress
A grenade in gilt or gilding-metal. Mounted on the ball a circlet inscribed *Quo fata vocant.* Within the circlet St. George and the Dragon.

White F.S. Helmet and Forage-cap
A grenade in gilt or gilding-metal; on the ball in silver St. George and the Dragon within a circlet inscribed *Northumberland Fusiliers.*

The Royal Warwickshire Regiment
Helmet-plate
On a black-velvet ground the Antelope in silver with gilt or gilding-metal collar and chain. On the universal scroll *The Royal Warwickshire Regiment.*

White F.S. Helmet and Forage-cap
In silver the Antelope with gilt collar and chain. On a scroll below *Royal Warwickshire.*

The Royal Fusiliers (City of London Regiment)
Full-dress Head-dress
In gilt or gilding-metal, a grenade; mounted on the ball the Garter surmounted by a crown. The Garter pierced with the motto; the ground of blue-enamel. Within the Garter the Rose; below the Garter, in silver, the White Horse.

White F.S. Helmet and Forage cap
As for full-dress head-dress but smaller; the Rose in Silver and the White Horse omitted.

The King's Regiment (Liverpool)
Helmet-plate
In silver, on a crimson-velvet ground, the White Horse, with scroll above inscribed in old English capitals *Nec Aspera Terrent.* On the universal scroll *The Liverpool Regiment.* Above the Garter a silver scroll inscribed *The King's.*

White F.S. Helmet and Forage-cap
In silver the White Horse. A gilt or gilding-metal scroll below inscribed in Old English *King's*.

The Norfolk Regiment
Helmet-plate
The figure of Britannia in silver on a black-velvet ground. On the universal scroll *The Norfolk Regiment*.

White F.S. Helmet and Forage-cap
In gilt or gilding-metal, the figure of Britannia; a tablet below inscribed *The Norfolk Regt* (Fig. 1956).

The Lincolnshire Regiment
Helmet-plate
In silver, on a black-velvet ground, the Sphinx over *Egypt*. On the universal scroll *The Lincolnshire Regt*.

White F.S. Helmet and Forage-cap
In gilt or gilding-metal, on a silver diamond-cut eight-pointed star, a circlet inscribed *Lincolnshire Regiment*, the letters pierced on a raised ground of blue-velvet. Within the circlet the Sphinx over *Egypt* in silver (Fig. 1957).

The Royal Lincolnshire Regiment
Forage-cap
In gilt or gilding-metal, on a silver diamond-cut eight-pointed star, a circlet inscribed *Royal Lincolnshire Regiment*. Within the circlet in silver the Sphinx superscribed *Egypt* on a ground of blue-enamel (Fig. 1958).

The Devonshire Regiment
Helmet-plate
The Castle of Exeter with scroll inscribed *Semper fidelis* in silver on a black-velvet ground. On the universal scroll *The Devonshire Regt*.

White F.S. Helmet and Forage-cap
In gilt or gilding-metal, on a silver eight-pointed star, a circlet surmounted by a crown. On the circlet *The Devonshire Regiment*; within, in silver, the Castle of Exeter with scroll inscribed *Semper fidelis* on a ground of blue-velvet.

The Suffolk Regiment
Helmet-plate
In silver on a black-velvet ground the Castle and Key with scroll above inscribed *Gibraltar* and scroll below inscribed *Montis insignia Calpe*. On the universal scroll *The Suffolk Regiment*.

White F.S. Helmet and Forage-cap
In silver, within a circlet inscribed *Montis insignia Calpe*, the Castle and Key surmounted by a scroll inscribed *Gibraltar*; above the circlet a crown; surrounding the circlet an oak-leaf wreath. Below the circlet, upon the wreath, a scroll inscribed *The Suffolk Regt*.

The Somerset Light Infantry (Prince Albert's)
Helmet-plate
In silver, on a black-velvet ground, a bugle with strings surmounted by a mural crown with scroll above inscribed *Jellalabad*; the Sphinx over *Egypt* within the strings of the bugle. On the scroll *Somerset Light Infantry.*

White F.S. Helmet and Forage-cap
In silver a bugle; within the strings the cypher of H.R.H. the late Prince Consort. Above the bugle a mural crown surmounted by a scroll inscribed *Jellalabad.*

The West Yorkshire Regiment (The Prince of Wales's Own)
Helmet-plate
In silver, on a scarlet-velvet ground, the White Horse with the motto *Nec aspera terrent* on a scroll above. On the universal scroll *The West Yorkshire Regiment.*

White F.S. Helmet and Forage-cap
In silver the White Horse, above a gilt or gilding-metal scroll inscribed *West Yorkshire.*

The East Yorkshire Regiment
Helmet-plate
In gilt or gilding-metal, on a ground of black-enamel, a laurel-wreath on an eight-pointed star. Within the wreath the White Rose in silver. On the universal scroll *The East Yorkshire Regiment.*

White F.S. Helmet and Forage-cap
In gilt or gilding-metal a badge, as for the centre of the helmet-plate, but larger; a scroll below inscribed *East Yorkshire.*

The Bedfordshire and Hertfordshire Regiment
Helmet-plate
In silver, on a black-velvet ground, an eight-pointed star; on the star, in gilt or gilding-metal, a Maltese cross. Within a gilt or gilding-metal circlet on a cross, in silver, a Hart crossing a ford; the Hart on a ground of blue enamel. On the universal scroll *The Bedfordshire Regiment.*

White F.S. Helmet and Forage-cap
In silver, a Maltese cross on a diamond-cut eight-pointed star. On the cross the Garter with motto. Within the Garter, the Hart (pierced) crossing a ford; below the star a scroll inscribed *Bedfordshire and Hertfordshire.*

The Leicestershire Regiment
Helmet-plate
On a black-velvet ground the Royal Tiger, in silver, with silver scroll above inscribed *Hindoostan.* On the universal scroll *The Leicestershire Regiment.*

White F.S. Helmet and Forage-cap
In gilt or gilding-metal the Tiger. In silver, above the Tiger, a scroll inscribed *Hindoostan*; below the Tiger another scroll inscribed *Leicestershire.*

The Green Howards (Alexandra, Princess of Wales's Own, Yorkshire Regiment)
Helmet-plate
On a black-velvet ground the Cypher of H.M. the late Queen Alexandra, as Princess of Wales, combined with the Dannebrog and surmounted by the coronet of the Princess, in silver metal. On the centre of the cross *1875* and *Alexandra.* On a scroll in silver metal *The Princess of Wales's Own Yorkshire Regiment.* The White Rose in the centre of the scroll.

White F.S. Helmet and Forage-cap
In silver metal the cypher of H.M. the late Queen Alexandra as Princess of Wales combined with the Dannebrog and surmounted by the coronet of the Princess. On the centre of the cross *1875* and *Alexandra.* On a scroll below *The Princess of Wales's Own Yorkshire Regiment.* In the centre of the scroll the White Rose.

The Lancashire Fusiliers
Full-dress Head-dress
A grenade in gilt or gilding-metal; mounted on the ball, in silver, the Sphinx over *Egypt* within a laurel-wreath.

White F.S. Helmet and Forage-cap
In gilt or gilding-metal a grenade; on the ball the Sphinx over *Egypt* within a laurel-wreath. Below the grenade a scroll inscribed *Lancashire Fusiliers.*

The Royal Scots Fusiliers
Fusilier cap
A grenade in gilt or gilding-metal; on the ball of the grenade, the Royal Arms.

Glengarry cap
As for fusilier cap, but smaller (Fig. 1959).

The Cheshire Regiment
Helmet-plate
In silver, on a black-velvet ground, an eight-pointed star. Within a gilt or gilding-metal circlet on the star, the Prince of Wales's plumes on a burnished-silver ground. The plumes in silver, the coronet in gilt or gilding-metal. On the universal scroll *The Cheshire Regiment.*

White F.S. Helmet and Forage-cap
In silver a diamond-cut eight-pointed star. On the star a circlet in gilt or gilding-metal inscribed *The Cheshire Regiment* surrounding the acorn with oak-leaves, filled below with green-enamel (Fig. 1960).

The Royal Welch Fusiliers
Full-dress Head-dress
A grenade in gilt or gilding-metal; the Prince of Wales's plumes and coronet mounted in silver on the ball.

White F.S. Helmet and Forage-cap
A grenade in gilt or gilding-metal; on the ball, in silver, a circlet (frosted) inscribed *Royal Welch Fusiliers.* Within the circlet the Prince of Wales's plumes and coronet in silver.

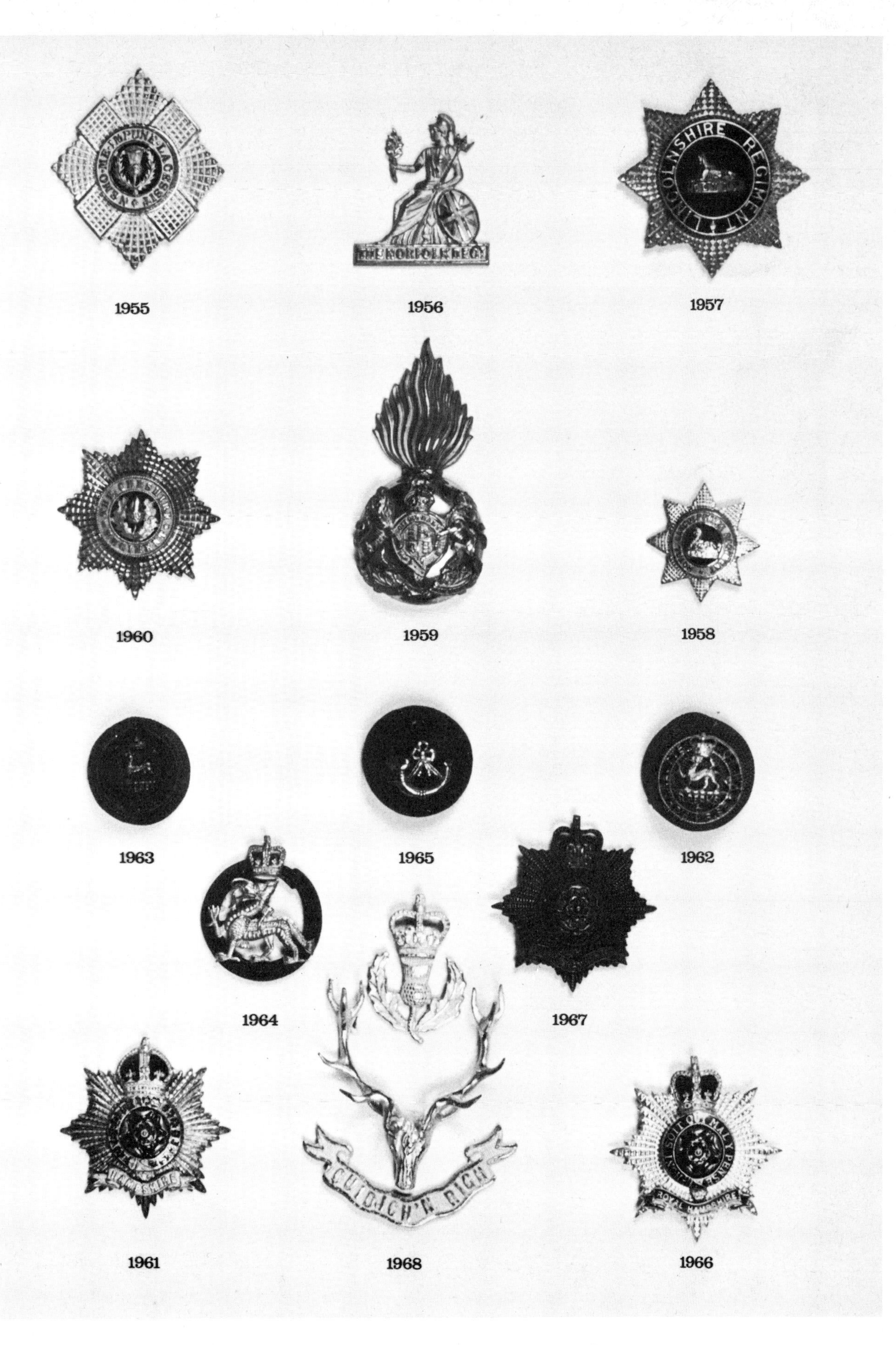
LINCOLNSHIRE REGIMENT
1955
1956
1957
1960
1959
1958
1963
1965
1962
1964
1967
CUIDICH'N RIGH
1961
1968
1966

The South Wales Borderers
Helmet-plate
In silver, on a black-velvet ground, the Welsh Dragon within a laurel-wreath. On the universal scroll *The South Wales Borderers.*

White F.S. Helmet and Forage-cap
In silver, within a wreath of laurel and immortelles, the Sphinx over *Egypt.* On the lower bend of the wreath *S.W.B.* in burnished silver.

The King's Own Scottish Borderers
Bonnet, White F.S. Helmet, Glengarry cap and Tam o' Shanter bonnet
In silver, a thistle-wreath; within the wreath a circlet pierced with the designation *King's Own Scottish Borderers.* Above the circlet a scroll surmounted by the Royal Crest. The scroll pierced with the motto *In veritate religionis confido.* Over the circlet the Cross of St. Andrew in burnished silver. On the Cross, the Castle of Edinburgh. On the wreath at the bottom of the circlet, a scroll with the motto in relief *Nisi Dominus frustra.*

The Cameronians (Scottish Rifles)
Shako
In bronze a bugle and strings; above the bugle a mullet on a black-corded boss.

White F.S. Helmet, Glengarry cap and Tam o' Shanter bonnet
In silver a thistle-wreath; within the wreath, in burnished silver, a mullet. On the bottom of the wreath a bugle with strings.

The Royal Inniskilling Fusiliers
Full-dress Head-dress
A grenade in gilt or gilding-metal; the Castle mounted in silver on the ball.

White F.S. Helmet and Forage-cap
As for full-dress head-dress but smaller. Below the Castle a scroll in silver inscribed *Inniskilling.*

The Gloucestershire Regiment
Helmet-plate
In silver, on a black-velvet ground, the Sphinx over *Egypt.* On the universal scroll *The Gloucestershire Regiment.*
Badge for the back of the helmet: in dead gilt or gilding-metal the Sphinx of *Egypt* within a laurel-wreath.

White F.S. Helmet and Forage-cap
In silver, within two twigs of laurel, the Sphinx over *Egypt.* On a scroll below *Gloucestershire.* Back-badge as for helmet.

The Worcestershire Regiment
Helmet-plate
On a black-velvet ground a silver eight-pointed elongated star. On the star, in gilt or gilding-metal, the Garter with motto. Within the Garter the Lion, in silver, on a black-velvet ground.

Below the Garter a scroll in gilt or gilding-metal inscribed *Firm*. On the universal scroll *The Worcestershire Regiment*.

White F.S. Helmet and Forage-cap
On an eight-pointed elongated silver star of 48 rays the Garter, oval-shaped, in gilt or gilding-metal. Within the Garter in silver on a pierced ground, upon a pedestal inscribed *Firm*, the Lion of the Royal Crest.

The East Lancashire Regiment
Helmet-plate
In silver, on a black-velvet ground, the Sphinx over *Egypt*. On the universal scroll *The East Lancashire Regiment*.

White F.S. Helmet and Forage-cap
In silver a laurel-wreath surmounted by a crown. Within the wreath the Sphinx over *Egypt*; on the lower part of the wreath a scroll inscribed *East Lancashire*. Below *Egypt*, and within the wreath, the Rose in gilt or gilding-metal.

The East Surrey Regiment
Helmet-plate
In silver, on a black-velvet ground, an eight-pointed diamond-cut star; on the star the Arms of Guildford in silver on a shield in frosted gilt or gilding-metal with burnished edges. On the universal scroll *The East Surrey Regt.*

White F.S. Helmet and Forage-cap
On a diamond-cut silver star the Arms of Guildford in silver on a shield, in frosted gilt or gilding-metal with burnished edges, surmounted by a gilt or gilding-metal crown. A scroll inscribed *East Surrey* in gilt or gilding-metal below the star.

The Duke of Cornwall's Light Infantry
Helmet-plate
In gilt or gilding-metal, on a ground of dark-green-velvet, a bugle with strings. On the strings of the bugle two red feathers set in gilt or gilding-metal. On the stem of the feathers, in silver, a turreted archway. On the universal scroll *The Duke of Cornwall's Lt. Infy.*

White F.S. Helmet and Forage-cap
In silver a bugle with strings surmounted by the coronet. Below the coronet a scroll inscribed *Cornwall*.

The Duke of Wellington's Regiment (West Riding)
Helmet-plate
In silver, on a black-velvet ground, the Duke of Wellington's Crest with motto on a scroll below *Virtutis fortuna comes*. On the universal scroll *The West Riding Regiment*. Above the Garter a silver scroll inscribed *Duke of Wellington's*.

White F.S. Helmet and Forage-cap
In silver a badge as for helmet-plate. A gilt or gilding-metal scroll below inscribed *The West Riding*.

The Border Regiment
Helmet-plate
In silver a laurel-wreath; on the wreath a Maltese cross with a lion between each division. On the divisions of the cross the honours of the Regiment. On the centre of the cross a raised circlet inscribed *Arroyo dos Molinos 1811*. Within the circlet, on a ground of red-enamel, the Dragon of China in gold and the word *China* on a gold ground. The upper part of the centre filled in with white-enamel. Below the wreath a scroll inscribed *The Border Regt.*

White F.S. Helmet and Forage-cap
In silver, on an eight-pointed diamond-cut star surmounted by a crown, a laurel-wreath. On the wreath a Maltese cross with a lion between each division. On the divisions of the cross the honours of the Regiment. On the centre of the cross a raised circlet inscribed *Arroyo dos Molinos 1811*. Within the circlet, on a ground of red-enamel, the Dragon of China in silver and the word *China* on a silver ground. Below the wreath a scroll inscribed *The Border Regt.*

The Royal Sussex Regiment
Helmet-plate
On a scarlet-velvet ground a Maltese cross, in gilt or gilding-metal, on a feather in silver; on the cross a wreath in silver and gold-enamel; on the wreath the Garter and motto in blue-enamel set with silver. Within the circle the Cross of St. George in red-enamel set with silver on a silver ground. On the universal scroll *The Royal Sussex Regiment.*

White F.S. Helmet and Forage-cap
In silver an eight-pointed star on a feather, the stem of the feather gilt. On the star the Garter and motto on a ground of blue-enamel. Within the Garter the Cross of St. George in red-enamel on a silver ground. A scroll below inscribed *The Royal Sussex Regt.*

The Hampshire Regiment
Helmet-plate
On a black-velvet ground the Royal Tiger, in gilt or gilding-metal, within a laurel-wreath in silver. On the universal scroll *The Hampshire Regt.*

White F.S. Helmet and Forage-cap
In silver an eight-pointed diamond-cut star; on the star the Garter, and motto pierced, ensigned with a crown in gilt metal; within the Garter the Rose. On the lower part of the star a scroll inscribed *Hampshire* (Fig. 1961).

The South Staffordshire Regiment
Helmet-plate
In silver, on a black-velvet ground, the Sphinx over *Egypt*. On the universal scroll *The South Staffordshire Regiment.*

White F.S. Helmet and Forage-cap
In silver the Stafford Knot, surmounted by a crown, with a scroll below in gilt or gilding-metal inscribed *South Staffordshire.*

The Dorsetshire Regiment
Helmet-plate
In silver, on a black-velvet ground, the Castle and Key. A scroll above the Castle inscribed *Primus in Indis* and one below inscribed *Montis insignia Calpe*. On the universal scroll *The Dorsetshire Regiment.*

White F.S. Helmet and Forage cap
In gilt or gilding-metal a laurel-wreath with a scroll inscribed *Dorsetshire*, the wreath and scroll forming a circle. Within the circle, in silver, the Castle and Key. Above the Castle the Sphinx resting on a tablet inscribed *Marabout*. Below the Castle a scroll with the words *Primus in Indis.*

The Prince of Wales's Volunteers (South Lancashire)
Helmet-plate
In silver, on a black-velvet ground, the Sphinx over *Egypt*. On the universal scroll *South Lancashire Regiment.*

White F.S. Helmet and Forage-cap
In silver the Sphinx over *Egypt*; above the Sphinx the Prince of Wales's plumes and motto, the coronet in gilt or gilding-metal. In gilt or gilding-metal, on either side, a spray of laurel; between the top-ends of the spray a scroll inscribed *South Lancashire*, between the bottom-ends another scroll inscribed *Prince of Wales's Vols.*

The Welch Regiment
Helmet-plate
In silver, on a black-velvet ground, the Prince of Wales's plumes with a scroll below inscribed *Gwell angau na chywilydd*. The coronet in gilt or gilding-metal. On the universal scroll *The Welch Regiment.*

White F.S. Helmet
The Prince of Wales's plumes in silver.

Forage-cap
In silver the Prince of Wales's plumes, the coronet in gilt or gilding-metal. Below, a scroll in gilt inscribed *The Welch.*

The Black Watch (Royal Highlanders)
Feather Bonnet
In gilt metal the Sphinx over *Egypt.*

White F.S. Helmet, Glengarry cap and Tam o' Shanter bonnet
In silver, diamond-cut, the Star of the Order of the Thistle; in gilt or gilding-metal, on the Star, a thistle-wreath. Within the wreath, in gilt or gilding-metal, an oval surmounted by a crown. The oval inscribed *Nemo me impune lacessit*. Within the oval, on a recessed seeded-ground, St. Andrew and Cross in silver. Below the wreath the Sphinx in gilt or gilding-metal. In silver, a half-scroll to the left of the crown inscribed *The Black*; another to the right inscribed *Watch*. A half-scroll to the left of the Sphinx inscribed *Royal*; another to the right inscribed *Highlanders.*

The Oxfordshire and Buckinghamshire Light Infantry
Helmet-plate
In silver, on a ground of black-enamel, a bugle with strings. On the universal scroll *The Oxfordshire and Buckinghamshire Lt. Infy.*

White F.S. Helmet and Forage-cap
In silver a bugle with strings.

The Essex Regiment
Helmet-plate
An oak-leaf wreath is substituted for the universal wreath. In silver, on a black-velvet ground, the Castle and Key with the Sphinx over *Egypt* above, and a scroll below inscribed *Montis Insignia Calpe.* On the universal scroll *The Essex Regt.*

White F.S. Helmet and Forage-cap
In silver the Castle and Key within an oak-leaf wreath. The Sphinx over *Egypt* above the Castle and a scroll inscribed *The Essex Regt* on the wreath below the Castle.

The Sherwood Foresters (Nottinghamshire and Derbyshire Regiment)
Helmet-plate
In the helmet-plate the Garter, with the motto, is omitted. Within the universal wreath a Maltese cross in silver. On the cross, in gilt or gilding-metal, an oak-leaf wreath; within the wreath, on a ground of blue-enamel, a stag lodged in silver. In gilt or gilding-metal, on the left division of the cross, the word *The*; on the right division, *Regt*; and on a scroll on the lower division *Notts and Derby.* A scroll of special pattern on the bottom of the universal wreath inscribed *Sherwood Foresters.*

White F.S. Helmet and Forage-cap
In silver a Maltese cross surmounted by a crown; within an oak-leaf wreath on the cross a stag lodged. A half-scroll on the left division of the cross inscribed *Sherwood*; another on the right division inscribed *Foresters.* On the lower division a scroll inscribed *Notts and Derby* in gilt or gilding-metal.

The Loyal Regiment (North Lancashire)
Helmet-plate
In silver, on a black-velvet ground, the Royal Crest. Below the Crest the Rose of Lancaster in silver, gilt and red-and-green-enamel. On the universal scroll *Loyal North Lancashire Regiment.*

White F.S. Helmet and Forage-cap
In silver the Royal Crest. In gilt or gilding-metal, below the crown, the Rose of Lancaster; below the Rose a scroll inscribed *The Loyal Regiment*

The Northamptonshire Regiment
Helmet-plate
In silver, on a black-velvet ground, the Castle and Key; on a scroll above *Gibraltar*, on a scroll below *Talavera.* On the universal scroll *The Northamptonshire Regiment.*

White F.S. Helmet and Forage-cap
In silver, within a laurel-wreath, the Castle and Key. Above the Castle a scroll, uniting the ends of the wreath, inscribed *Gibraltar*; beneath, a scroll inscribed *Talavera.* On the lower bend of the wreath, in gilt or gilding-metal, a scroll inscribed *Northamptonshire.*

The Royal Berkshire Regiment (Princess Charlotte of Wales's)
Helmet-plate
In silver, on a scarlet-cloth ground, a stag under an oak. On the universal scroll *Royal Berkshire Regiment.*

White F.S. Helmet and Forage-cap
(1) On a scarlet-cord boss a gilt circlet pierced and inscribed *Princess Charlotte of Wales's*; within the circlet the China Dragon and above the Dragon an Imperial crown. Worn up to c. 1920.
(2) As (1) but circlet inscribed *Ps Charlotte of Wales's* and, below the Dragon, *R. Berks.*
(3) As (2) but *s* omitted after *P* and with St. Edward's crown (Fig. 1962).

Service-dress cap
As for forage-cap but on a khaki-cord boss and with a scarlet-cloth patch behind the central device (Fig. 1963).

Beret
(1) On a coil of rope, in bronze, the China Dragon surmounted by an Imperial crown in silver-plate with red-enamel in the crown.
(2) As (1) but with St. Edward's crown (Fig. 1964).

The Queen's Own Royal West Kent Regiment
Helmet-plate
In silver, on a black-velvet ground, the White Horse of Kent above a scroll inscribed *Invicta.* Above the horse another scroll with the motto *Quo fas et gloria ducunt.* On the universal scroll *The Royal West Kent Regiment.*

White F.S. Helmet and Forage-cap
In silver the White Horse of Kent above a scroll inscribed *Invicta.* On another scroll below *Royal West Kent.*

The King's Own Yorkshire Light Infantry
Helmet-plate
In silver, on a black-enamel ground, a French horn with the White Rose in the centre. On the universal scroll *The King's Own Yorkshire Light Infantry.*

White F.S. Helmet and Forage-cap
In gilt or gilding-metal, a French horn; within the horn the White Rose in silver on a ground of black-enamel.

The King's Shropshire Light Infantry
Helmet-plate
In silver, on a ground of dark-green enamel, a bugle with strings. In gilt or gilding-metal, within the strings of the bugle, the cypher *KLI.* On the universal scroll *King's Shropshire Lt Infty.*

White F.S. Helmet and Forage-cap
In silver a bugle with strings. Within the strings the letters *KSLI* in gilt or gilding-metal.

The Middlesex Regiment (Duke of Cambridge's Own)
Helmet-plate
In silver, on a black-velvet ground, a laurel-wreath; within the wreath the Prince of Wales's plumes; below the plumes the coronet and cypher of H.R.H. the late George, Duke of Cambridge. On the bottom of the wreath a scroll inscribed *Albuhera.* On the universal scroll *The Middlesex Regiment.*

White F.S. Helmet and Forage-cap
In silver a laurel-wreath; within the wreath the Prince of Wales's plumes; below the plumes the coronet and cypher of H.R.H. the late George, Duke of Cambridge. On the lower bend of the wreath *Albuhera.* A scroll below inscribed *Middlesex Regiment.*

The King's Royal Rifle Corps
Busby
In black metal a Maltese cross surmounted by a tablet inscribed *Celer et Audax.* On the cross a circlet inscribed *The King's Royal Rifle Corps*; within the circlet a bugle with strings. On the divisions of the cross the honours of the regiment. On the boss, a crown.

F. S. Helmet
On a scarlet-cloth ground a Maltese cross as worn on the busby. The centre pierced; the whole surmounted by a crown.

Forage cap
In silver, a bugle with strings on a scarlet-cord boss (Fig. 1965).

The Wiltshire Regiment (Duke of Edinburgh's)
Helmet-plate
On a black-velvet ground, a cross patée in lined gilt or gilding-metal with burnished edges. On the cross a circular convex plate. On the plate, in silver, the cypher of H.R.H. the late Alfred, Duke of Edinburgh, surmounted by the coronet. On the universal scroll *The Wiltshire Regiment.*

White F.S. Helmet and Forage-cap
As for helmet-plate, but with the cypher and coronet in gilt or gilding-metal; a scroll beneath inscribed *The Wiltshire Regiment*; above the cross the coronet.

The Manchester Regiment
Helmet-plate
In silver, on a black-velvet ground, Arms with the motto of the City of Manchester. On the universal scroll *The Manchester Regiment.*

White F.S. Helmet and Forage-cap
In silver the Fleur-de-Lys.

The North Staffordshire Regiment (The Prince of Wales's)
Helmet-plate
In silver, on a black-velvet ground, the Prince of Wales's plumes. On the universal scroll *The North Staffordshire Regiment.*

White F.S. Helmet and Forage-cap
The Stafford Knot surmounted by the Prince of Wales's plumes; the Knot and coronet in gilt or gilding-metal, the plumes and scroll in silver. Below the Knot, in silver, a scroll inscribed *North Stafford.*

The York and Lancaster Regiment
Helmet-plate
In silver and gilt or gilding-metal, on a black-velvet ground, the Union Rose. On the universal scroll *The York & Lancaster Regiment.*

White F.S. Helmet and Forage-cap
In gilt or gilding-metal the Tiger within a scroll inscribed *York and Lancaster* upon a laurel-wreath. Between the ends of the wreath a coronet in silver; below the coronet the Union Rose in gilt or gilding-metal and silver.

The Durham Light Infantry
Helmet-plate
In silver, on a dark-green-velvet ground, a bugle with strings. On the universal scroll *The Durham Light Infantry.*

White F.S. Helmet and Forage-cap
In silver a bugle ornamented with laurel-leaves. Upon the strings a crown. Within the strings *DLI.*

The Highland Light Infantry (City of Glasgow Regiment)
Shako
In silver the Star of the Order of the Thistle. On the Star a silver horn. In the centre of the horn the monogram *HLI* in gilt or gilding-metal. Above the horn in gilt or gilding-metal a crown with crimson-enamel. Below the horn a scroll, in gilt or gilding-metal, inscribed *Assaye*; under the scroll in gilt or gilding-metal the Elephant. A black boss is worn with a gilt thistle mount.

White F.S. Helmet, Glengarry cap and Tam o' Shanter bonnet
As for shako, but without the boss.

The Seaforth Highlanders (Ross-shire Buffs, The Duke of Albany's)
Feather Bonnet
As for Glengarry cap, but without the coronet and cypher.

White F.S. Helmet, Glengarry cap and Tam o' Shanter bonnet
In silver, a stag's head; above, the coronet and cypher of H.R.H. Leopold, the late Duke of Albany; below a scroll inscribed *Cuidich'n Righ.*

The Gordon Highlanders
Feather Bonnet
In silver the crest of the Marquis of Huntly within an ivy-wreath. On the bottom of the wreath *Bydand.*

White F.S. Helmet, Glengarry cap and Tam o' Shanter bonnet
As for feather bonnet.

The Queen's Own Cameron Highlanders
Feather Bonnet
In silver a thistle-wreath; within the wreath the figure of St. Andrew with Cross, with a scroll on the lower bend of the wreath inscribed *Cameron.*

White F.S. Helmet, Glengarry cap and Tam o' Shanter bonnet
As for feather bonnet.

The Royal Ulster Rifles
Busby
In black-metal the Harp and crown; below the Harp a scroll inscribed *Quis separabit.* On a round boss, the Sphinx over *Egypt*; below the Sphinx a bugle with strings.

F.S. Helmet
A badge as for busby.

Forage-cap
A green-cord boss with a Harp and crown in silver across which is a scroll inscribed *Royal Ulster Rifles.*

The Royal Irish Fusiliers (Princess Victoria's)
Full-dress Head-dress
A grenade in gilt or gilding-metal. In silver, on the ball, the eagle with a wreath of laurel. Below the eagle a small tablet inscribed with the figure *8.*

White F.S. Helmet and Forage-cap
1st badge: the Coronet of H.R.H. the Princess Victoria. 2nd badge: a gilt or gilding-metal grenade with the Harp surmounted by the plumes and coronet of the Prince of Wales in silver on the ball. The 1st badge is worn over the 2nd.

Service-dress cap
As for forage-cap, but 2nd badge only in bronze.

The Argyll and Sutherland Highlanders (Princess Louise's)
Feather Bonnet
In silver a thistle-wreath; within the wreath a circlet inscribed *Argyll and Sutherland.* Within the circlet the double cypher of H.R.H. the Princess Louise. To the left of the cypher the Boar's Head; to the right the Cat. Above the cypher, and on the circlet, the coronet of the Princess.

White F.S. Helmet, Glengarry cap and Tam o' Shanter bonnet
As for feather bonnet.

The Rifle Brigade (Prince Consort's Own)
Busby
In black metal a bugle; on the boss, a crown.

White F.S. Helmet and Forage cap
In silver a wreath of laurel intertwined with a scroll bearing some of the battle honours of the regiment. Within the wreath a Maltese cross with a lion between each division. On the divisions the other battle honours of the regiment. On the centre of the cross a circlet inscribed *The Rifle Brigade*; within the circlet a bugle with strings surmounted by a crown. Above the cross a crown on a tablet inscribed *Waterloo*; below the cross two scrolls inscribed *France and Flanders, 1914–18, Macedonia, 1915–18.* On the lower part of the wreath a scroll inscribed *Prince Consort's Own.*

The following are the authorised head-dress badges contained in *Pamphlet No. 5* of the *Dress Regulations for Officers of the Army, 1973.*

The Royal Scots (The Royal Regiment)
The Star of the Order of the Thistle in silver-plate; on the Star a raised circle inscribed with the motto of the Order *Nemo me impune lacessit* in gilt or gilding-metal; within the circle on a ground of green-enamel, the thistle in gilt or gilding-metal.

The Queen's Regiment
The Dragon in rhodium-plate, surmounted by the Prince of Wales's Plume and coronet also in rhodium-plate, surrounded by the Garter inscribed *Honi soit qui mal y pense* in hard gold and, below, a scroll inscribed *Queen's* also in hard gold.

The King's Own Royal Border Regiment
The Lion of England in silver within a laurel-wreath ensigned with the crown all in gold.

The Royal Regiment of Fusiliers
Forage-cap: the grenade fired in gold-embroidery, the case ensigned with an embroidered crown in colour. On the case of the grenade St. George and the Dragon within a wreath of laurel both in silver-plate.
The beret: the grenade and crown in anodised gilt. St. George and the Dragon within a wreath of laurel both in silver-plate.

The King's Regiment
The White Horse of Hanover superimposed on a fleur-de-lys. Below, a scroll inscribed *King's* in old English lettering. The White Horse in silver-plate and the remainder in gilt.

The Royal Anglian Regiment
Upon a rhodium star of eight points the Castle and Key of Gibraltar; underneath, a scroll inscribed *Royal Anglian* in gold-plate.

The Devonshire and Dorset Regiment
In front of the Castle of Exeter, ensigned with a scroll inscribed *Semper fidelis*, the Sphinx upon a plinth inscribed *Marabout;* beneath the whole a scroll inscribed *Primus in Indis*. The Castle in silver, remainder gold.

The Light Infantry
A bugle-horn stringed in silver-plate.

The Prince of Wales's Own Regiment of Yorkshire
Upon a mount inscribed *Yorkshire* a Horse Courant. All in silver.

The Green Howards (Alexandra, Princess of Wales's Own Yorkshire Regiment)
The Cypher of H.R.H. Alexandra, Princess of Wales, interlaced with the Dannebrog inscribed with the date *1875*; the Roman numerals *XIX* below; the whole surmounted by the Coronet of the Princess; below, a scroll inscribed *The Green Howards*. In silver-plate.

The Royal Highland Fusiliers (Princess Margaret's Own Glasgow and Ayrshire Regiment)
A grenade fired in gold, thereon the monogram *HLI* surmounted by the crown. In silver and gilt.
No. 2 Dress: as above but in bronze.

The Cheshire Regiment
In silver-plate a faceted eight-pointed star. On the star a circle in gilt or gilding-metal inscribed *The Cheshire Regiment* surrounding the acorn with oak-leaves, filled below with green-enamel.

The Royal Welch Fusiliers
A grenade in gold-embroidery, on the case a dragon in silver-plate.
S.D. Cap: in bronze a grenade; on the ball a circle inscribed *Royal Welch Fusiliers*; within the circle the Prince of Wales's plumes and coronet.

The Royal Regiment of Wales
The plumes of the Prince of Wales; below, the motto inscribed *Ich Dien*. In silver embroidery.
No. 2 Dress: as above but in silver-plate.

The King's Own Scottish Borderers
Bonnet: in silver-plate a thistle-wreath; within the wreath a circle pierced with the designation *King's Own Scottish Borderers*; above the circle a scroll surmounted by the Royal Crest. The scroll pierced with the motto *In veritate religionis confido*. Over the circle the Cross of St. Andrew in burnished silver-plate. On the Cross, the Castle of Edinburgh. On the wreath, at the bottom of the circle, a scroll with the motto in relief *Nisi Dominus frustra*.

The Royal Irish Rangers
A harp in silver rhodium-plate ensigned with a gilt crown; beneath, a gilt scroll inscribed *Royal Irish Rangers*.

The Gloucestershire Regiment
No. 1 Dress: in gold-embroidery a sphinx upon a plinth inscribed *Egypt* above two sprays of laurel; underneath, a scroll inscribed *Gloucestershire*.
Back-badge: the sphinx upon a plinth inscribed *Egypt* with a wreath around the sphinx.
No. 2 Dress: as above but in bronze.

The Worcestershire and Sherwood Foresters Regiment
A Maltese cross charged with the Garter in gold, encircling a stag in silver; underneath, a plinth inscribed *Firm* in gold. The whole upon an elongated star of eight points in silver.

The Queen's Lancashire Regiment
The Rose of Lancaster ensigned with the Crown, the whole upon an oval annulet inscribed *The Queen's Lancashire Regiment*; underneath a scroll inscribed *Loyally I Serve*. All in gold except the Rose which is in red-enamel with seeds and petals fimbriated gold.

The Duke of Wellington's Regiment (West Riding)
In silver-plate the Duke of Wellington's crest with the motto on a scroll below *Virtutis fortuna comes*. A gilt or gilding-metal scroll below inscribed *The West Riding*.

The Royal Hampshire Regiment
An eight-pointed silver-plated star on the centre of which the Garter with motto, on a ground of blue-enamel, surmounted by a crown in gilt which displaces the uppermost point of the star. Within the Garter the Hampshire Rose in gilt and red-enamel. On the lower part of the star a scroll inscribed *Royal Hampshire* on a ground of blue-enamel (Fig. 1966).
No. 2 Dress: as above but in bronze (Fig. 1967).

The Staffordshire Regiment (The Prince of Wales's)
The Stafford Knot ensigned with the plumes of the Prince of Wales; the feathers and scrolls, inscribed *Ich Dien*, in silver, remainder in gold.

The Black Watch (Royal Highland Regiment)
In silver-plate, diamond-cut, the Star of the Order of the Thistle; in gilt or gilding-metal, on the Star, a thistle-wreath. Within the wreath, in gilt or gilding-metal, an oval surmounted by a crown. The oval inscribed *Nemo me impune lacessit*. Within the oval on a recessed seeded-ground St. Andrew and Cross in silver-plate. Below the wreath, the Sphinx in gilt or gilding-metal.

The Duke of Edinburgh's Royal Regiment (Berkshire and Wiltshire)
The China dragon, in rhodium, within two coils of rope surmounted by a ducal coronet in hard gold superimposed on a cross patée in lined rhodium with burnished edges. On a red-cloth backing.

Queen's Own Highlanders (Seaforth and Camerons)
A thistle ensigned with the crown within the attires of a stag's head caboshed. Underneath, a scroll inscribed *Cuidich'n Righ*. All in silver (Fig. 1968).

The Gordon Highlanders
In silver-plate the Crest of the Marquis of Huntly within an ivy-wreath. On the bottom of the wreath the motto *Bydand*.

The Argyll and Sutherland Highlanders (Princess Louise's)
In silver-plate a thistle-wreath; within the wreath a circle inscribed *Argyll and Sutherland*; within the circle the double cypher of H.R.H. the Princess Louise. To the left of the cypher the Boar's Head, to the right, the Cat. Above the cypher and on the circle the Coronet of the Princess.

The Royal Green Jackets
A Maltese cross inscribed with selected battle honours. Thereon a bugle-horn stringed and encircled with the title of the regiment. All within a wreath of laurel ensigned with the crown resting upon a plinth inscribed *Peninsula*. Across the tie a naval crown ensigned with a scroll inscribed *Copenhagen 2nd April 1801*. All in silver.

CHAPTER 5

Infantry of the Line: Other-ranks

Throughout this chapter regiments will be referred to by their new titles as set out in the Army Order of 1920.

In some instances there was no change from the existing designation and in many others it was confined to the removal of brackets or the re-arrangement of the sequence of wording. One major change was in the title of Alexandra, Princess of Wales's Own (Yorkshire Regiment) which now became The Green Howards with its former title added in brackets.

These alterations in title had little effect on the design of cap-badges and the majority remained unchanged until amalgamations took place except that, in 1952, those which had the Imperial crown in their design replaced it with the St. Edward's crown on the accession of Queen Elizabeth II.

Below are enumerated those changes which occurred between 1920 and 1970, some of which entailed changes in design: others, like the disbandments, resulted simply in obsolescence.

1920 The spelling of 'Welsh' altered to 'Welch' in The Royal Welch Fusiliers and the Welch Regiment (A.O. 56/1920).

1921 An alteration to the order of 1920:
The King's Royal Rifles to be The King's Royal Rifle Corps (A.O. 69/1921).
The Royal West Kent Regiment (Queen's Own) to be The Queen's Own Royal West Kent Regiment (A.O. 183/1921).

1922 The following Irish Regiments were disbanded (A.O. 78/1922):
The Royal Irish Regiment
The Connaught Rangers
The Prince of Wales's Leinster Regiment (Royal Canadians)
The Royal Munster Fusiliers
The Royal Dublin Fusuliers

1923 The Highland Light Infantry assumed the additional title of (City of Glasgow Regiment) (A.O. 221/1923).
The Manchester Regiment changed its badge from the Arms of the City of Manchester to a Fleur-de-lys.

1934 The Black Watch (Royal Highlanders) became The Black Watch (Royal Highland Regiment) (A.O. 256/1934).

1935 In honour of the Silver Jubilee of H.M. King George V the following infantry regiments received the 'Royal' designation and their titles altered as follows (A.O. 110/1935):
The Buffs (Royal East Kent Regiment)

The Royal Northumberland Fusiliers
The Royal Norfolk Regiment
The East Yorkshire Regiment (The Duke of York's Own)

1938 The Prince of Wales's Volunteers (South Lancashire) to be The South Lancashire Regiment (The Prince of Wales's Volunteers) (A.O. 244/1938).

1942 17th January: The Lowland Regiment and The Highland Regiment formed.

1946 The following regiments were awarded the 'Royal' designation for their services during the Second World War and their titles changed accordingly (A.O. 167/1946):
The Royal Lincolnshire Regiment
The Royal Leicestershire Regiment
The Royal Hampshire Regiment

1949 The Lowland Regiment and The Highland Regiment disbanded (A.O. 150/1949).

1951 Change of title of The Dorsetshire Regiment to The Dorset Regiment.

1952 Accession of Queen Elizabeth II. All badges which bore the Imperial crown altered to St. Edward's crown.

1958 Following the publication of the White Paper on Defence, in July 1957, the whole of the infantry was grouped into fourteen regional brigades: all regiments in a brigade to wear a common cap-badge. The brigades were:
Lowland, Home Counties, Lancastrian, Fusilier, Midland (afterwards Forester), East Anglian, Wessex, Light Infantry, Yorkshire, Mercian, Welsh, North Irish, Highland and Green Jackets.
1st April: The Oxfordshire and Buckinghamshire Light Infantry title changed to 1st Green Jackets (43rd and 52nd).
25th April: The West Yorkshire Regiment (The Prince of Wales's Own) and The East Yorkshire Regiment (The Duke of York's Own) amalgamated to form The Prince of Wales's Own Regiment of Yorkshire.
17th May: The Devonshire Regiment and The Dorset Regiment amalgamated to form The Devonshire and Dorset Regiment.
2nd June: The Bedfordshire and Hertfordshire Regiment and The Essex Regiment amalgamated to form 3rd East Anglian Regiment (16th/44th Foot).
1st July: The East Lancashire Regiment and The South Lancashire Regiment (The Prince of Wales's Volunteers) amalgamated to form The Lancashire Regiment (Prince of Wales's Volunteers).
1st September: The King's Regiment (Liverpool) and The Manchester Regiment amalgamated to form The King's Regiment (Manchester and Liverpool).
7th November: Title of The King's Royal Rifle Corps changed to 2nd Green Jackets (The King's Royal Rifle Corps).
7th November: Title of The Rifle Brigade (Prince Consort's Own) changed to 3rd Green Jackets (The Rifle Brigade).

1959 20th January: The Royal Scots Fusiliers and The Highland Light Infantry (City of Glasgow Regiment) amalgamated to form The Royal Highland Fusiliers (Princess Margaret's Own Glasgow and Ayrshire Regiment).
31st January: The South Staffordshire Regiment and The North Staffordshire Regiment (The Prince of Wales's) amalgamated to form The Staffordshire Regiment (The Prince of Wales's).
9th June: The Royal Berkshire Regiment (Princess Charlotte of Wales's) and The Wiltshire Regiment (Duke of Edinburgh's) amalgamated to form The Duke of Edinburgh's Royal Regiment (Berkshire and Wiltshire).

29th August: The Royal Norfolk Regiment and The Suffolk Regiment amalgamated to form 1st East Anglian Regiment (Royal Norfolk and Suffolk).
1st October: The King's Own Royal Regiment (Lancaster) and The Border Regiment amalgamated to form The King's Own Royal Border Regiment.
6th October: The Somerset Light Infantry (Prince Albert's) and The Duke of Cornwall's Light Infantry amalgamated to form the Somerset and Cornwall Light Infantry.
14th October: The Queen's Royal Regiment (West Surrey) and The East Surrey Regiment amalgamated to form The Queen's Royal Surrey Regiment.

1960 1st June: The Royal Lincolnshire Regiment and The Northamptonshire Regiment amalgamated to form 2nd East Anglian Regiment (Duchess of Gloucester's Own Royal Lincolnshire and Northamptonshire).

1961 7th February: Seaforth Highlanders (Ross-shire Buffs, The Duke of Albany's) and The Queen's Own Cameron Highlanders amalgamated to form Queen's Own Highlanders (Seaforth and Camerons).
1st March: The Buffs (Royal East Kent Regiment) and The Queen's Own Royal West Kent Regiment amalgamated to form The Queen's Own Buffs, Royal Kent Regiment.

1963 1st May: The Forester Brigade dispersed. The Royal Leicestershire Regiment being posted to the East Anglian Brigade; The Sherwood Foresters, to the Mercian Brigade; and The Royal Warwickshire Regiment to the Fusilier Brigade with change of title to The Royal Warwickshire Fusiliers.

1964 1st September: The Royal Anglian Regiment formed from the 1st, 2nd and 3rd East Anglian Regiments and The Royal Leicestershire Regiment. Titles on formation were:
1st (Norfolk and Suffolk) Battalion
2nd (Duchess of Gloucester's Own Lincolnshire and Northamptonshire) Battalion
3rd (16th/44th Foot) Battalion
4th (Leicestershire) Battalion

1966 1st January: The Royal Green Jackets formed from the Green Jackets Brigade. Titles on formation were:
1st Bn. The Royal Green Jackets (43rd and 52nd)
2nd Bn. The Royal Green Jackets (The King's Royal Rifle Corps)
3rd Bn. The Royal Green Jackets (The Rifle Brigade)
31st December: The Queen's Regiment formed from the Home Counties Brigade:
1st Bn. formerly The Queen's Royal Surrey Regiment
2nd Bn. formerly The Queen's Own Buffs, Royal Kent Regiment
3rd Bn. formerly The Royal Sussex Regiment
4th Bn. formerly The Middlesex Regiment (Duke of Cambridge's Own)

1968 23rd April: The Royal Regiment of Fusiliers formed from the Fusilier Brigade:
1st Bn. formerly The Royal Northumberland Fusiliers
2nd Bn. formerly The Royal Warwickshire Fusiliers
3rd Bn. formerly The Royal Fusiliers (City of London Regiment)
4th Bn. formerly The Lancashire Fusiliers
14th May: The Cameronians (Scottish Rifles) disbanded.
1st July: The Royal Irish Rangers (27th (Inniskilling), 83rd and 87th) formed from the regiments of the North Irish Brigade: The Royal Inniskilling Fusiliers, The Royal Ulster Rifles and The Royal Irish Fusiliers (Princess Victoria's).

1st July: The sub-titles omitted from the designations of The Queen's Regiment, The King's Regiment, The Royal Anglian Regiment and The Royal Green Jackets.
1st July: The Infantry re-organized into five divisions:
The Scottish Division
The Queen's Division
The King's Division
The Prince of Wales's Division
The Light Division
Brigade head-dress badges to be replaced by individual regimental badges.
10th July: The Light Infantry formed from the regiments of the Light Infantry Brigade:
1st Bn. formerly The Somerset and Cornwall Light Infantry
2nd Bn. formerly The King's Own Yorkshire Light Infantry
3rd Bn. formerly The King's Shropshire Light Infantry
4th Bn. formerly The Durham Light Infantry.
14th December: The York and Lancaster Regiment disbanded.

1969 11th June: The South Wales Borderers and The Welch Regiment amalgamated to form The Royal Regiment of Wales.

1970 28th February: The Worcestershire Regiment and The Sherwood Foresters (Nottinghamshire and Derbyshire Regiment) amalgamated to form The Worcestershire and Sherwood Foresters Regiment (29th/45th Foot).
25th March: The Lancashire Regiment (Prince of Wales's Volunteers) and The Loyal Regiment (North Lancashire) amalgamated to form The Queen's Lancashire Regiment.

THE BADGES

Details of the badges follow: those which appeared in Volume 1 carry their original figure-numbers and those which appear now, for the first time, have new figure-numbers.

Where the date of the sealed pattern is known this information is added.

The Royal Scots (The Royal Regiment)

The Star of the Order of the Thistle in white-metal. In the centre St. Andrew and Cross above a scroll inscribed *The Royal Scots* in gilding-metal with a voided centre to show a red-cloth backing (Fig. 589). Also anodised.

The Queen's Royal Regiment (West Surrey)

(1) The Paschal Lamb in gilding-metal above a scroll inscribed *The Queen's* in white-metal. In this pattern the flag is swallowed-tailed (Fig. 590).
(2) The Paschal Lamb standing on an heraldic-torse. In gilding-metal. In this pattern the flag is square-ended (Fig. 1969). Sealed 5th June 1924.
(3) A smaller version of (2) for wear on the beret. In gilding-metal, sealed 10th June 1949; in gold-anodised, sealed 18th August 1961 (Fig. 1970).

The Buffs (East Kent Regiment)

Royal East Kent Regiment after 1935

The Dragon above a scroll inscribed *The Buffs*. Sealed 14th July 1896. All in gilding-metal (Fig. 591). Also anodised, sealed 14th January 1964.

The King's Own Royal Regiment (Lancaster)

(1) The Lion of England on a bar inscribed *The King's Own.* All in gilding-metal (Fig. 592). Pattern sealed 16th March 1897.

(2) The Lion of England on a solid tablet inscribed *The King's Own.* In gold-anodised (Fig. 1971). Sealed 17th October 1954.

The Northumberland Fusiliers

Royal Northumberland Fusiliers after 1935

(1) A fused grenade. On the ball a circlet inscribed *Northumberland Fusiliers.* In the centre St. George and the Dragon. All in gilding-metal (Fig. 593).

(2) A fused grenade. On the ball a circlet inscribed *Quo fata Vocant.* In the centre St. George and the Dragon. Sealed 3rd May 1937. The grenade in gilding-metal, remainder in white-metal (Fig. 1972).

The Royal Warwickshire Regiment

Royal Warwickshire Fusiliers after 1963

The Antelope ducally chained and gorged standing on an heraldic-torse. Below, a wavy scroll inscribed *Royal Warwickshire.* Sealed 28th July 1896. The Antelope in white-metal, title-scroll in gilding-metal (Fig. 594).

The Royal Fusiliers (City of London Regiment)

(1) A fused grenade. On the ball the Garter proper surmounted by an Imperial crown. In the centre a Rose. Sealed 28th May 1902. All in gilding-metal (Fig. 597).

(2) As (1) but with St. Edward's crown. In gilding-metal, sealed 6th May 1955. Also gold-anodised (Fig. 1973).

The King's Regiment (Liverpool)

(1) The White Horse of Hanover standing on ground in white-metal. Below, a scroll inscribed *The King's* in gilding-metal (Fig. 598).

(2) The White Horse of Hanover standing on an heraldic-torse in white metal. Below, a scroll inscribed *King's* in old English lettering in gilding-metal. Sealed 20th January 1927 (Fig. 1974).

(3) As (2) in same metals but smaller size for the beret, sealed 13th April 1950. Also gold- and silver-anodised, sealed 22nd November 1971 (Fig. 1975).

The Norfolk Regiment

Royal Norfolk Regiment after 1935

(1) The figure of Britannia holding a sprig of olive in her right hand, a trident in her left hand resting against her left shoulder; below her left arm an oval shield bearing the Great Union. The whole enclosed by a laurel-wreath. All in white-metal. Below, a scroll inscribed *The Norfolk Regt.* in gilding-metal (Fig. 599).

(2) The figure of Britannia only, as above. Sealed 21st April 1937. In gilding-metal (Fig. 1976).

(3) As (2), but smaller size for wear on the beret. In gilding-metal, sealed 10th January 1950 (Fig. 1977). Also anodised, sealed 21st April 1964.

The Lincolnshire Regiment

Royal Lincolnshire Regiment after 1946

(1) The Sphinx superscribed *Egypt*, in old English characters, in white-metal. Below, a scroll inscribed *Lincolnshire* in gilding-metal (Fig. 600).

(2) The Sphinx superscribed *Egypt*, in roman characters, in white-metal. Below, a scroll inscribed *Royal Lincolnshire Regiment* in gilding-metal, sealed 17th March 1948 (Fig. 1978). Also anodised, same size, sealed 11th March 1965.

The Devonshire Regiment

(1) An eight-pointed star the topmost point displaced by an Imperial crown. On this a circlet inscribed *The Devonshire Regiment*. In a voided centre the Castle of Exeter. Sealed 19th August 1903. Star and Castle in white-metal, remainder in gilding-metal (Fig. 602).

(2) As above but with St. Edward's crown and the Castle on a solid centre. Sealed 10th October 1955. Also in gold- and silver-anodised (Fig. 1979).

The Suffolk Regiment

(1) The Castle and Key of Gibraltar, with a scroll above inscribed *Gibraltar*, within a circlet inscribed *Montis Insignia Calpe* surmounted by an Imperial crown, the whole within a wreath of oak. All in white-metal. Below, a scroll inscribed *The Suffolk Regt* in gilding-metal. Sealed 29th October 1901 (Fig. 605).

(2) As above but with St. Edward's crown, sealed 8th November 1955 (made but never issued). Also anodised.

The Somerset Light Infantry (Prince Albert's)

(1) A bugle surmounted by a mural crown and above this a scroll inscribed *Jellalabad*. Within the strings of the bugle the letters *PA*. In white-metal (Fig. 607).

(2) Similar design to above but smaller. In white-metal (Fig. 1981).

The West Yorkshire Regiment (The Prince of Wales's Own)

The White Horse of Hanover on ground in white-metal. Below, a scroll inscribed *West Yorkshire* in gilding-metal. Sealed 1st December 1896 (Fig. 608). Also anodised, same size.

The East Yorkshire Regiment

An eight-pointed star. On this a laurel-wreath and within it a Rose. Below the star a scroll inscribed *East Yorkshire*. Sealed 22nd August 1898. The Rose in white-metal, remainder in gilding-metal (Fig. 609).

The Bedfordshire and Hertfordshire Regiment

(1) A Maltese cross superimposed on an eight-pointed star. On this the Garter proper and in the centre a Hart crossing a ford. Below, a scroll inscribed *Bedfordshire*. Star and scroll in gilding-metal, remainder in white-metal (Fig. 610).

(2) As above but scroll inscribed *Bedfordshire & Hertfordshire* set below bottom-point of the star. Pattern sealed in 1924. All in white-metal (Fig. 611).

The Leicestershire Regiment

Royal Leicestershire Regiment after 1946

(1) The Royal Tiger superscribed *Hindoostan* resting on a scroll inscribed *Leicestershire*.

589 590 1969 1970

591 592 1971 593

1972 594 597 1973

598 1974 1975 599

1976 1977 600 1978

The Tiger in gilding-metal, remainder in white-metal. Sealed 15th June 1897 (Fig. 612).

(2) As (1) but the scroll altered to read *Royal Leicestershire*. In same metals, sealed 12th June 1951 (Fig. 1982).

(3) As (2) but smaller size for wear on the beret. In the same metals, also anodised, sealed 11th July 1968 (Fig. 1983).

The Green Howards (Alexandra, Princess of Wales's Own Yorkshire Regiment).

(1) The letter *A* and Dannebrog surmounted by a coronet and in these the date *1875* and *Alexandra* all resting on a tablet inscribed *Yorkshire*. Below, a scroll inscribed *The Princess of Wales's Own Regt*. Below the word *of* is a Rose. Sealed 12th October 1903. All in white-metal (Fig. 616).

(2) As (1) but the letter *A* is not voided and is surmounted by an Imperial crown. In white-metal (Fig. 617).

(3) The letter *A* and Dannebrog, all voided, surmounted by a coronet and on these the date *1875*. Below, a scroll inscribed *The Green Howards*. In white-metal, sealed 27th July 1950 (Fig. 1984). Also anodised, same size.

(4) The letter *A* and Dannebrog, partly voided, surmounted by a coronet and on these the date *1875*, all resting on the roman numerals *XIX*. Below, a scroll inscribed *The Green Howards*. In white-metal (Fig. 1985). Also anodised, same size.

The Lancashire Fusiliers

A fused grenade. On the ball a laurel-wreath and within this the Sphinx superscribed *Egypt*. In gilding-metal. Below, a scroll inscribed *The Lancashire Fusiliers* in white-metal. Sealed 14th September 1897 (Fig. 618).

The Royal Scots Fusiliers

(1) A fused grenade. On the ball the Royal Arms with both the Royal Crest and the lion with Imperial crowns. In gilding-metal (Fig. 620). Also gold-anodised.

(2) As (1) but with the Royal Crest and the lion with St. Edward's crown. In gilding-metal (Fig. 1986). Also anodised, same size, sealed 11th July 1957.

The Cheshire Regiment

On an eight-pointed star, in white-metal, a gilding-metal circlet inscribed *The Cheshire Regiment* with, in a voided centre, an acorn with oak-leaves (Fig. 1987). Also anodised, same size, sealed 26th May 1966.

The Royal Welch Fusiliers

A fused grenade. On the ball a circlet inscribed *Royal Welch Fusiliers*. In the centre the Prince of Wales's plumes, coronet and motto. The grenade and coronet in gilding-metal, remainder in white-metal (Fig. 623). Also anodised, same size, sealed 27th April 1962.

The South Wales Borderers

An unbroken wreath of Immortelles on the base of which the letters *SWB*. In the centre the Sphinx superscribed *Egypt*. Sealed 8th September 1896. The wreath in gilding-metal, remainder in white-metal (Fig. 625). Also anodised, sealed 8th April 1964.

602 1979 605 607

1981 608 609 610

611 612 1982 1983

616 617 1984 1985

618 620 1986 1987

The King's Own Scottish Borderers

(1) A circlet inscribed *King's Own Scottish Borderers*, thereon the Cross of St. Andrew and, within the circlet, the Castle of Edinburgh with three turrets, a flag flying to the left of each; above the circlet a scroll inscribed *In veritate religionis confido* and below the circlet another scroll inscribed *Nisi Dominus frustra*. Outside the circlet a wreath of thistles, the whole ensigned with the Royal Crest with the Imperial crown. In white-metal (Fig. 629).

(2) As above but with the St. Edward's crown in the Royal Crest. Sealed 27th September 1955 (Fig. 1988). Also in silver-anodised.

The Cameronians (Scottish Rifles)

(1) A mullet above a bugle stringed and enclosed by a spray of thistles. Sealed 12th September 1906. In white-metal (Fig. 631). Also anodised, same size.

(2) A larger version of the above worn by Sergeants. In white-metal (Fig. 1989).

The Royal Inniskilling Fusiliers

(1) A fused grenade. On the ball the Castle of Inniskilling with St. George's flag flying to the left from the central turret. Below, a scroll inscribed *Inniskilling*. Grenade and flames in gilding-metal, remainder in white-metal, sealed 30th June 1921 (Fig. 632). Also found with the flag flying to the right. An anodised version with the flag flying to the right was sealed 27th April 1967.

(2) The Castle of Inniskilling with St. George's flag flying to the right from the central turret. Above, a scroll inscribed *Inniskilling*. In white-metal (Fig. 1990).

The Gloucestershire Regiment

(1) The Sphinx superscribed *Egypt* above two sprays of laurel. Below, a scroll inscribed *Gloucestershire*. Sealed 14th July 1896. In white-metal (Fig. 634). Also anodised, same size.

(2) Back-badge: the Sphinx superscribed *Egypt* within a complete laurel wreath. In gilding-metal (Fig. 635). Also anodised, same size, sealed 20th March 1967.

The Worcestershire Regiment

(1) An eight-pointed star. On this the Garter proper and within this the Lion of England. At the base of the star a small tablet inscribed *Firm*. Below, a scroll inscribed *Worcestershire*. In gilding-metal (Fig. 636).

(2) An elongated eight-pointed star. On this the Garter proper and within this the Lion of England standing on a tablet inscribed *Firm*. The Garter in gilding-metal, remainder in white-metal (Fig. 1991). Also anodised, same size.

The East Lancashire Regiment

(1) The Sphinx superscribed *Egypt* and below this the Rose; all within a laurel-wreath surmounted by an Imperial crown. Resting on the base of the wreath a scroll inscribed *East Lancashire*. Sealed 8th November 1930. The Rose in gilding-metal, remainder in white-metal (Fig. 638).

(2) As above but with St. Edward's crown, sealed 9th August 1954 (Fig. 1992). Also anodised, same size, sealed 26th May 1966.

KINGS
INNISKILLING
EGYPT
GLOUCESTERSHIRE
WORCESTERSHIRE
EAST SURREY
CORNWALL
623
625
629
1988
631
1989
632
1990
634
635
636
1991
638
1992
640
1993
1994
1995
641
642
645

The East Surrey Regiment

(1) An eight-pointed star, the topmost point displaced by an Imperial crown which rests on a shield bearing the Arms of Guildford. Below, a scroll inscribed *East Surrey*. Sealed 21st January 1902. Crown, shield and scroll in gilding-metal, remainder in white-metal (Fig. 640).

(2) As above, but smaller size for wear on the beret. Sealed 27th September 1951 (Fig. 1993).

(3) As (1) but with St. Edward's crown. Sealed in metal, 6th December 1954. Also anodised (Fig. 1994).

(4) As (2) but with St. Edward's crown (Fig. 1995).

The Duke of Cornwall's Light Infantry

A bugle with strings. Resting on each end of the bugle a scroll inscribed *Cornwall*. Above the scroll a coronet. Sealed 7th June 1891. In white-metal (Fig. 641). Also anodised, sealed 4th February 1964.

The Duke of Wellington's Regiment (West Riding)

The crest and motto of the Duke of Wellington above a scroll inscribed *The West Riding*. The crest and motto in white-metal, remainder in gilding-metal. Sealed 9th January 1897. (Fig. 642). Also anodised, same size, sealed 7th April 1970.

The Border Regiment

(1) An eight-pointed star, the topmost point displaced by an Imperial crown. On the star a cross, similar to that of the Order of the Bath, on the four arms of which are inscribed battle honours. The cross is superimposed on a laurel-wreath. In the centre of the cross a circlet inscribed *Arroyo dos Molinos 1811* and in the centre a Dragon superscribed *China* on a ground of one-third white (above) and two-thirds red (below). On the lower points of the star a scroll inscribed *The Border Regt.* Sealed 5th July 1905. In white-metal except the lower two-thirds of the centre which is red cloth (Fig. 645).

(2) As above but with St. Edward's crown. Sealed 6th March 1956. (Fig. 1996). Also anodised, same size.

The Royal Sussex Regiment

The Star of the Order of the Garter over the Roussillon plume with a scroll below inscribed *The Royal Sussex Regt.* Sealed 23rd August 1898. The scroll in gilding-metal, remainder in white-metal (Fig. 646). Also anodised, sealed 4th May 1954.

The Hampshire Regiment

Royal Hampshire Regiment after 1946

(1) The Hampshire Rose, above which the Royal Tiger standing on an heraldic-torse, the whole enclosed by a laurel-wreath. On the base of the wreath a scroll inscribed *Hampshire*. The Rose and scroll in gilding-metal, remainder in white-metal (Fig. 647).

(2) The Hampshire Rose, above which the Royal Tiger standing on an heraldic-torse and surmounted by an Imperial crown, surrounded by a laurel-wreath. On the base of the wreath a scroll inscribed *Royal Hampshire*. The Rose and scroll in gilding-metal, remainder in white-metal. Sealed 26th January 1949 (Fig. 1997).

(3) As (2) but with St. Edward's crown (Fig. 1998). Also anodised, same size, sealed 12th May 1971.

The South Staffordshire Regiment

(1) The Stafford Knot surmounted by an Imperial crown. Below the Knot a scroll inscribed *South Staffordshire*. Sealed 12th November 1901. The scroll in gilding-metal, remainder in white-metal (Fig. 649).

(2) As above but with St. Edward's crown and with a backing of brown holland. Sealed 18th October 1955 (Fig. 1999). Also anodised, sealed 21st January 1966.

The Dorsetshire Regiment

Dorset Regiment after 1951

(1) The Castle and Key of Gibraltar. Above, the Sphinx superscribed *Marabout*. Below the Castle, a scroll inscribed *Primus in Indis*. A laurel-wreath encloses the Castle and motto and is continued below the Castle by a scroll inscribed *Dorsetshire*. Sealed 18th October 1901. Wreath and title-scroll in gilding-metal, remainder in white-metal (Fig. 651).

(2) As above but wording on title-scroll altered to read *Dorset*. Sealed 4th October 1956. (Fig. 2000). Also anodised.

The Prince of Wales's Volunteers (South Lancashire)

South Lancashire Regiment (The Prince of Wales's Volunteers) after 1938

(1) The Prince of Wales's plumes, coronet and motto. Below, the Sphinx superscribed *Egypt*. Above the plumes a scroll inscribed *South Lancashire* and below the Sphinx a scroll inscribed *Prince of Wales's Vols*. Branches of laurel connect the ends of the scrolls. The plumes, motto and Sphinx over *Egypt* in white-metal, remainder in gilding-metal. (Fig. 652). Also anodised sealed 17th October 1963.

(2) As above, but smaller for wear on the beret. Sealed in metal, 24th August 1950 (Fig. 2001). Also anodised, sealed 22nd February 1965.

The Welch Regiment

The Prince of Wales's plumes, coronet and motto. Below, a scroll inscribed *The Welch*. Sealed 11th May 1920. The plumes and motto in white-metal, remainder in gilding-metal (Fig. 654). Also anodised, same size, sealed 24th August 1964.

The Black Watch (Royal Highlanders)

The Black Watch (Royal Highland Regiment) after 1934

(1) The Star of the Order of the Thistle. On the Star a thistle-wreath. Within the wreath an oval inscribed *Nemo me impune lacessit* surmounted by an Imperial crown. Within the oval St. Andrew and Cross. Below the wreath the Sphinx. Across the top of the wreath scrolls inscribed *The Royal Highlanders*; at the base, on either side of the Sphinx, scrolls inscribed *Black Watch*. All in white-metal (Fig. 657).

(2) General design as above but with the scrolls at top and bottom extended to edge of star. Worn by Sergeants. St. Andrew and Cross, title-scrolls and Star in white-metal, remainder in gilding-metal (Fig. 656).

(3) As (1) but omitting the title-scrolls. All in white-metal (Fig. 2002). Sealed 4th March 1938.

(4) As (2) but omitting the title-scrolls. St. Andrew and Cross in white-metal, remainder in gilding-metal (Fig. 2003).

(5) As (3) but with St. Edward's crown. Sealed 23rd January 1956 (Fig. 2004). Also anodised, same size.
(6) As (4) but with St. Edward's crown.

The Oxfordshire and Buckinghamshire Light Infantry
(1) A bugle-horn with strings. Sealed 12th October 1898. In white-metal (Fig. 658).
(2) As above but smaller for wear on the beret. In white-metal, sealed 1st April 1950 (Fig. 2005). Also anodised, same size, sealed 28th August 1964.

The Essex Regiment
The Castle and Key of Gibraltar. Above the Castle the Sphinx superscribed *Egypt*. The whole, except the Sphinx, enclosed in a wreath of oak. On the base of the wreath a scroll inscribed *The Essex Regt.* The Sphinx and title-scroll in white-metal, remainder in gilding-metal (Fig. 660). Also anodised, same size, sealed 1st February 1966.

The Sherwood Foresters (Nottinghamshire and Derbyshire Regiment)
(1) A Maltese cross surmounted by an Imperial crown. In the centre of the cross a wreath of oak and, within the wreath, a stag lodged. On the left arm of the cross and across the left branch of the wreath a half-scroll inscribed *Sherwood*, and on the right arm of the cross and across the right branch of the wreath a half-scroll inscribed *Foresters*. Below the cross a scroll inscribed *Notts & Derby*. Sealed 14th December 1903. Title-scroll in gliding-metal, remainder in white-metal (Fig. 662).
(2) As above but with St. Edward's crown. Sealed 1st February 1955 (Fig. 2006). Also anodised, same size.

The Loyal Regiment (North Lancashire)
(1) The Royal Crest, with Imperial crown, above the Rose of Lancaster. Below the Rose a scroll inscribed *Loyal North Lancashire*. The Royal Crest in white-metal, remainder in gilding-metal (Fig. 664).
(2) The Royal Crest, with Imperial crown, above the Rose of Lancaster. Below the Rose a scroll inscribed *The Loyal Regiment*. The Royal Crest in white-metal, remainder in gilding-metal. Sealed 16th October 1935 (Fig. 665).
(3) As above but with St. Edward's crown in the Royal Crest. Sealed in metal, 2nd August 1956. Also anodised (Fig. 2007).

The Northamptonshire Regiment
The Castle and Key of Gibraltar within a laurel-wreath. Above the Castle a scroll inscribed *Gibraltar* and below the Castle a scroll inscribed *Talavera*. On the base of the wreath a scroll inscribed *Northamptonshire*. Sealed 15th October 1901. All in white-metal except the title-scroll which is in gilding-metal (Fig. 2008). Also anodised, same size, sealed 6th May 1965.

The Royal Berkshire Regiment (Princess Charlotte of Wales's)
The China Dragon on a bar above a scroll inscribed *Royal Berkshire*. Sealed 26th July 1896. In gilding-metal (Fig. 667). Also anodised, same size.

The Queen's Own Royal West Kent Regiment
The White Horse of Kent on a scroll inscribed *Invicta* in old English lettering. Below the motto-scroll another scroll inscribed *Royal West Kent*. Sealed 21st June 1898. In white-metal (Fig. 668). Also anodised, same size, sealed 2nd November 1964.

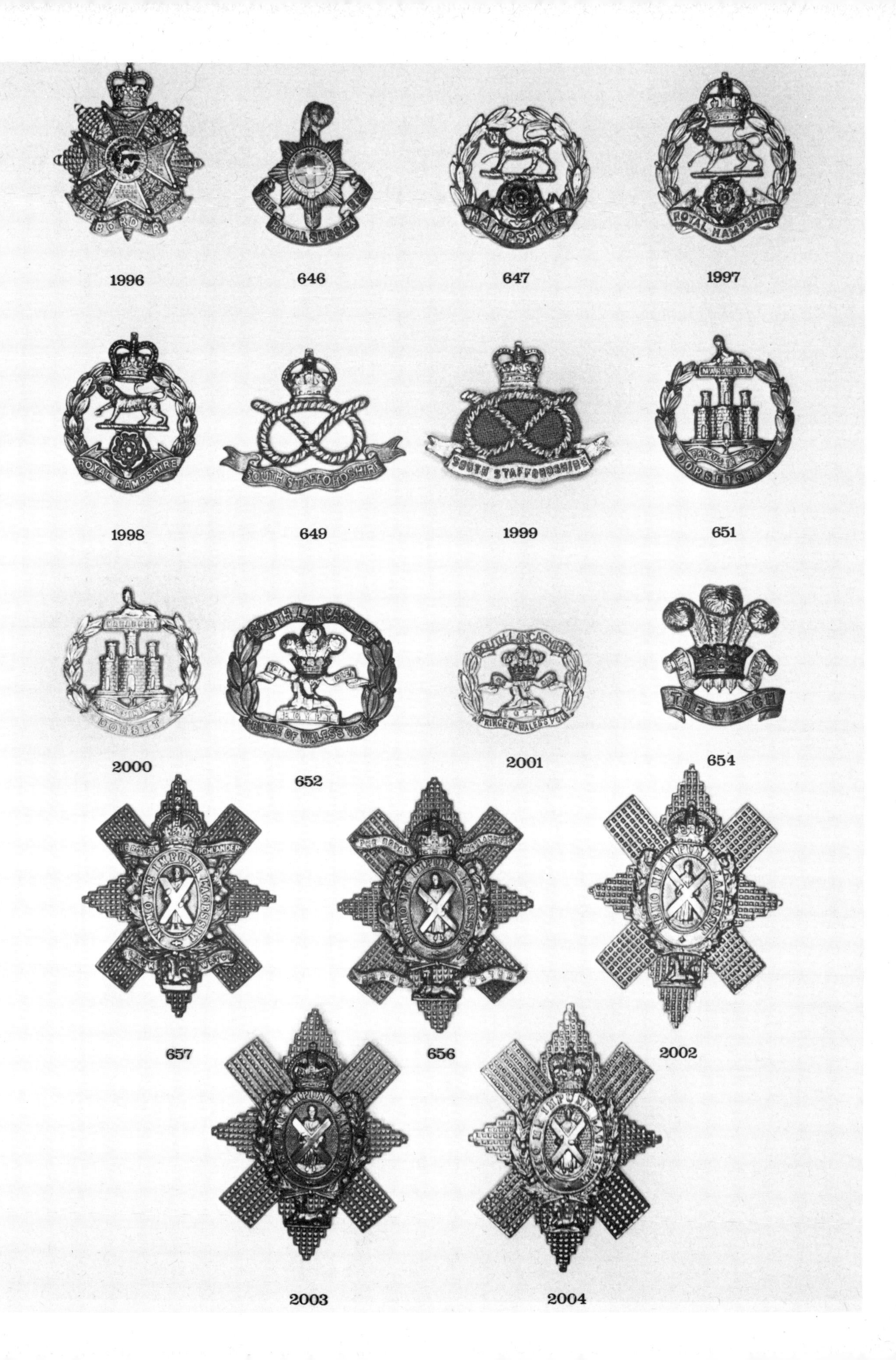

1996 646 647 1997

1998 649 1999 651

2000 652 2001 654

657 656 2002

2003 2004

The King's Own Yorkshire Light Infantry

(1) A French horn with the White Rose of York in the twist. The Rose in white-metal, the French horn in gilding-metal (Fig. 670).

(2) As above but all in white-metal (Fig. 2009). Sealed 29th June 1938. Also anodised, same size, sealed 25th April 1951.

The King's Shropshire Light Infantry

(1) A strung bugle-horn, the strings tied in three bows. Within the bend of the bugle, and below the strings on bars, the letters *KSLI* in gilding-metal (Fig. 671).

(2) As above but smaller for wear on the beret (Fig. 2010). Also anodised, same size, sealed 14th August 1963.

The Middlesex Regiment (Duke of Cambridge's Own)

The Prince of Wales's plumes, coronet and motto. Below, the coronet and cypher of the Duke of Cambridge interlaced and reversed. All within a laurel-wreath. Across the base of the wreath a scroll inscribed *Albuhera*. Below the wreath a scroll inscribed *Middlesex Regt.* Sealed 8th September 1896. The plumes, motto and title-scroll in white-metal, remainder in gilding-metal (Fig. 672). Also anodised, sealed 22nd June 1964. After the Second World War this badge was worn in all white-metal by Warrant Officers and Sergeants.

The King's Royal Rifle Corps

(1) A Maltese cross. On the top arm a tablet inscribed *Celer et Audax* and above the tablet an Imperial crown. In the centre of the cross a circlet inscribed *The King's Royal Rifle Corps*. Within the circlet a bugle with strings. Battle honours on each arm of the cross. In black-metal. Sealed 13th December 1905 (Fig. 2011). Worn with a red-cloth backing.

(2) As above but with St. Edward's crown. Worn with a red-cloth backing. In black-plastic. Sealed 19th September 1955 (Fig. 2012).

The Wiltshire Regiment (Duke of Edinburgh's)

(1) A cross patée lined with burnished edges. On the cross a circular convex plate and thereon the cypher *AEA* of Alfred Ernest Albert, Duke of Edinburgh. Above the cross a coronet. Below, a scroll inscribed *The Wiltshire Regiment*. All in gilding-metal (Fig. 676). Also anodised, same size.

(2) As above but with the cypher of Prince Philip, Duke of Edinburgh. In gilding-metal. Sealed 5th June 1956 (Fig. 2013). Also anodised, same size, sealed 26th August 1964.

The Manchester Regiment

A fleur-de-lys in gilding-metal (Fig. 2014). Also in white-metal, sealed 10th February 1949, and anodised, sealed 24th August 1964.

The North Staffordshire Regiment (The Prince of Wales's)

The Stafford Knot with the Prince of Wales's plumes, coronet and motto above and a scroll inscribed *North Stafford* below. The coronet and knot in gilding-metal, remainder in white-metal (Fig. 678). Also anodised, same size, sealed 26th April 1966.

The York and Lancaster Regiment

The Royal Tiger with the Union Rose above and surmounted by a coronet. Below the Tiger, a scroll inscribed *York and Lancaster* with laurel-sprays continuing the scroll to the coronet.

658
2005
THE ESSEX REGT
660
NOTTS & DERBY
662
NOTTS & DERBY
2006
ROYAL NORTH LANCASHIRE
664
THE LOYAL REGIMENT
665
THE LOYAL REGIMENT
2007
GIBRALTAR
TALAVERA
NORTHAMPTONSHIRE
2008
ROYAL BERKSHIRE
667
ROYAL KENT WEST
668
670
2009
KSLI
671
KSLI
2010
MIDDLESEX
672
2011
2012
676
THE WILTSHIRE REGIMENT
2013

Sealed 28th October 1897. The coronet in white-metal; the Rose in white-metal with gilding-metal centre; remainder in gilding-metal (Fig. 679). An anodised version, same size, was sealed 1st November 1963.

The Durham Light Infantry

(1) A bugle with strings taken upwards into the base of an Imperial crown. Within the strings the letters *DLI.* Sealed 20th October 1903. All in white-metal (Fig. 681).
(2) As above but smaller size for wear on the beret. Sealed 21st September 1950 (Fig. 2015).
(3) As (2) but with St. Edward's crown. Sealed 12th February 1955 (Fig. 2016). Also anodised, same size.

The Highland Light Infantry (City of Glasgow Regiment)

(1) The Star of the Order of the Thistle, thereon a bugle-horn. In the twist of the horn the monogram *HLI.* Above the horn an Imperial crown and below it the Elephant superscribed *Assaye* on a scroll. All in white-metal (Fig. 684). Also anodised, same size.
(2) As above but with St. Edward's crown (Fig. 2017). Also anodised, same size.

Seaforth Highlanders (Ross-shire Buffs, Duke of Albany's)

A stag's head caboshed above a scroll inscribed *Cuidich'n Righ.* In white-metal (Fig. 685). Also anodised, same size, sealed 6th November 1964.

The Gordon Highlanders

The Crest of the Marquis of Huntly, viz. a stag's head issuant from a ducal coronet within a wreath of ivy. On the base of the wreath a scroll inscribed *Bydand.* In white-metal (Fig. 687). Also anodised, same size.

The Queen's Own Cameron Highlanders

St. Andrew with Cross within a wreath of thistles. On the base of the wreath a scroll inscribed *Cameron.* Sealed 25th May 1897. In white-metal (Fig. 688). Also anodised, same size, sealed 8th January 1965.

The Royal Ulster Rifles

(1) A Harp surmounted by an Imperial crown. Below the Harp a scroll inscribed *Quis separabit.* Sealed in 1913. In white-metal (Fig. 691).
(2) As above but with St. Edward's crown. Sealed 2nd September 1954 (Fig. 2018). An anodised version, same size, sealed 28th May 1964.

The Royal Irish Fusiliers (Princess Victoria's)

A fused grenade in gilding-metal. On the ball in white-metal a Harp surmounted by the Prince of Wales's plumes, coronet and motto. Above this, as a separate badge, a coronet in white-metal. Sealed 13th February 1914 (Fig. 694). Also anodised, same size.

The Argyll and Sutherland Highlanders (Princess Louise's)

A circlet inscribed *Argyll and Sutherland.* Within the circlet the letter *L*, cypher of H.R.H. the late Princess Louise, interlaced and reversed. Within the circlet and to the left of the cypher the Boar's Head and on the right of the cypher the Cat. Above the cypher the

NORTH STAFFORD
YORK AND LANCASTER
CUIDICH 'N RICH
BYDAND
CAMERON
2014
678
679
681
2015
2016
684
2017
685
687
688
691
2018
694
698
705
2019
2020

Princess's coronet. The whole within a wreath of thistles. In white-metal (Fig. 698). Also anodised, same size.

The Rifle Brigade (Prince Consort's Own)

(1) A cross based on that of the Order of the Bath, thereon a circlet inscribed *Rifle Brigade* enclosing a bugle surmounted by an Imperial crown; the cross enclosed with a laurel-wreath on which are fourteen battle-honour scrolls. The upper ends of the wreath connected by a tablet inscribed *Waterloo* surmounted by an Imperial crown. Battle honours on each arm of the cross. Below the cross a scroll inscribed *Peninsula.* In white-metal (Fig. 705).

(2) Similar to (1) but with *The Rifle Brigade* inscribed on the circlet, and below the cross two battle-honour scrolls inscribed *France & Flanders 1914–18* and *Macedonia 1915–18*, and across the base of the wreath a scroll inscribed *Prince Consort's Own.* This pattern was sealed on 26th August 1927. In white-metal (Fig. 2019). Also anodised, same size.

(3) A cross based on that of the Order of the Bath, thereon a circlet inscribed *Rifle Brigade* enclosing a bugle surmounted by St. Edward's crown. The cross enclosed by a laurel-wreath the upper ends of which connected by a tablet inscribed *Waterloo* surmounted by a Guelphic crown. Battle honours on each arm of the cross. Below the cross a Naval crown with above it the wording *Copenhagen 2 April 1801.* In white-metal, sealed 10th October 1956 (Fig. 2020). Also anodised, same size.

11th (Royal Militia Island of Jersey) Battalion, The Hampshire Regiment

On the 19th June 1940, ten officers and a hundred and ninety-three men of The Royal Militia of the Island of Jersey paraded in Jersey and the commanding officer, Lieutenant-Colonel H. M. Vatcher M.C., informed them that the Channel Islands were to be demilitarised and invited any men who wished to leave Jersey with him and fight from England to step forward. All did so and the party arrived in Southampton the following evening, becoming the nucleus of a new battalion designated as above. After war service the battalion was disbanded in April 1946.

Upon a saltire a shield bearing the Arms of Jersey (three lions leopardé in pale) surmounted by an Imperial crown. In gilding-metal (Fig. 2021).

The Lowland Regiment

St. Andrew's Cross, thereon a thistle; below the thistle and turned round the lower portion of the Cross a scroll in two parts: the upper part inscribed *Lowland* and the lower part *Regiment.* In white-metal. Sealed 9th June 1942 (Fig. 2022).

The Highland Regiment

A cross resembling St. Andrew's Cross but sharpened at each point; on the cross a circular strap with the buckle on the left side level with the centre of the cross, on the opposite side a thistle; the strap inscribed at the top *Highland* and on the bottom *Regiment.* On the arms of the cross and within the strap, two claymores, points uppermost; in the centre a Scottish targe or shield. In white-metal (Fig. 2023).

The Lowland Brigade

Upon a saltire a thistle within a circlet inscribed *Nemo me impune lacessit.* All in silver-anodised. Sealed 17th November 1958 (Fig. 2024).

The Home Counties Brigade
A Saxon crown enfiled with a sword point-upwards. Underneath and over the hilt a scroll inscribed *Home Counties*. All in silver-anodised. Sealed 22nd May 1958 (Fig. 2025).

The Lancastrian Brigade
The Rose of Lancaster gules garnished gold-anodised, ensigned with the Royal Crest in silver-anodised and within a wreath of laurel. Underneath, a scroll inscribed *Lancastrian* in gold-anodised (Fig. 2026).

The Fusilier Brigade
A grenade fired, the case ensigned with St. Edward's crown, all gold-anodised and bearing St. George and the Dragon within a wreath of laurel in silver-anodised. Sealed 5th September 1958 (Fig. 2027).

The Forester Brigade
A Maltese cross voided, the points pommelled, and thereon, on a mount, an antelope-statant gorged with a ducal coronet and chained, within the Garter. The whole encircled with a chaplet of oak-leaves issuant from a scroll inscribed *Forester Brigade* and ensigned with, upon a mount, a Tiger passant gardant. The Garter and oak-chaplet silver-anodised, remainder gold-anodised. Sealed 14th April 1959 (Fig. 2028).

The East Anglian Brigade
Upon a star of eight points the Castle and Key of Gibraltar. Below, a scroll inscribed *East Anglia*. The star silver-anodised, remainder gold-anodised. Sealed 22nd May 1958 (Fig. 2029). Minor differences are found in manufacture.

The Wessex Brigade
The Wessex Wyvern on a plinth inscribed *Wessex*. All in gold-anodised (Fig. 2030).

The Light Infantry Brigade
A bugle-horn stringed in silver-anodised (Fig. 2031).

The Yorkshire Brigade
The White Rose of York in silver-anodised ensigned with St. Edward's crown in gold-anodised. Underneath, a scroll inscribed *Yorkshire* in gold-anodised (Fig. 2032). Minor differences are found in manufacture.

The Mercian Brigade
A double-headed Eagle displayed, in silver-anodised, ensigned with a Saxon crown in gold-anodised (Fig. 2033).

The Welsh Brigade
The Prince of Wales's plumes, coronet and motto all in silver-anodised (Fig. 2034).

The North Irish Brigade
A Harp in silver-anodised ensigned with St. Edward's crown in gold-anodised. Below, a scroll inscribed *North Irish Brigade* in gold-anodised. Sealed 8th December 1958 (Fig. 2035).

The Highland Brigade
A stag's head superimposed on St. Andrew's Cross with a scroll below inscribed *Cuidich'n Righ.* All in silver-anodised (Fig. 2036).

The Green Jackets Brigade
Upon a Maltese cross a bugle-horn stringed; the whole within a wreath of laurel and ensigned with St. Edward's crown resting on a plinth inscribed *Peninsula.* All in silver-anodised. Sealed 7th October 1958 (Fig. 2037).

The Queen's Regiment
The Dragon surmounted by the Prince of Wales's plumes and coronet in silver-anodised, all surrounded by the Garter proper with, below, a scroll inscribed *Queen's* in gold-anodised. Sealed 10th July 1966 (Fig. 2038).

The King's Own Royal Border Regiment
The Lion of England in silver-anodised within a laurel-wreath surmounted by St. Edward's crown in gold-anodised (Fig. 2039).

The Royal Regiment of Fusiliers
A grenade fired, the case ensigned with St. Edward's crown all gold-anodised and bearing St. George and the Dragon within a wreath of laurel in silver-anodised (Fig. 2027).

The King's Regiment
A fleur-de-lys in gold-anodised, thereon the White Horse of Hanover in silver-anodised. Below, a scroll inscribed in old English lettering *King's* in gold-anodised (Fig. 2041).

The Royal Anglian Regiment
Upon a silver-anodised star of eight points, the Castle and Key of Gibraltar. Underneath, a scroll inscribed *Royal Anglian* in gold-anodised. Sealed 25th March 1954 (Fig. 2042).

The Devonshire and Dorset Regiment
In front of the Castle of Exeter in silver-anodised the Sphinx, its plinth inscribed *Marabout.* Above the Castle a scroll inscribed *Semper fidelis* and underneath a scroll inscribed *Primus in Indis* all in gold-anodised (Fig. 2043).

The Light Infantry
A bugle-horn stringed in silver-anodised (Fig. 2031).

The Prince of Wales's Own Regiment of Yorkshire
The White Horse of Hanover on ground, on which is inscribed the word *Yorkshire*, in silver-anodised (Fig. 2044).

The Royal Highland Fusiliers (Princess Margaret's Own Glasgow and Ayrshire Regiment)
A fused grenade in gold-anodised; thereon the monogram *HLI* surmounted by St. Edward's crown in silver-anodised (Fig. 2045).

The Royal Regiment of Wales (24th/41st Foot)
The Prince of Wales's plumes, coronet and motto all in silver-anodised (Fig. 2046).

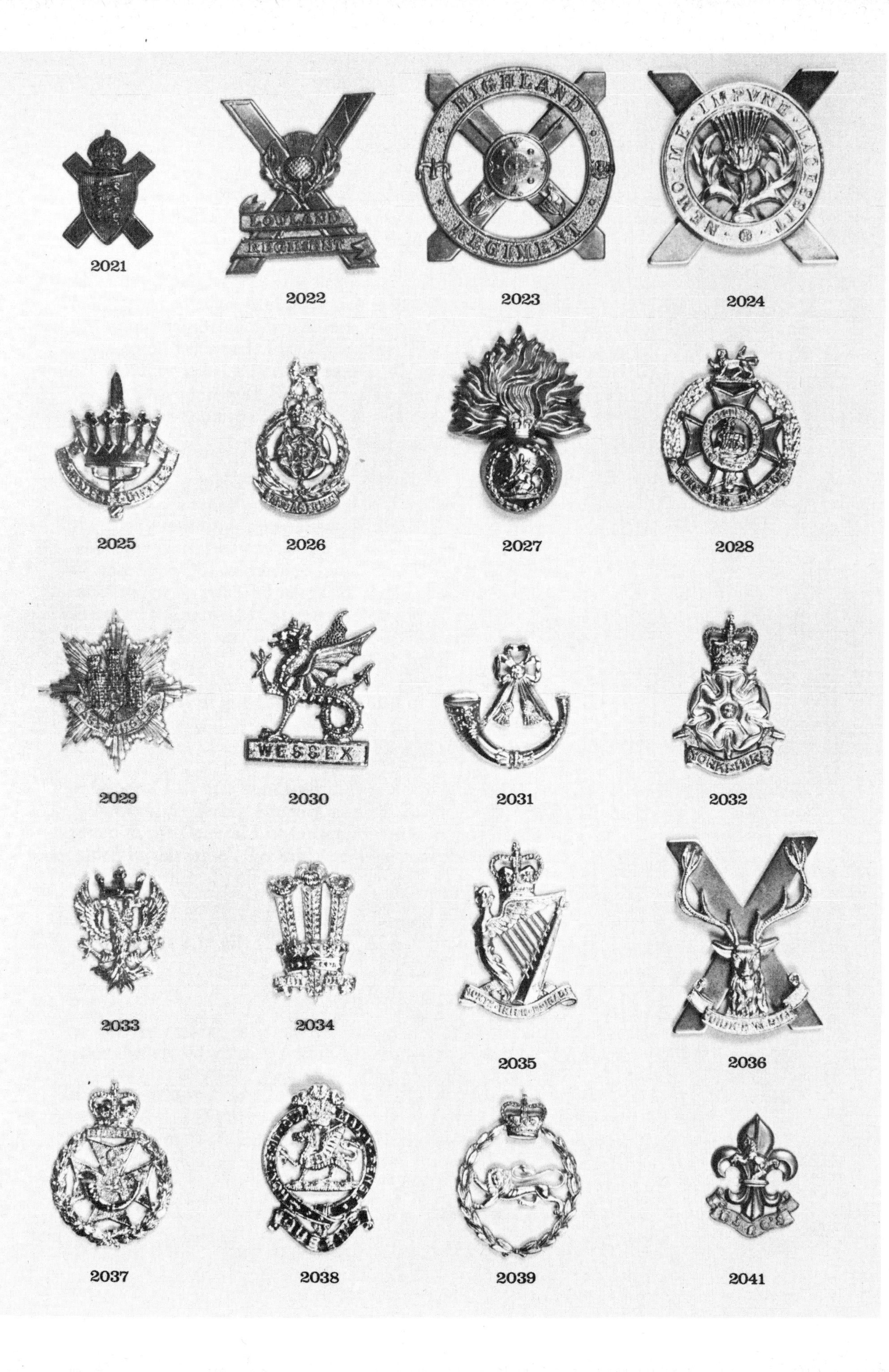

LOWLAND
HIGHLAND
REGIMENT
NEMO ME IMPUNE LACESSIT
WESSEX
2021
2022
2023
2024
2025
2026
2027
2028
2029
2030
2031
2032
2033
2034
2035
2036
2037
2038
2039
2041

The Royal Irish Rangers (27th (Inniskilling), 83rd and 87th)
A Harp in silver-anodised ensigned with St. Edward's crown in gold-anodised. Below, a scroll inscribed *Royal Irish Rangers* in gold-anodised (Fig. 2047).

The Worcestershire and Sherwood Foresters Regiment (29th/45th Foot)
An elongated eight-pointed star in silver-anodised. On this, in gold-anodised, a Maltese cross with the Garter superimposed. Within the Garter a stag lodged in silver-anodised. Below the cross a gold-anodised tablet inscribed *Firm* (Fig. 2048).

The Queen's Lancashire Regiment
An oval inscribed *The Queen's Lancashire Regiment* and, in a voided centre, a Rose surmounted by St. Edward's crown. Below the oval a scroll inscribed *Loyally I Serve.* All gold-anodised (Fig. 2049).

The Staffordshire Regiment (The Prince of Wales's)
The Stafford Knot in gold-anodised surmounted by the Prince of Wales's plumes and motto in silver-anodised, the coronet gold-anodised, on a backing of brown-holland material (Fig. 2050).

The Duke of Edinburgh's Royal Regiment (Berkshire and Wiltshire)
The China Dragon in silver-anodised, within two coils of rope surmounted by a ducal coronet in gold-anodised, superimposed on a cross patée lined with burnished edges in silver-anodised (Fig. 2051).

Queen's Own Highlanders (Seaforth and Camerons)
The Thistle surmounted by St. Edward's crown. Below, and separately, a stag's head caboshed and below this a scroll inscribed *Cuidich'n Righ.* All silver-anodised (Fig. 2052).

The Royal Green Jackets
A Maltese cross and thereon a circlet inscribed *The Royal Green Jackets* enclosing a bugle-horn stringed; battle honours are on each arm of the cross; the whole enclosed in a laurel-wreath surmounted by St. Edward's crown resting on a plinth inscribed *Peninsula.* On the lower portion of the wreath a Naval crown superscribed *Copenhagen 2nd April 1801.* In silver-anodised (Fig. 2053).

2042 2043 2031 2044

2045 2046 2047 2048

2049 2050 2051 2053

2052

CHAPTER 6

Airborne Forces

Army Air Corps

(1) Within a laurel-wreath surmounted by an Imperial crown an Eagle facing right resting on the letters *A.A.C.* within bars. Worn from 1942 until 1950 when the Corps was disbanded. In white-metal sealed 27th May 1942 (Fig. 2054). Also in hall-marked silver for officers.

(2) As (1) but in red cloth (Fig. 2055).

(3) Within a laurel-wreath surmounted by St. Edward's crown an Eagle facing left. In anodised-silver (Fig. 2056). Also in silver-plate for officers. The Army Air Corps was reformed in 1957 (Army Order 82/57).

(4) Officers' beret-badge: same design as (2) but embroidered silver on a dark-blue background.

The Glider Pilot Regiment

The Glider Pilot Regiment was included originally in the Army Air Corps but, when the latter was disbanded in 1950, it was formed as a separate regiment and wore its own badge. When the present Army Air Corps was formed in 1957 the Glider Pilot Regiment was incorporated in it and ceased to wear its individual badge.

(1) An Eagle facing left within a scroll inscribed *Glider Pilot Regiment* and surmounted by an Imperial crown. In white-metal (Fig. 2057). Also in silver-plate for officers. Sealed in anodised-silver, 10th November 1950.

(2) As above but with St. Edward's crown (Fig. 2058). In white-metal and also in silver-plate for officers. Sealed in anodised-silver, 12th October 1955.

The Parachute Regiment

(1) Upon a spread of wings an open parachute. Above, the Royal Crest. In white-metal. Sealed 25th March 1943 (Fig. 2059). Also in silver-plate for officers. Sealed in anodised-silver, 11th September 1959.

(2) As above but with St. Edward's crown in the Royal Crest (Fig. 2060). In white-metal. Sealed 28th September 1954. Also anodised, sealed 18th April 1966, and for officers in silver-plate.

Special Air Service Regiment

(1) A winged dagger striking downwards. On the lower part of the dagger a scroll inscribed *Who Dares Wins*. The dagger in white-metal, remainder in gilding-metal (Fig. 2061). Sealed 27th May 1953. Officers in silver and gilt. Also anodised.

(2) Beret-badge for soldiers: as above but in embroidered cloth (Fig. 2062).

(3) Beret-badge for officers: as above but in silver-thread and silk (Fig. 2063).

2054 2055 2056

2059 2057 2058 2060

2062 2061 2063

2064 2065 2066

2068 2069 2070

2067 2071 2072

CHAPTER 7

Special Service Forces: Second World War

No. 2 Commando

(1) A dagger point-downwards with the letters *S S* either side of the hilt. In white-metal (Fig. 2064).

(2) As above in silver-embroidery on black-velvet (Fig. 2065). Worn by officers.

Nos. 50, 51 and 52 Commandos

A knuckleduster-knife point-downwards. In brass (Fig. 2066).

Long Range Desert Group

Within a circle a scorpion above the letters *LRDG*. In brass (Fig. 2067). Also in bronze, and silver, for officers.

No. 1 Demolition Squadron (Popski's Private Army)

(1) An astrolobe. In silver (Fig. 2068). For officers.

(2) As above but slightly different design. In bronze (Fig. 2069). For officers.

(3) As (2) in cast white-metal (Fig. 2070). For other-ranks.

Raiding Support Regiment

A winged-gauntlet clasping a bare hand reaching from a representation of the fortress of Europe. Above, the letters *RSR*. Below, a scroll inscribed *Quit you like men*. All embroidered: the winged-gauntlet in light-blue edged red, motto in black, remainder in white edged red, on dark-blue cloth (Fig. 2071). The original badges were made by Italian nuns in a North African convent.

'V' Force

The Roman numeral *V* superimposed on crossed daggers, points-upwards. Below, a scroll inscribed *Force* (Fig. 2072). In cast bronzed-brass. Officers: in cast silver, not hall-marked. A combined British and Indian Force which operated in the Arakan.

CHAPTER 8

The Brigade of Gurkhas

In 1947, following the division of the Indian Army between India and Pakistan, a tripartite agreement was reached by Britain, India and Nepal whereby eight battalions of Gurkhas would be transferred to the British Army; the 1st and 2nd Battalions of the 2nd, 6th, 7th and 10th Gurkhas became the new British Brigade of Gurkhas as from the 1st January 1948.

The original intention was to have a self-contained Gurkha Division and, for a short period, the 7th Gurkha Rifles became the 101st and 102nd Field Regiments, R.A. but reverted to an infantry-role when this project was abandoned.

Gurkha Engineer and Signal units were formed. The 67 Gurkha Field Squadron, R.E. was raised in 1948 and the Gurkha Engineers became a unit in their own right on 28th September 1955. A Gurkha Signal Training Wing was started in 1950 and the Gurkha Signals, too, became a unit in their own right on the same date in 1955.

The Gurkha Army Service Corps was formed with effect from 1st July 1958 (A.O. 67/1958) subsequently changing its title to Gurkha Transport Regiment in 1965 when the Royal Corps of Transport was formed.

The Gurkha Military Police had a brief existence, becoming an integral part of the Brigade of Gurkhas on 28th September 1955, but were disbanded on 1st January 1965. There was also a Gurkha Independent Parachute Company from 1965 to 1971.

Changing Defence needs have reduced the number of Gurkha units required and there are now only five battalions of infantry; the 6th, 7th and 10th having been reduced to one battalion each.

2nd King Edward VII's Own Gurkha Rifles (The Sirmoor Rifles)

Forage-cap: British officers only

The Prince of Wales's plumes, coronet and motto. In silver-plate worn on a scarlet-cord boss $\frac{3}{4}''$ deep and $1\frac{1}{4}''$ diameter (Fig. 2073).

Field Service cap: all officers and Warrant Officers

As above but scarlet-cord boss is $\frac{9}{16}''$ deep and $1''$ diameter.

Beret: all officers and Warrant Officers

As above but scarlet-cord boss is $\frac{3}{8}''$ deep and $1\frac{1}{8}''$ diameter.

Beret: other-ranks
The Prince of Wales's plumes, coronet and motto. In blackened-brass with scarlet-cloth backing (Fig. 2074).

Field Service cap: other-ranks
As above.

Kilmarnock cap: other ranks
As above but without the scarlet backing. Also worn by Gurkha officers.

6th Queen Elizabeth's Own Gurkha Rifles
(Granted the above title on 1st January 1959)

Forage-cap: British officers only
(1) A pair of crossed kukris, cutting-edges downwards and crossed right-over-left, with the numeral *6* below and separate. All in silver-plate on a black-cord boss $\frac{3}{4}$″ deep and 1$\frac{1}{8}$″ diameter (Fig. 2075).
(2) As above but surmounted by St. Edward's crown (Fig. 2077).

Field Service cap: all officers
As above but black-cord boss $\frac{1}{2}$″ deep and 1″ diameter.

Beret: all officers
(1) As above but larger and not worn on a boss. 1$\frac{1}{4}$″ high and 1$\frac{3}{8}$″ wide. In silver-plate (Fig. 2076).
(2) As above but surmounted by St. Edward's crown (Fig. 2078).

Kilmarnock cap: Gurkha officers only
As beret-badge.

Beret: other-ranks
(1) As officers' (1) but in white-metal, sealed 31st December 1951, also in anodised-silver.
(2) As officers' (2). In same metals.

Kilmarnock cap: other-ranks
As beret-badge.

7th Duke of Edinburgh's Own Gurkha Rifles
(Granted the above title on 1st January 1959)

Forage-cap: British officers only
(1) A pair of crossed kukris, cutting-edges upwards and crossed left-over-right, with the numeral *7* above and resting on the kukris. All in silver-plate on a black-cord boss $\frac{3}{4}$″ deep and 1$\frac{1}{4}$″ diameter (Fig. 2079).
(2) As (1) but surmounted by the Duke of Edinburgh's coronet and cypher (Fig. 2080).

Field Service cap: all officers
As above but black-cord boss $\frac{1}{2}$″ deep and 1$\frac{3}{4}$″ diameter.

2073

2075

2077

2074

2076

2078

2079

2080

2081

2082

2083

2084

2085

2086

Beret: all officers

(1) As above but not worn on a boss: $1\frac{3}{8}''$ high and $1''$ wide. In silver-plate.
(2) As above but surmounted by the Duke of Edinburgh's coronet and cypher. The cypher is voided.

Beret: other-ranks

(1) As officers' (1) but in white-metal. Sealed 21st July 1951 (Fig. 2081). Also in silver-anodised.
(2) As officers' (2) but cypher not voided (Fig. 2082). In same metals. Sealed in white-metal, 11th October 1960.

Kilmarnock cap: other ranks

As beret-badge.

Gurkha hat: all ranks

As other-ranks' beret-badge, worn on a rectangular patch of Cameron of Erracht tartan.

10th Princess Mary's Own Gurkha Rifles

(Granted above title by Army Order 135 of 1949)

Forage-cap: British officers only

(1) A bugle-horn with strings, mouthpiece to the right; a kukri interlaced with the bugle, handle to the left behind the bell, blade to the right in front of the bugle, cutting-edge of the kukri downwards. Above the kukri and below the bugle-strings the numerals *10*. All in silver-plate on a black-cord boss $\frac{3}{4}''$ deep and $1\frac{1}{4}''$ diameter (Fig. 2083).
(2) As (1) but the numeral *10* between the bugle and the cutting-edge of the kukri, and the cypher of the Princess Royal between the bugle-strings and the top-edge of the kukri. All in silver-plate on a black-cord boss $\frac{3}{4}''$ deep and $1\frac{1}{4}''$ diameter (Fig. 2084).

Field Service cap: all officers

As above but black-cord boss $\frac{1}{2}''$ deep and $1''$ diameter.

Beret: all officers

As above (2) but slightly larger and not worn on a boss. $1''$ high and $1\frac{1}{8}''$ wide. In silver-plate.

Beret: other-ranks

(1) As officers' (2) in white-metal, sealed 22nd September 1955. In anodised-silver, sealed 18th October 1961.
(2) As officers' (2) but with the addition of a scroll below the bugle inscribed *Princess Mary's Own*. In white-metal, sealed 11th July 1951 (Fig. 2085). Also in anodised-silver with the cypher not voided, sealed 30th June 1961.

Kilmarnock cap: other-ranks

As beret-badge.

Gurkha hat: officers
As beret-badge (2) but larger, measuring $1\frac{1}{2}''$ high and $1\frac{1}{4}''$ in width, and with the addition of a scroll below the bugle inscribed *Princess Mary's Own*. In silver-plate (Fig. 2086). Other-ranks wore the same badge in anodised-silver on a rectangular patch of Hunting Stuart tartan.

The Queen's Gurkha Engineers
(Awarded prefix 'Queen's' in 1977)

Forage-cap: British officers only
A pair of crossed kukris, cutting-edges downwards and crossed left-over-right, surmounted by a fused grenade. Across the handles of the kukris a scroll inscribed *Ubique*. The kukris in silver-plate, remainder in gilt, worn on a scarlet-cord boss $\frac{3}{4}''$ deep and $1\frac{1}{4}''$ diameter.

Service-dress cap: British officers only
As Forage-cap badge above but worn on a dark-blue cord boss (Fig. 2087).

Field Service cap: all officers
As Forage-cap badge but larger: $1\frac{1}{4}''$ high and $1''$ wide. Not worn on a boss. Also found all in silver-plate.

Beret: all officers
As Field Service cap-badge. Also worn on Kilmarnock cap by Gurkha officers.

Beret: other-ranks
As officers' but in white- and gilding-metal (Fig. 2088). Also in anodised-silver, sealed 19th November 1958.

Kilmarnock cap: other-ranks
As beret-badge.

Gurkha hat: all ranks
As other-ranks' beret-badge, worn on a rectangular dark-blue-cloth patch.

The Queen's Gurkha Signals
(Awarded prefix 'Queen's' in 1977)

Forage-cap: British officers only
The figure of Mercury on a Globe surmounted by St. Edward's crown. Below, a two-part scroll inscribed *Certa Cito*. Superimposed, a pair of crossed kukris, crossing over the Globe, cutting-edges upwards and crossing left-over-right. The crown and motto-scrolls in gilt, Mercury and kukris in silver-plate (Fig. 2089). Also worn on Kilmarnock cap by Gurkha officers.

Service-dress cap: British officers only
As Forage-cap.

Field Service cap: all officers
Same design as above but in gold, silver, blue and green wire embroidery.

Beret: all officers
Same as Field Service cap-badge.

Beret: other-ranks
As officers' Forage-cap badge but in white- and gilding-metal.

Kilmarnock cap: other-ranks
As beret-badge.

Gurkha hat: all ranks
As other-ranks' beret-badge, worn on a rectangular patch of Royal Stuart tartan.

Gurkha Transport Regiment
Forage-cap: British officers only

(1) On an eight-pointed star a three-part scroll inscribed *Gurkha Army Service Corps*. A wreath behind and above the scroll on which is the Royal cypher and crown; overall a pair of crossed kukris, cutting-edges downwards and crossed left-over-right, the handles dividing the scroll into three parts, the points crossing the laurel-wreath. The star and kukri-blades in silver-plate, remainder in gilt (Fig. 2090).

(2) As above but scroll inscribed *Gurkha Transport Regiment* (Fig. 2091).

Also worn by Gurkha officers on the Kilmarnock cap.

Field Service cap: all officers
As above but smaller: in fact a collar-badge is worn.

Beret: all officers
Same as Field Service cap-badge.

Beret: other-ranks

(1) As officers' Forage-cap badge (1) but in gold- and silver-anodised. Sealed 14th June 1960.

(2) As officers' Forage-cap badge (2) but in gold- and silver-anodised.

Field Service cap: other-ranks
An other-ranks' collar-badge is worn.

Kilmarnock cap: other-ranks
As beret-badge.

Gurkha hat: all ranks
Officers' is as Forage-cap badge; other-ranks', as beret-badge.

Gurkha Military Police
Forage-cap: British officers only

(1) A pair of crossed kukris, crossed right-over-left and cutting-edges upwards, with the Royal cypher surmounted by St Edward's crown between the blades. At the base a scroll inscribed *Gurkha Military Police*. All in flat silver-chrome (Fig. 2092).

2089

2087

2088

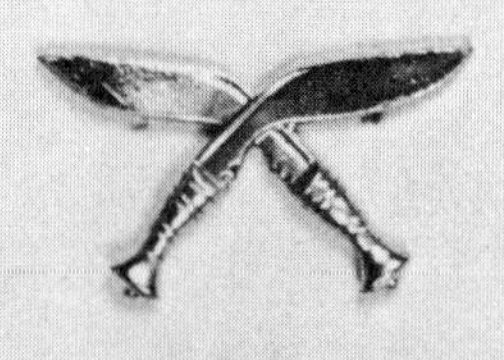

2094

2093

2095

2090

2092

2091

(2) Within a wreath of laurel, a pair of crossed kukris crossed left-over-right and cutting-edges upwards, above which the Royal cypher surmounted by St. Edward's crown. Below the wreath a scroll inscribed *Gurkha Military Police.* All in silver-plate.

Service-dress cap: British officers only
As Forage-cap badge.

Kilmarnock cap: all Gurkha ranks
As officers' Forage-cap badge but in gilding-metal. Also anodised (Fig. 2093). Sealed 23rd June 1959.

Gurkha hat: all Gurkha ranks
Same as Kilmarnock cap-badge.

Staff Band, The Brigade of Gurkhas
Beret: all Gurkha ranks
A pair of crossed kukris, crossed left-over-right and cutting-edges downwards. In white-metal. Also anodised (Fig. 2094).
Note: For some years, from raising in 1955, the 6th Gurkhas' badge without the numeral was worn. The kukris are crossed right-over-left.

Kilmarnock cap
Same as beret-badge.

Boys Company, The Brigade of Gurkhas
Beret: Gurkha ranks
A pair of crossed kukris, crossed left-over-right and cutting-edges downwards, with a scroll between the handles inscribed *Boys.* All in white-metal, sealed 19th January 1954 (Fig. 2095). Also anodised.

Kilmarnock cap
Same as beret-badge.

Gurkha Independent Parachute Company
Beret: all ranks
The badge of the Parachute Regiment worn on a rectangular patch of Gurkha Brigade ribbon (green, black, red, black, green). Worn from 1964 to 1971.
Note: the original badge designed and approved for wear was never issued. It was a pair of crossed kukris, crossing left-over-right, cutting-edges downwards, with a parachute set above the intersection. All in flat-white silver-chrome.

CHAPTER 9

The Royal Marines

The Royal Marine Artillery and The Royal Marine Light Infantry were amalgamated in 1923 to form The Royal Marines.

Helmet-plate

(1) Officers: an eight-pointed star, the topmost-point displaced by an Imperial crown. On the star a laurel-wreath and within the wreath a voided strap inscribed *Per mare per terram*. In the centre, the Globe. Above the strap a scroll inscribed *Gibraltar*. Below the wreath the 'Fouled Anchor'. Blue-enamel backing to the strap, the Globe in silver-and-gilt, remainder in gilt (Fig. 1099). Worn from 1923 to 1954.

(2) Other-ranks: similar design to the officers' pattern but with the motto on a circlet instead of a strap. All in gilding-metal (Fig. 1100). In gilt-finish for Senior N.C.O.s. Worn from 1904 to 1954.

(3) As (1) but with St. Edward's crown (Fig. 2096). Worn from 1954 to date.

(4) As (2) but with St. Edward's crown (Fig. 2097). Worn from 1954 to date.

Officers' cap-badge

(1) The Globe (sea in silver, land in gilt) within a gilt laurel-wreath. Above, and separate, the Royal Crest in gilt (Fig. 2098). Worn from 1923 to 1954.

(2) As above but with St. Edward's crown on the Royal Crest. Worn from 1954 to date.

Quartermaster-Sergeants' cap-badge

(1) As officers' (1) above but all in gilt. Worn from 1923 to 1954.

(2) As officers' (2) above but in all gilt and with St. Edward's crown in the Royal Crest (Fig. 2099). Worn from 1954 to date.

Other-ranks' cap-badge

(1) The Globe surmounted by the Royal Crest within a laurel-wreath. In gilding-metal (Fig. 2100). In gilt-finish for Sergeants. Worn from 1923 to 1954.

(2) As above but with St. Edward's crown in the Royal Crest (Fig. 2101). Worn from 1954 to date.

Royal Marine Police cap-badge

The Royal Marine Police were formed in 1922.
The Globe within a laurel-wreath in white-metal (Fig. 2102).

THE ROYAL MARINES BANDS

Portsmouth Division

Helmet-plate

(1) In 1923 this Band adopted the helmet-plate previously worn by the R.M.A. Band, who had been authorised to wear the Royal Cypher by General Order, Royal Marines 44 of 1912 to commemorate their attendance on King George v on his voyage to India. On the helmet-plate a silver cypher of King George v was mounted above the 'Fouled Anchor' and below the Globe. The plate itself of the same pattern as shown in Fig. 1100 (Fig. 2103).

(2) To commemorate the Royal Tour of the Commonwealth in 1953/54 the combined cyphers of Queen Elizabeth II and H.R.H. Prince Philip in silver were placed below the crown (Royal Marines Routine Order 360 of 1955) (Fig. 2104).

(3) As (2) but with St. Edward's crown (Fig. 2105).

Cap-badge

(1) Within a laurel-wreath a fused grenade with the Royal Cypher of King George v mounted on the ball. The cypher in silver, remainder in gilt (Fig. 1113). This badge was worn by the R.M.A. from 1912 to 1923.

(2) As above but with St. Edward's crown above King George's cypher and above, and separately, the combined cyphers of Queen Elizabeth II and Prince Philip surmounted by St. Edward's crown in silver (Fig. 2106).

Plymouth Division

Helmet-plate

(1) The same pattern as shown in Fig. 1100. On this, above the circlet, the Prince of Wales's plumes, coronet and motto in gilt with silver plumes for Senior N.C.O.s. In brass with silver plumes for the rank-and-file (Fig. 1117). General Order, Royal Marines 206 of 1920 authorised the wearing of the Prince of Wales's plumes for their attendance on H.R.H. The Prince of Wales on his voyage to Canada, Australia, New Zealand and other British Possessions. Worn until 1952 when their designation was changed to Plymouth Group, Royal Marines.

(2) As above but with St. Edward's crown.

Cap-badge

(1) In three pieces. The Globe within a laurel-wreath: above, the Prince of Wales's plumes, coronet and motto; above this the Royal Crest. In silver-and-gilt for Sergeants, in gilding-metal and silver for other-ranks. Also anodised with silver plumes.

(2) As above but with St. Edward's crown in the Royal Crest (Fig. 2107).

Chatham Division

Helmet-plate

The same pattern as shown in Fig. 1100. On this, between the Globe and the 'Fouled Anchor', a Rose. In gilt with silver Rose for Senior N.C.O.s. In gilding-metal with silver Rose for the rank-and-file (Fig. 1118). General Order, Royal Marines 31 of 1902 authorised the wearing of the White Rose of York to commemorate the bands' attendance on H.R.H. The Duke of York (later King George v) on his voyage to the Colonies in 1901.
The Chatham Division was disbanded in 1950.

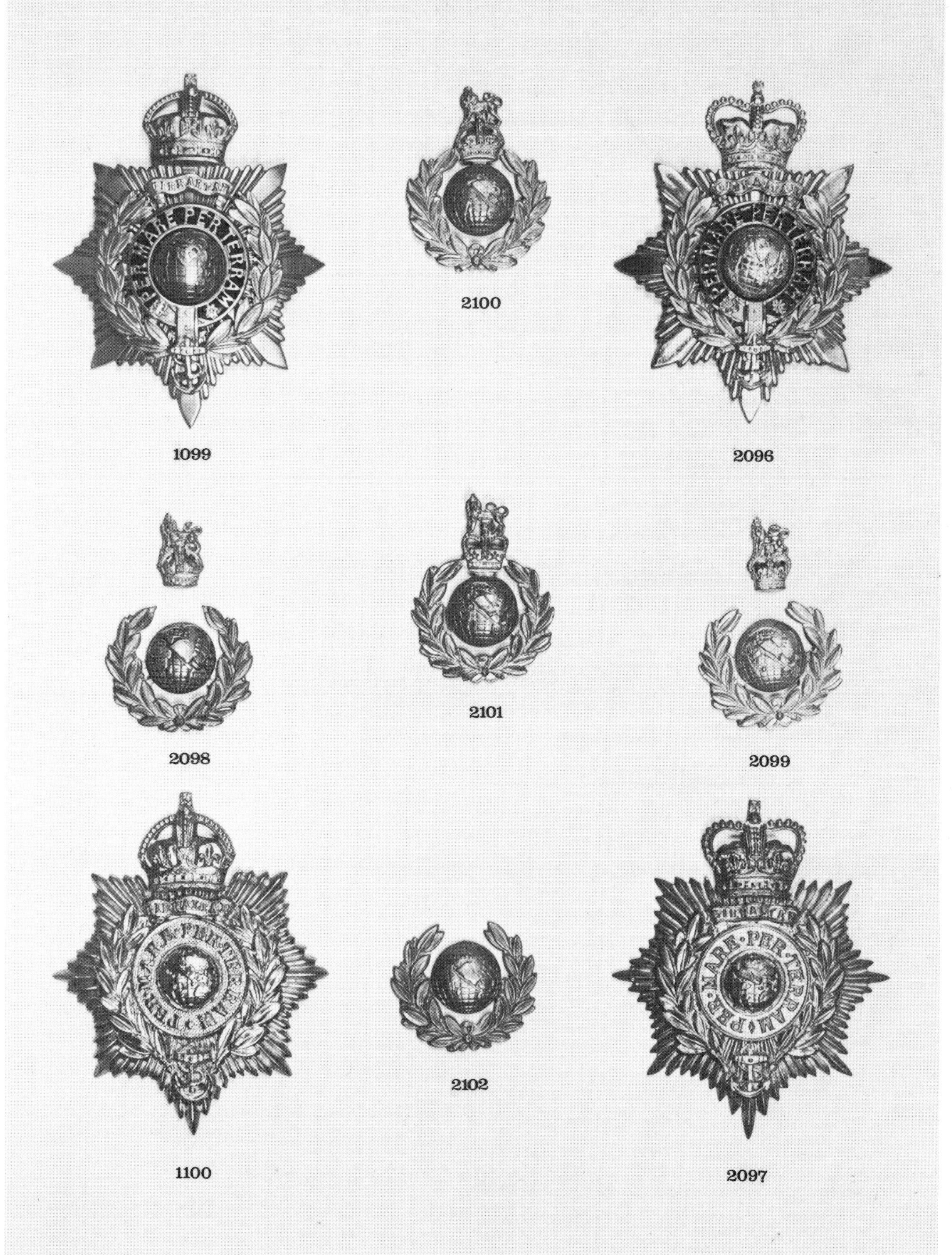

1099 2100 2096

2098 2101 2099

1100 2102 2097

Cap-badge

In three pieces: the Globe within a laurel-wreath; above this the White Rose of York; and above this the Royal Crest (Fig. 2108). In silver-and-gilt for Sergeants, in gilding-metal and silver for other-ranks.

Royal Marines School of Music

Cap-badge

(1) The Globe within a laurel-wreath surmounted by a lyre. In gilding-metal (Fig. 2109).
(2) As above but different design of lyre (Fig. 2110).

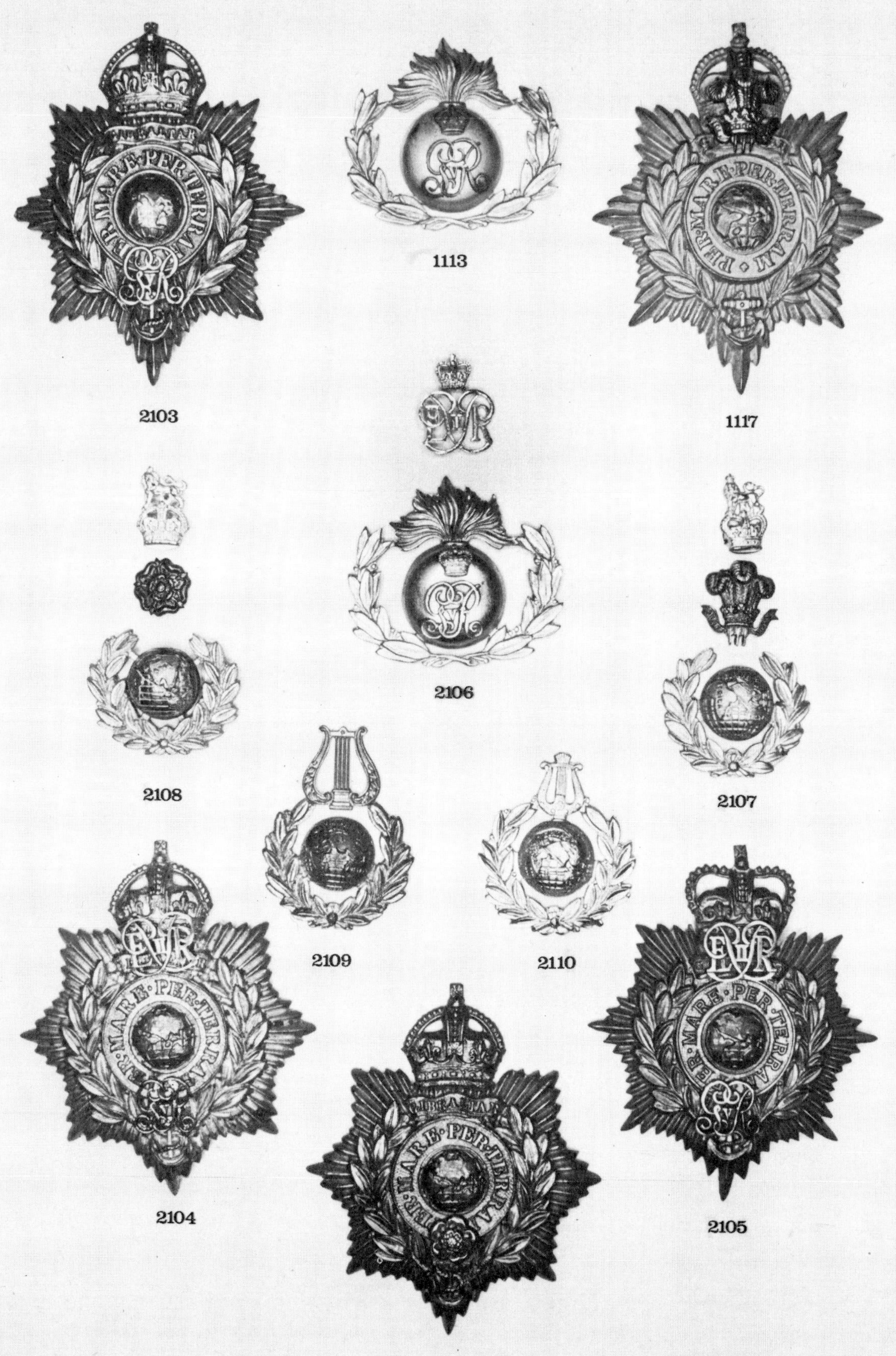

2103 1113 1117

2108 2106 2107

2109 2110

2104 1118 2105

CHAPTER 10

Department and Corps

Royal Army Chaplains Department

Christian Chaplains:

(1) A cross surmounted by an Imperial crown. In silver. Pattern worn up to 1922 (Fig. 973).

(2) A cross, surmounted by an Imperial crown, voided between the arms of the cross. In silver, also in black-metal (Fig. 974).

(3) A wreath, half of oak and half of laurel, surmounted by an Imperial crown. On the wreath a silver-plated Maltese cross with, at its centre, a gilt-lined blue-enamel circlet inscribed in gilt *In this sign conquer.* Within the circlet a voided gilt quatrefoil on a ground of blue-enamel (Fig. 2110). Also in black-metal for Service-dress cap. Sealed 12th December 1939.

(4) As (3) but with St. Edward's crown (Fig. 2111).

Jewish Chaplains:

(1) The Star of David surmounted by an Imperial crown in black-metal (Fig. 976).

(2) The Star of David in silver-plate enclosing a quatrefoil in gilt on blue-enamel. The whole within an oak- and laurel-wreath surmounted by an Imperial crown in gilt (Fig. 2112). In black-metal for Service-dress cap.

(3) As (2) but with St. Edward's crown (Fig. 2113).

Army Scripture Readers

Within a laurel-wreath the letters *ASR* on a bar. The wreath in gilding-metal, remainder in white-metal (Fig. 2114). First worn in all-brass but latterly in gold- and silver-anodised.

Royal Army Service Corps

(1) An eight-pointed star, the topmost-point displaced by an Imperial crown resting on the Garter and, in a voided centre, the Royal cypher of King George v. Below the Garter a scroll inscribed *Royal Army Service Corps* with laurel-sprays from each end of the scroll to meet the crown. In gilding-metal (Fig. 992). Officers': in gilt with blue-enamel ground to the Garter and red-enamel to the cypher.

(2) As above, but with the cypher of King Edward VIII (Fig. 2115).

(3) As above, but with the cypher of King George VI (Fig. 2116).

(4) Similar design but crown raised leaving a space between the base of the crown and the top of the Garter. Sealed 12th February 1949 (Fig. 2117).

(5) As (4) but with St. Edward's crown and cypher of Queen Elizabeth II. Sealed 5th February 1953 (Fig. 2118). Also anodised, sealed 16th August 1961.

973 974 976 2114

2110 2112 2111 2113

992 2115 2116 2117

2118

2120 2121

2119

Royal Corps of Transport

Formed 15th July 1965

A star of eight points in silver-anodised. Thereon a scroll terminating in sprigs of laurel and inscribed *Royal Corps of Transport*, all in gold-anodised, encircling the Garter proper. In a voided centre the Royal Cypher of Queen Elizabeth II in gold-anodised, all ensigned with St. Edward's crown in silver-anodised (Fig. 2119). Officers': in silver-and-gilt with a crimson ground to the Royal Cypher.

R.A.S.C. Fleet

Now the Army Department Fleet (Royal Corps of Transport)

(1) An embroidered Imperial crown with, below, the letters *R.A.S.C.* all within a gold-embroidered laurel-wreath on a navy-blue-cloth ground (Fig. 2120). Sealed 3rd March 1945.

(2) As above but with St. Edward's crown (Fig. 2121). Sealed 9th March 1954.

(3) As (2) but omitting the letters *R.A.S.C.* Sealed 11th June 1965.

Royal Army Medical Corps

(1) A laurel-wreath surmounted by an Imperial crown. In the centre the rod of Aesculapius with a serpent twined round it. Below, a scroll inscribed *Royal Army Medical Corps.* In gilding-metal (Fig. 1007). Officers': in gilt, also in bronze.

(2) As above but scroll inscribed *In arduis fidelis.* The scroll in white-metal, remainder in gilding-metal. Sealed 22nd September 1950. (Fig. 2122).

(3) As (2) but with St. Edward's crown (Fig. 2123). Officers' service-dress: bronze. Full-dress: gilt-and-silver. At first, only the scroll was in silver but later patterns have both scroll and serpent in silver. Sealed 20th April 1954.

Royal Army Ordnance Corps

(1) The Garter surmounted by an Imperial crown. Within the Garter a shield bearing the arms of the Board of Ordnance. Below the Garter a scroll inscribed *Royal Army Ordnance Corps.* In gilding-metal (Fig. 1025).

(2) As above but scroll inscribed *Sua tela tonanti.* In gilding-metal (Fig. 2124). Worn from March 1947 to November 1949. Sealed 14th March 1947.

(3) Within the Garter the shield of the arms of the Board of Ordnance and, above, an Imperial crown the base of which rests on the inner rim of the Garter. Below the Garter a scroll inscribed *Sua tela tonanti.* The shield in white-metal, remainder in gilding-metal (Fig. 2125). Also anodised. Adopted November 1949. Sealed 19th September 1949.

(4) As (3) but with St. Edward's crown (Fig. 2126). Sealed 2nd November 1954.

Royal Electrical and Mechanical Engineers

Formed 1st October 1942

(1) Four shields, each bearing one of the initials of the Corps title, placed on a laurel-wreath in the form of a cross with a pair of calipers in the centre, the whole ensigned with the Imperial crown. In gilding-metal. Sealed 22nd June 1942 (Fig. 2127). Officers': in gilt, also in bronze.

(2) Upon a flash-of-lightning a horse forcene with a coronet of four fleurs-de-lys round its neck, a chain attached to the back of the coronet and falling down its near-side to a globe on which the horse is standing on its near-side hind-leg. Above the horse

a scroll inscribed *R.E.M.E.* ensigned with an Imperial crown. The horse, coronet, chain and globe in white-metal; remainder in gilding-metal. Sealed 14th August 1947 (Fig. 2128). Also anodised. Officers': gilt-and-silver.

(3) As (2) but with St. Edward's crown. Sealed 9th June 1954 (Fig. 2129). Also anodised, sealed 25th September 1963.

Corps of Royal Military Police

Granted title of 'Royal' in 1946

(1) Within a laurel-wreath the cypher of King George v surmounted by an Imperial crown. Below the wreath a scroll inscribed *Military Police*. In gilding-metal (Fig. 1031).
(2) As above but with cypher of King George vi (Fig. 2130).
(3) As (2) but scroll inscribed *Royal Military Police*. Sealed 14th May 1948 (Fig. 2131).
(4) As (3) but with cypher of Queen Elizabeth ii and with St. Edward's crown (Fig. 2132). In gilding-metal, sealed 4th June 1953. Also anodised. Officers': in gilt, also in silver-plate.

Royal Army Pay Corps

(1) The monogram *RAPC* surmounted by the Royal Crest with Imperial crown. In gilding-metal (Fig. 1036). For officers: in gilt, also in bronze.
(2) The Royal Crest with Imperial crown over a scroll inscribed *Fide et fiducia*. The Royal Crest in gilding-metal, remainder in white-metal (Fig. 2133).
(3) Same design as (2) but with Royal Crest in brass and scroll in gilding-metal (Fig. 2134). Produced during the Second World War.
(4) As (2) but smaller (Fig. 2135).
(5) As (4) but smaller still for wear on the beret (Fig. 2136). Also anodised, sealed 19th October 1950.
(6) As (2) but with St. Edward's crown (Fig. 2137). Sealed 8th September 1954. Also anodised.
(7) As (5) but with St. Edward's crown (Fig. 2138). Also anodised.

Royal Army Veterinary Corps

(1) A Centaur (voided) within a wreath of laurel ensigned with an Imperial crown. Below the wreath a scroll inscribed *Royal Army Veterinary Corps*. The Centaur in white-metal, remainder in gilding-metal. Officers': in silver-plate and gilt, also in bronze (Fig. 1044).
(2) As above but with St. Edward's crown. Sealed 18th March 1955 (Fig. 2139). Also anodised.

Small Arms School Corps

The Small Arms School, Hythe, and Machine Gun School, Netheravon, were formed into the above Corps in 1929.

(1) A Vickers machine-gun and thereon a pair of crossed rifles with bayonets fixed with an Imperial crown within the angle formed by the rifles above the machine-gun. The whole within a wreath of laurel and, on the wreath, scrolls inscribed: on the left side *Small*, on the bottom *Arms*, on the right side *School*. In gilding-metal. Sealed 13th October 1930. (Fig. 2140). Also in bronze and later in chrome
(2) As above but with St. Edward's crown. Sealed in chrome, 6th September 1956 (Fig. 2141). Also anodised, sealed 6th September 1956.

Military Provost Staff Corps

(1) A laurel-wreath surmounted by an Imperial crown. Within this the cypher of King George v. In gilding-metal (Fig. 1054).
(2) The cypher of King George vi ensigned with an Imperial crown. In gilding-metal (Fig. 2142).
(3) The cypher of Queen Elizabeth ii ensigned with St. Edward's crown. Below, a scroll inscribed *Military Provost Staff Corps*. In gilding-metal. Sealed 16th October 1953 (Fig. 2143). Also anodised.

Royal Army Educational Corps

Granted 'Royal' title in 1946 (Army Order of 28th November)

(1) An open book superimposed on crossed lances and rifles. Below, a scroll inscribed *Army Educational Corps*. In gilding-metal. Sealed 16th August 1927 (Fig. 1056). Officers': in gilt, also in bronze.
(2) An open book surmounted by an Imperial crown superimposed on crossed rifles and lances. Below, a scroll inscribed *R.A.E.C.* The book in white-metal, remainder in gilding-metal (Fig. 2144). Trial-pattern only.
(3) A fluted-flambeau of five flames and theron, below the flames, an Imperial crown and, below the crown, a scroll inscribed *R.A.E.C.* The crown and scroll in gilding-metal, remainder in white-metal (Fig. 2145). Sealed 9th February 1951.
(4) As (3) but with St. Edward's crown. Sealed 28th February 1955 (Fig. 2146). Also anodised.

Royal Army Dental Corps

Granted title of 'Royal' in 1946 (A.O. 167/1946)

(1) A laurel-wreath surmounted by an Imperial crown. Within the wreath the monogram *ADC*. In gilding-metal. Sealed 11th August 1921 (Fig. 1057). Officers': in gilt, also in bronze.
(2) A dragon's head, with a sword in its mouth within a wreath of laurel ensigned with an Imperial crown. On the lower portion of the wreath a scroll inscribed *Ex dentibus ensis*. The head of the dragon and the blade of the sword in white-metal, remainder in gilding-metal. Sealed 16th January 1948 (Fig. 2147).
(3) As (2) but with St. Edward's crown. Sealed 21st June 1954 (Fig. 2148). Also anodised.

Royal Pioneer Corps

Auxiliary Military Pioneer Corps when raised in October 1939, Pioneer Corps under Army Order 200/1940, and 'Royal' title granted in 1946 (Army Order 176/1946)

(1) A 'pile' consisting of a pick, head downwards, placed centrally with a rifle crossing it in front from the left and a shovel crossing it between the rifle and pick from the right. On the 'pile' a wreath of laurel pointing downwards; above the 'pile' an Imperial crown and, below, a scroll inscribed *Labor omnia vincit.* In gilding-metal (Fig. 2149). Also in white-metal.
(2) As above but smaller size for wear on the beret. In gilding-metal. Sealed 31st October 1947 (Fig. 2150).
(3) As (2) but with St. Edward's crown. In gilding-metal. Sealed 27th July 1954 (Fig. 2151). Officers': in silver-plate.

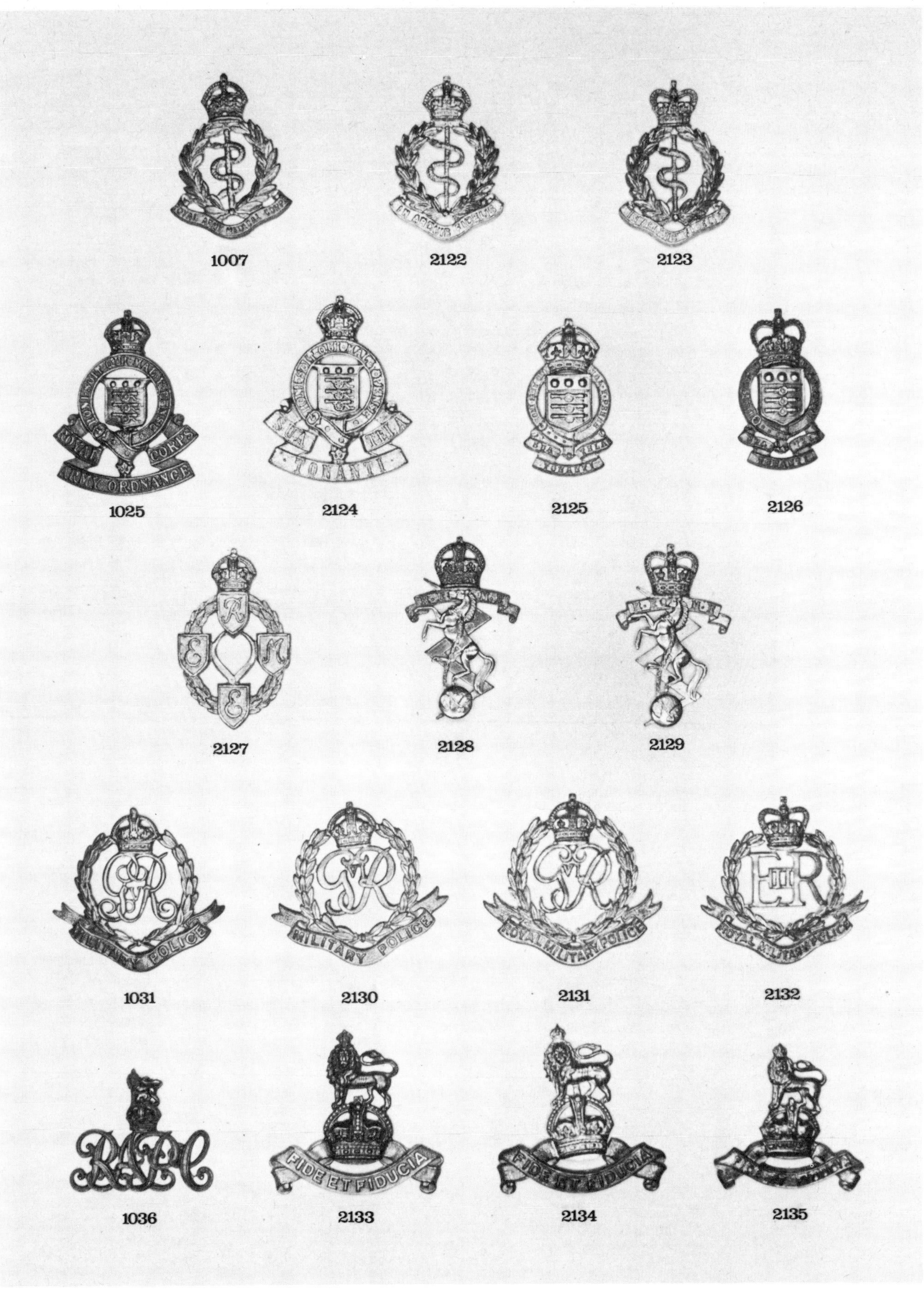
1007
2122
2123
ROYAL CORPS
ARMY ORDNANCE
1025
SUA TELA
TONANTI
2124
2125
2126
2127
2128
2129
MILITARY POLICE
1031
MILITARY POLICE
2130
ROYAL MILITARY POLICE
2131
ROYAL MILITARY POLICE
2132
1036
FIDE ET FIDUCIA
2133
FIDE ET FIDUCIA
2134
2135

Intelligence Corps
Raised in 1940 (Army Order 112/1940)
(1) A rose ensigned with the Imperial crown within two branches of laurel. Below the laurel a scroll inscribed *Intelligence Corps*. In gilding-metal. Sealed 11th August 1940 (Fig. 2152). Also anodised.
(2) As above but with St. Edward's crown. In gilding-metal. Sealed 10th June 1955 (Fig. 2153). Also anodised. Officers': in silver-plate.

Army Physical Training Corps
The Army School of Physical Training became a 'Corps' in September 1940
(1) Crossed swords surmounted by an Imperial crown. In gilding-metal (Fig. 1060).
(2) As above but in white-metal (Fig. 2154).
(3) As above but with St. Edward's crown. Sealed 26th October 1954 (Fig. 2155). Officers': in silver-plate.

Army Catering Corps
Formed in March 1941 (Army Order 35/1941)
(1) An ancient Grecian brazier within a circlet inscribed *Army Catering Corps* ensigned with an Imperial crown. In gilding-metal. Sealed 28th May 1941 (Fig. 2156).
(2) As above but with brazier in white-metal (Fig. 2157). Also anodised, sealed 12th March 1951.
(3) As (2) but with St. Edward's crown. Sealed 12th October 1954 (Fig. 2158). Also anodised, sealed 2nd April 1963.
(4) As (3) but with the addition of a scroll below the circlet inscribed *We sustain* (Fig. 2159). Also anodised.

Mobile Defence Corps
The Mobile Defence Corps was formed under Army Order 33 of 1955 and disbanded in 1959
A Phoenix arising from flames superimposed upon crossed swords surmounted by St. Edward's crown, with a scroll below inscribed *Mobile Defence Corps*. The Phoenix and flames in gilding-metal, remainder in white-metal. Sealed 9th December 1955 (Fig. 2160). Also anodised.

Royal Defence Corps (later National Defence Company)
(1) A circlet inscribed *Royal Defence Corps*. In the centre the cypher of King George v surmounted by an Imperial crown. In gilding-metal (Fig. 1063).
(2) A circlet inscribed *National Defence Company*. In the centre the cypher of King Edward VIII surmounted by an Imperial crown. In gilding-metal (Fig. 2161).
(3) Within a circlet inscribed *National Defence Company* the Royal cypher of King George VI in a voided-centre and surmounted by an Imperial crown. In gilding-metal (Fig. 2162). Also in bronze.

Non-Combatant Corps
Non-Combatant Labour Corps from July 1939 to April 1940
(1) The letters *NCLC*. In gilding-metal.
(2) The letters *NCC*. In gilding-metal (Fig. 2163).

2136 2137 2138

1044 2139 2140 2141

1054 2142 2143

1056 2144 2145 2146

1057 2147 2148

General Service Corps

(1) The Royal Arms in gilding-metal (Fig. 1084). Also in gilt and in bronze.
(2) As (1) but smaller size and with St. Edward's crown. Sealed 18th June 1963 (Fig. 2166). Also in gilt for officers.

The following was worn by the personnel of certain Training Battalions during 1944 and 1945:

(3) The Royal Crest with an Imperial crown superimposed on crossed swords. Below the Royal Crest a scroll inscribed *Deus Vult*. Below the scroll a decorative motif incorporating the rose, thistle, leek and shamrock. In gilding-metal, sealed 8th May 1944 (Fig. 2164). Officers' version in bronze.

The following is worn by Infantry only of the Junior Leaders Training Regiments: all others wear the cap-badge of their own arm.

(4) As (3), but with St. Edward's crown, in gilding metal. Sealed 12th November 1958 (Fig. 2165). Also anodised.

Army Legal Services

Badge granted in 1958: the blindfolded figure of Justice, holding a sword in the right hand and scales in the left hand, standing before a globe showing a map of Europe, Asia and Africa. Crossed swords points-upward behind the globe which is ensigned with the Royal Crest. All within a circlet inscribed *Army Legal Services*. Below the circlet a scroll inscribed *Justitia in Armis*. In silver-plate with red-enamel in the cushion of the crown and black-enamel behind the globe (Fig. 2767).

2149
2150
2151
2152
2160
2153
1060
2154
2155
ARMY CATERING CORPS
2156
ARMY CATERING CORPS
2157
ARMY CATERING CORPS
2158
2159
ROYAL DEFENCE CORPS
1063
2162
NCC
2163
NATIONAL DEFENCE COMPANY
2161
2166
2167
1084
2164
2165

CHAPTER 11

Schools and Miscellaneous

ROYAL MILITARY ACADEMY

The Academy was established by Royal Warrant of 30th April 1741 and trained officer-cadets for the Royal Regiment of Artillery and the Corps of Royal Engineers. It was amalgamated with the Royal Military College in 1947.

Officer-cadets' cap-badge: 1902 to 1947
A circlet inscribed *Royal Military Academy* surmounted by an Imperial crown. In the centre a gun. In gilding-metal (Fig. 1068). Also in gilt, and bronze.

ROYAL MILITARY COLLEGE

In 1802 the first college for Army Cadets was opened at Great Marlow. Meanwhile the permanent home at Sandhurst was being built and was completed in 1812. Officer-cadets from Sandhurst were commissioned into the Cavalry, Foot Guards, Infantry and the Departmental Corps.

Officer-cadets' cap-badge: 1911 to 1937

(1) A circlet inscribed *Vires acquirit eundo* surmounted by an Imperial crown. In the centre the cypher of King George v. In gilding-metal with the cypher in white-metal (Fig. 1075). Also in bronze.

(2) As above but all in white-metal (Fig. 1076).

Officer-cadets' cap-badge: 1937 to 1947

(1) A circlet inscribed *Vires acquirit eundo* surmounted by an Imperial crown. In the centre the cypher of King George vi. In gilding-metal with the cypher in white-metal (Fig. 2168). Also in bronze.

(2) As above but all in gilding-metal (Fig. 2169).

ROYAL MILITARY ACADEMY SANDHURST

The Royal Military Academy and The Royal Military College were amalgamated in 1947 and now trains officer-cadets for all Arms of the Services.

1068
1075
1076
2168
2169
2170
2171
2172
1077
2173
2174
2175
2176
2177
1083
1084

Officer-cadets' cap-badge: 1947 to 1953
A circlet inscribed *Royal Military Academy Sandhurst* surmounted by an Imperial crown. In the centre the cypher of King George VI. Below, a scroll inscribed *Serve to Lead.* In white-metal (Fig. 2170). Sealed 14th November 1946.

Officer-cadets' cap-badge: 1953 to date
A circlet inscribed *Royal Military Academy Sandhurst* surmounted by St. Edward's crown. In the centre the cypher of Queen Elizabeth II. Below, a scroll inscribed *Serve to Lead.* In white-metal (Fig. 2171). Sealed 22nd September 1953.

MONS OFFICER CADET SCHOOL

Mons Officer Cadet School was formed as a school for all arms, except Infantry, in 1949. The School took over infantry-training on the closing of Eaton Hall in 1958. It was absorbed by the Royal Military Academy Sandhurst in 1972.

Head-dress badge to 1972
The Royal Crest, above a scroll inscribed *Leadership*, all within a complete laurel-wreath joined at the head by a tablet inscribed *Mons.* The Royal Crest and motto silver-anodised, remainder gold-anodised (Fig. 2172).

ROYAL MILITARY SCHOOL OF MUSIC

A Military Music Class was established at Kneller Hall in March 1857. It was designated *The Military School of Music* and granted the title *Royal* in 1887.

Student Bandmasters cease to wear their regimental badges on joining the School and wear the badge described below which was taken into use on 10th October 1907. On the accession of Queen Elizabeth the crown was changed.

Student Bandmasters' Head-dress badge

(1) The monogram *RMSM* surmounted by an Imperial crown. In gilding-metal (Fig. 1077).
(2) As above but with St. Edward's crown (Fig. 2173).

ROYAL HOSPITAL, CHELSEA

The badge described below was introduced in 1945 for the Royal Hospital Staff. It is not worn by the pensioners.

Staff Head-dress badge

(1) Within the Garter proper, surmounted by an Imperial crown, the Rose and Thistle conjoined on one stalk. Below, a scroll inscribed *Royal Hospital Chelsea.* In gilding-metal (Fig. 2174). Sealed 7th December 1943.
(2) As above, but with St. Edward's crown in gold-anodised (Fig. 2175). Sealed 11th August 1954.

ARMY APPRENTICES SCHOOL

This title covered several institutions whose purpose was to train for the Regular Army tradesmen for such trades as armourers, fitters, electricians, etc. During the 1950s the group-title was changed to Army Apprentices College and all Junior Tradesmen, as the students are called, now wear the cap-badge of their particular arm.

School cap-badge

(1) A pierced cog-wheel on which is superimposed a cross, two swords in saltire and a fluted-flambeau of five flames, the whole surmounted by an Imperial crown. Below, a scroll inscribed *Army Apprentices School.* In gilding-metal (Fig. 2176). Sealed 1st January 1947. Pipers' version in white-metal.

(2) As above but with St. Edward's crown (Fig. 2177). Sealed 21st July 1954. Pipers' in silver-anodised.

EXTRA-REGIMENTALLY EMPLOYED LIST

The Extra-Regimentally Employed List originated as part of the re-organisation of the Staff of the Army resulting from the report of the Esher Committee in 1904.

The List was in two parts. Part I included the names of officers of the Judge Advocate's Staff and Staff Quartermasters; the latter being officers employed at Training Establishments, etc., or on establishments not applicable to any particular arm of the Service. Part II included the names of Quartermasters supernumerary to their regimental establishment.

The E.R.E. List was re-organised and divided into three categories in 1953.

Cap-badge

The Royal Crest in gilt (Fig. 1083). Also in bronze.

GENERAL LIST

The General List first appeared in *The Army List* in October 1914, its title being *General List, Infantry, for Service Battalions*, and it included the names of 'officers who have been gazetted to the General List for service with Service Battalions but whose allocation is not included in this issue'. To this was added, in February 1915, the names of officers 'who are holding other appointments'.

Cap-badge

The Royal Arms in gilt (Fig. 1084). Also in bronze.

MISCELLANEOUS

War Correspondents

Gold-embroidered letter *C* within a circular chain on gold cloth. Sealed 11th May 1956.

War Department Constabulary

Renamed Army Department Constabulary in 1964 without change of badge.

(1) The cypher of King George VI within a circlet inscribed *War Dept Constabulary* and surmounted by an Imperial crown. In white-metal (Fig. 2178).

(2) As above but with the cypher of Queen Elizabeth II and the St. Edward's crown.

(3) An eight-pointed star the topmost-point displaced by St. Edward's crown. On the star a circlet inscribed *War Dept Constabulary* and in the centre the cypher of Queen Elizabeth II. In silver plate. Also chrome, sealed 13th January 1953. Introduced in 1962 for Sub-Inspectors and above.

Ministry of Defence Police

On 1st October 1971 the police-forces of the Navy, Army and Air Force were amalgamated.

(1) Officers': a silver-plated eight-pointed star, the topmost-point displaced by St. Edward's crown. On this a blue-enamelled circlet inscribed *Ministry of Defence Police*. On a frosted-centre the cypher of Queen Elizabeth II.

(2) Sergeants' and Constables': a laurel-wreath surmounted by St. Edward's crown. Within this a circlet inscribed *Ministry of Defence Police*. In a voided-centre an eight-pointed star with a frosted-centre bearing the cypher of Queen Elizabeth II. In white-metal (Fig. 2179).

Army Depot Police Cyprus

Formerly War Dept Police (Cyprus), it was formed to guard the Sovereign Base areas following the granting of independence to Cyprus.

(1) On a circular shield the Arms of Cyprus, two lions passant gardant one above the other, surmounted by St. Edward's crown. Below, a scroll inscribed *War Dept Police (Cyprus)*. In white-metal (Fig. 2180). Also anodised, sealed 28th March 1962. Officers' in silver-plate.

(2) As above but scroll altered to read *Army Depot Police Cyprus*. In silver-anodised.

Army Department Fire Service

(1) The Royal cypher of Queen Elizabeth II within a circlet inscribed *Fire Service* at top and *W.D.* at bottom surmounted by St. Edward's crown. Chromed, sealed 20th January 1954 and in silver-anodised, sealed 25th March 1962 (Fig. 2181).

(2) As above but the circlet inscribed Army Fire Service, in silver-anodised.

Crown Film Unit

A circlet inscribed *Crown Film Unit* and within this an Imperial crown. In bronze (Fig. 2182).

War Office Messengers

A scroll inscribed *The War Office* surmounted by St. Edward's crown. In gilding-metal (Fig. 2183). Sealed 1st October 1953. Senior Messengers': the same badge but chromed, was sealed 1st October 1953.

Control Commission Germany

Within a laurel-wreath, the monogram *CCG*. In brass (Fig. 2184). Officers' in gilt.

Control Commission Germany: Police

An eight-pointed star, the topmost-point displaced by an Imperial crown. On this the cypher of King George VI. In silver-plate (Fig. 2185). Worn by officers.

The Allied Control Commission for Austria

Cap-badge: the crusader-shield of the Eighth Army with a tablet above inscribed *A.C.A.* In metal and enamels: both shield and cross in white-enamel outlined in gold; the tablet in white-enamel outlined and inscribed in gold; the space between the shield and the tablet in blue-enamel. Fitted at the back with a pin-brooch fastener.

2178

2179

2180

2181

2182

2183

2184

2185

CHAPTER 12

Women's Services

Queen Alexandra's Royal Army Nursing Corps
Formed 1st February 1949 (Army Order 5/1949). Other ranks included 1st July 1950 (A.C.I. 455/1950)

(1) The Dannebrog, thereon in the centre a circle enclosing the letter *A*, the cypher of Queen Alexandra; above, and resting on the top arm of the cross, an Imperial crown; on either side of the cross a wreath of laurel. On the lower portion of the left branch a scroll inscribed *Sub Cruce* and on the lower portion of the right branch a scroll inscribed *Candida.* Below the cross, and on the bottom of the branches, a scroll inscribed *Q.A.R.A.N.C.* The bottom-scroll in white-metal, remainder in gilding-metal (Fig. 2186). Worn on a backing of scarlet-cloth. Officers': in silver-and-gilt.
(2) As above but with St. Edward's crown (Fig. 2187). In same metals, also anodised. Officers': in gilt-and-silver.
(3) Officer's beret-badge: embroidered in gold and silver, with a red cap to the crown, on grey-cloth.

Auxiliary Territorial Service
Formed 9th September 1938 by Royal Warrant.
The letters *A TS* within a laurel-wreath surmounted by an Imperial crown. In gilding-metal (Fig. 2188). Officers': in gilt, also in bronze.

Women's Royal Army Corps
Formed 1st February 1949 (Army Order 6/1949).

(1) Within a laurel-wreath a lioness rampant surmounted by an Imperial crown. The lioness in white-metal, remainder in gilding-metal (Fig. 2189). Officers': in silver-and-gilt.
(2) As above but with St. Edward's crown (Fig. 2190). Worn on a beech-brown backing. Also anodised. Officers': in silver-and-gilt.
(3) Officers' beret-badge: embroidered in gold, silver and red on bottle-green cloth.

First Aid Nursing Yeomanry
This organisation was formed in 1907 as a corps of horsewomen, trained in first-aid, for mobile service. By 1914 it had become mechanised and during the Great War served in France and Flanders with the British, French and Belgian Armies. It was the first women's service to be mechanised and staffed, and ran self-contained ambulance units.

By Army Order 94 of 31st March 1927 it was re-designated *First Aid Nursing Yeomanry (Ambulance Car Corps)* and again changed in 1933 to *Women's Transport Service (F.A.N.Y.)*

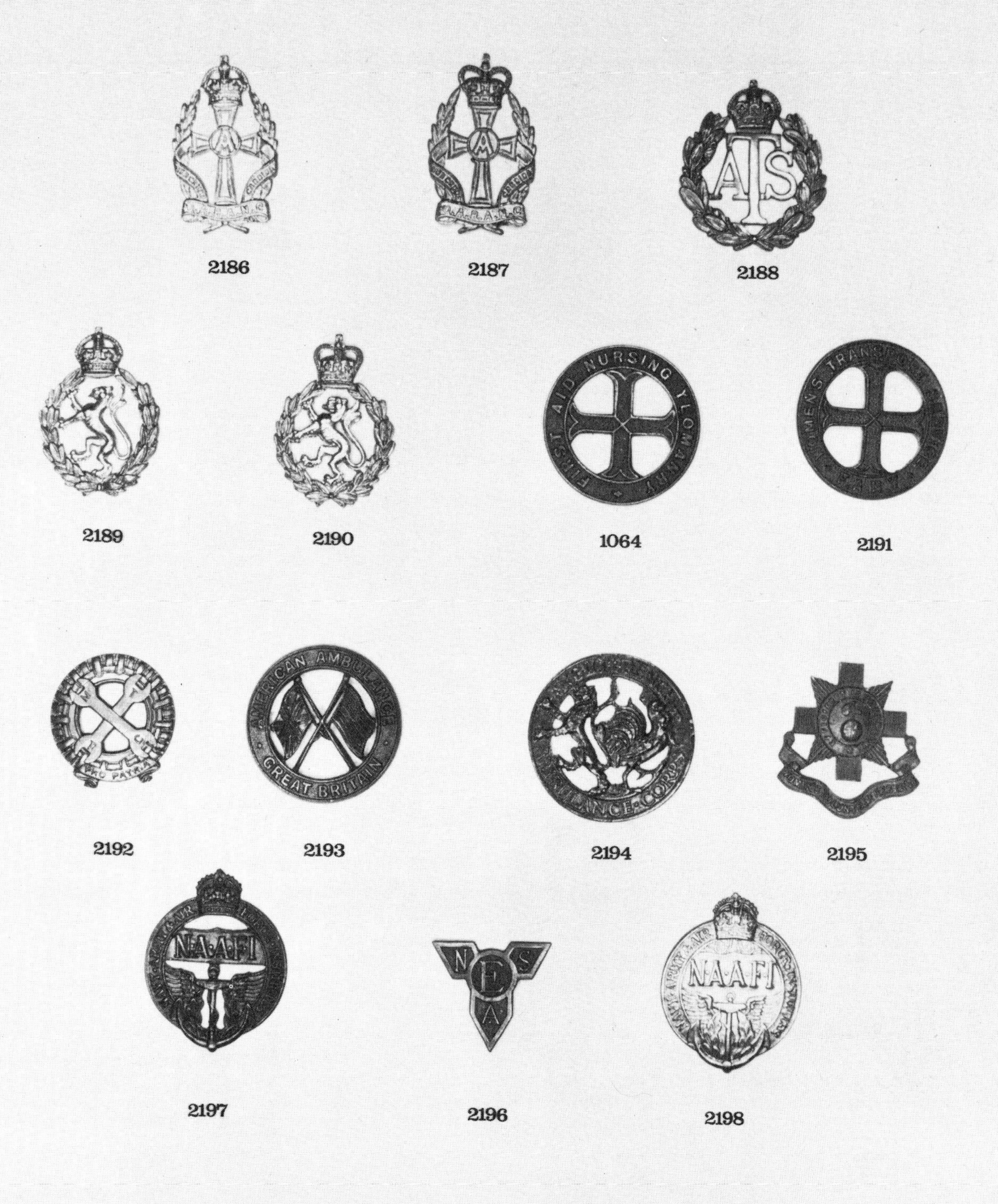
2186
2187
ATS
2188
2189
2190
FIRST AID NURSING YEOMANRY
1064
2191
PRO PATRIA
2192
AMERICAN AMBULANCE
GREAT BRITAIN
2193
2194
2195
N·A·A·F·I
2197
N F S A
2196
N·A·A·F·I
2198

Badge
A circlet inscribed *First Aid Nursing Yeomanry* with, in the centre, a cross moline. In bronze (Fig. 1064).

Women's Transport Service (F.A.N.Y.)
A circlet inscribed *Women's Transport Service F.A.N.Y.* with, in the centre, a cross moline. In bronze (Fig. 2191).

Mechanised Transport Training Corps
Formed in February 1939. Trained drivers for Government departments and allocated drivers for those departments and branches of the Services. Later, the word *Training* was omitted from the title. When H.R.H. The Princess Elizabeth was commissioned into the A.T.S. she attended No. 1 Training Centre at Aldershot.

Badge
Superimposed on a motor-tyre two open-ended spanners in saltire. On either end of the two spanners are the letters *M.T.T.C.* Below, a scroll inscribed *Pro Patria.* In bronze (Fig. 2192).

American Ambulance in Great Britain
Staffed by British personnel and financed from 1940 through the British War Relief Society of the U.S.A.

Badge
A circlet inscribed *American Ambulance Great Britain.* In a voided-centre crossed flags: the Great Union on the left and the Stars and Stripes on the right. In bronze (Fig. 2193).

Anglo-French Ambulance Corps
A circlet inscribed *Anglo-French Ambulance Corps.* In a voided-centre the British Lion rampant on the left and the Gallic Cock on the right. In bronze (Fig. 2194).

Women's Volunteer Reserve
St. George's Cross superimposed on a four-pointed star. On this a circlet inscribed *Efficiency is Strength.* In the centre a globe surmounted by a pennant bearing the Cross of St. George. Below, a scroll inscribed *Women's Volunteer Reserve.* In bronze (Fig. 2195).

Entertainments National Service Association
Triangular in shape with the letters *N* and *S* top-left and top-right, the letter *E* in a circle in the centre, and the letter *A* below. The letter *E* and outer border in blue-enamel, and circle surrounding the *E* in red and the letters *N.S.A.* in gilt, all on a white background. Also in bronze (Fig. 2196).

Navy, Army and Air Force Institutes
(1) A Fouled Anchor with a slip of laurel and wings either side. Above, the letters *N.A.A.F.I.* all within a circlet inscribed *Navy Army & Air Force Institutes* and surmounted by an Imperial crown. The centre voided. In black-metal (Fig. 2197).
(2) As above but non-voided. In silver-plate (Fig. 2198).

CHAPTER 13

The Plastic Badges of the Second World War

Plastic badges were introduced into the British Army early in 1942. Unlike the case of the all-brass badges of 1916, there was no question of saving labour: at this later time in our history metal-for-munitions was of paramount importance.

Householders had been exhorted by leaflet, and through the medium of radio, to surrender-up all unwanted metal; they were informed how many saucepans or kettles would make an essential part for a Spitfire or tank; and their local parks and gardens were denuded systematically of iron gates and railings. So the least that the Government of the day could do was to economise on the manufacture of badges by finding a suitable substitute for metal.

At that time, new forms of plastic materials were being developed and even simple things like cardboard containers for cosmetics and razor-blades were being ousted in favour of delicate little boxes made in coloured plastics; so what better material to try.

The colours chosen were silver-grey, light-bronze, chocolate-brown, and black, but those of The Royal Marines, The King's Royal Rifle Corps, and the Buckinghamshire Batallion are the only examples known in the last-named colour.

The fasteners on the reverse were mainly two thin brass strips and we suggest that, when mounting these badges, collectors bend the strips back both in the same direction; not towards each other. This will reduce wear and avoid possible fracture if subsequent mounting is required. Only a very few had a single slider but that type is found in later issues of the Royal Artillery 'gun'-pattern and of The Army Physical Training Corps.

Although this book deals only with British Army badges, collectors might be interested to know that plastic badges were also issued to the Royal Air Force, The Air Training Corps, The King's Own Malta Regiment and the Polish Army in Britain.

The following is a list of all those issued with, where known, the date the pattern was sealed.

Royal Armoured Corps

A mailed gauntlet for the right hand, fist clenched, palm to the front, with a billet on the wrist inscribed *RAC*; issuing from the wrist upwards, two concentric circles barbed; the whole ensigned with the Imperial crown. In light-bronze (Fig. 2199). Sealed 31st January 1943.

Royal Tank Regiment

Within a laurel-wreath, surmounted by the Imperial crown, an early-model tank; on the bottom of the wreath a scroll inscribed *Fear Naught.* In light-bronze (Fig. 2200). Sealed 12th February 1943.

Reconnaissance Corps
A vertical spear, point uppermost, on each side forked-lightning; on the base of the spear and lightning, a scroll inscribed *Reconnaissance Corps*. In chocolate-brown (Fig. 2201). Sealed 31st August 1942.

The Royal Regiment of Artillery
(1) Above a gun a scroll inscribed *Ubique* surmounted by an Imperial crown. Below the gun a scroll inscribed *Quo fas et gloria ducunt*. In chocolate-brown (Fig. 2202).
(2) A grenade of seven flames with a scroll below inscribed *Ubique*. In chocolate-brown (Fig. 2203).

Corps of Royal Engineers
The Royal Cypher of King George VI within the Garter and surmounted by an Imperial crown, the whole surrounded by a laurel-wreath. Across the base of the wreath a scroll inscribed *Royal Engineers*. In chocolate-brown (Fig. 2204).

Royal Corps of Signals
An oval inscribed *Royal Corps of Signals* with, in the bottom-centre, the Globe with a sprig of laurel either side. The oval surmounted by an Imperial crown. In the centre the figure of Mercury, holding a caduceus in his left hand, his right hand held aloft, poised on the Globe with his left foot. In chocolate-brown (Fig. 2205).

Grenadier Guards
A fused grenade. In light-bronze (Fig. 2206).

Coldstream Guards
The Star of the Order of the Garter. In light-bronze.

Scots Guards
The star of the Order of the Thistle in light-bronze (Fig. 2207).

The Royal Scots (The Royal Regiment)
The Star of the Order of the Thistle. In a voided-centre St. Andrew and Cross on a red background, below which a scroll inscribed *The Royal Scots*. In light-bronze (Fig. 2208). Sealed 25th August 1943.

The Queen's Royal Regiment (West Surrey)
The Paschal Lamb. In light-bronze (Fig. 2209).

The Buffs (Royal East Kent Regiment)
A Dragon above a scroll inscribed *The Buffs*. In light-bronze (Fig. 2210). Sealed 3rd September 1943.

The King's Own Royal Regiment (Lancaster)
The Lion of England on a bar inscribed *The King's Own*. In light-bronze (Fig. 2211). Sealed 13th August 1943.

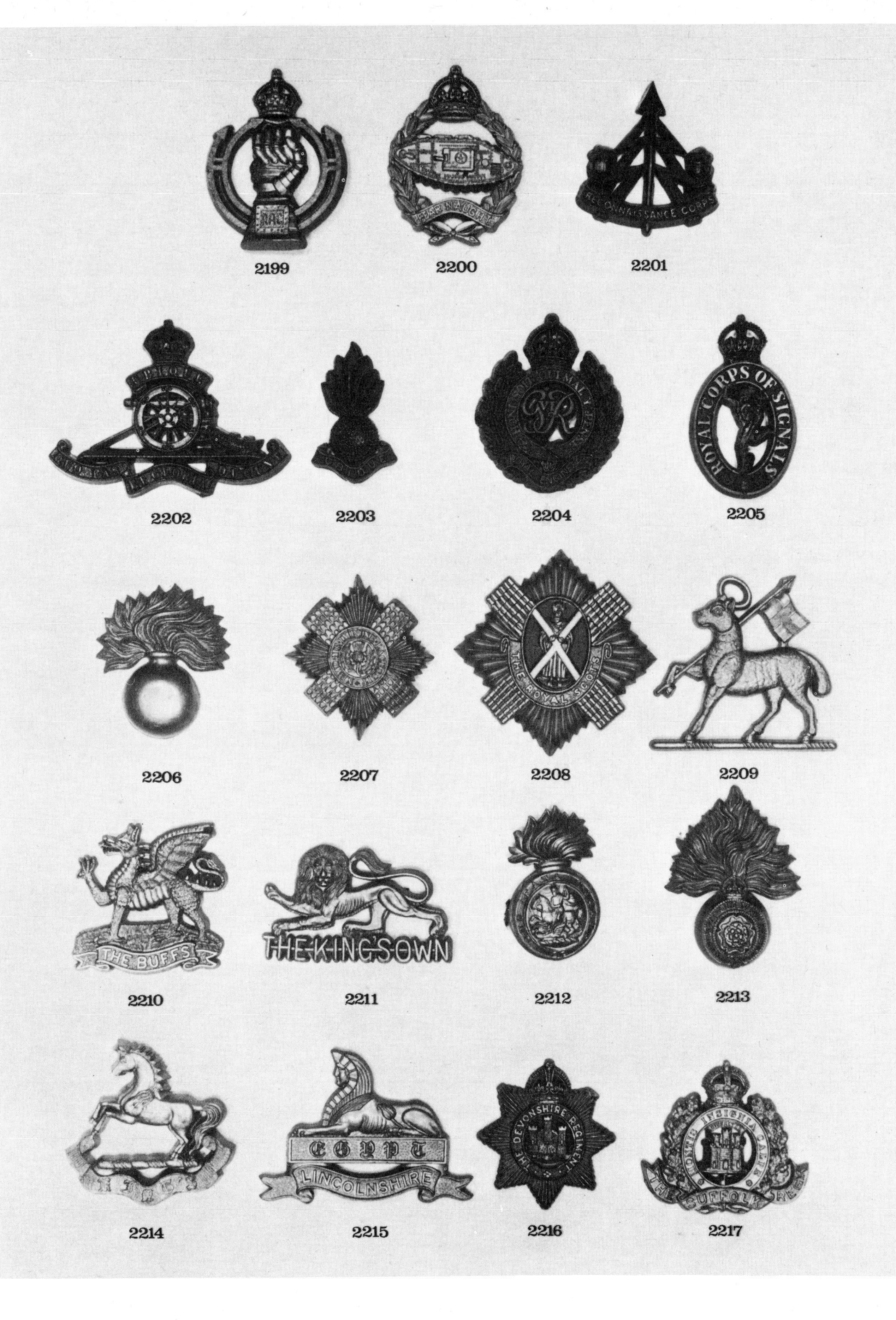

2199 2200 2201

2202 2203 2204 2205

2206 2207 2208 2209

2210 2211 2212 2213

2214 2215 2216 2217

The Royal Northumberland Fusiliers
A grenade. On the ball a circlet inscribed *Quo Fata Vovant*; within the circlet St. George and the Dragon. In light-bronze (Fig. 2212). Sealed 9th July 1943.

The Royal Fusiliers (City of London Regiment)
A fused grenade. On the ball the Garter proper with the Imperial crown superimposed. In the centre a Rose. In light-bronze (Fig. 2213). Sealed 17th March 1945.

The King's Regiment (Liverpool)
The White Horse of Hanover standing on an heraldic-horse; below this a scroll inscribed *King's* in Old English lettering. In light-bronze (Fig. 2214).

The Lincolnshire Regiment
The Sphinx resting on a tablet inscribed *Egypt* in Old English lettering. Below this a scroll inscribed *Lincolnshire*. In light-bronze (Fig. 2215).

The Devonshire Regiment
An eight-pointed star, the topmost-point displaced by an Imperial crown. On the Star a circlet inscribed *The Devonshire Regiment*. Within the circlet the Castle of Exeter inscribed with the motto *Semper fidelis*. In light-bronze (Fig. 2216). Sealed 13th August 1943.

The Suffolk Regiment
The Castle and Key of Gibraltar, with a scroll above inscribed *Gibraltar*, within a circlet inscribed *Montis Insignia Calpe* surmounted by an Imperial crown, the whole within a wreath of oak. Below, a scroll inscribed *The Suffolk Regt*. In light-bronze (Fig. 2217). Sealed 9th October 1942.

The West Yorkshire Regiment (The Prince of Wales's Own)
The White Horse of Hanover on ground. Below, a scroll inscribed *West Yorkshire*. In light-bronze (Fig. 2218). Sealed 9th October 1942.

The East Yorkshire Regiment (The Duke of York's Own)
An eight-pointed star, with the White Rose of York in the centre, surrounded by a laurel-wreath. Below, a scroll inscribed *East Yorkshire*. In light-bronze (Fig. 2219). Sealed 14th November 1943.

The Bedfordshire and Hertfordshire Regiment
A Maltese cross superimposed on an eight-pointed star. On this the Garter proper and in the centre a Hart crossing a ford. Below, a scroll inscribed *Bedfordshire & Hertfordshire*. In silver-grey (Fig. 2220). Sealed 3rd May 1943.

The Leicestershire Regiment
The Royal Tiger superscribed *Hindoostan*. A scroll below inscribed *Leicestershire*. In light-bronze (Fig. 2221).

The Green Howards (Alexandra, Princess of Wales's Own Yorkshire Regiment)
The letter *A*, cypher of the late Queen Alexandra, with *Alexandra* inscribed on the cross-bar of the cypher; combined with the cypher is the Dannebrog inscribed *1875* on the cross;

below are two scrolls: the top one inscribed *The Yorkshire Regiment* and the bottom one *Princess of Wales's Own.* A Rose below the centre of the bottom scroll; the whole ensigned with a coronet. In silver-grey (Fig. 2222).

The Lancashire Fusiliers
A fused grenade. On the ball a laurel-wreath and within this the Sphinx superscribed *Egypt.* Below, a scroll inscribed *The Lancashire Fusiliers.* In light-bronze (Fig. 2223). Sealed 1st March 1944.

The Cheshire Regiment
An eight-pointed star. On this a circlet inscribed *The Cheshire Regiment.* In the centre an acorn with oak-leaves. In light-bronze (Fig. 2224). Sealed 16th April 1943.

The Royal Welch Fusiliers
A fused grenade. On the ball a circlet inscribed *Royal Welch Fusiliers.* In the centre the Prince of Wales's plumes, coronet and motto. In light-bronze (Fig. 2225). Sealed 10th April 1943.

The South Wales Borderers
An unbroken wreath of Immortelles on the base of which the letters *SWB.* In the centre the Sphinx superscribed *Egypt.* In light-bronze (Fig. 2226). Sealed 18th January 1943.

The Royal Inniskilling Fusiliers
A fused grenade. On the ball the Castle of Inniskilling with St. George's flag flying to the right from the central turret. Below the Castle a scroll inscribed *Inniskilling.* In light-bronze (Fig. 2227). Sealed 12th January 1944.

The Gloucestershire Regiment
(1) The Sphinx superscribed *Egypt* above two sprays of laurel. Below, a scroll inscribed *Gloucestershire.* In silver-grey (Fig. 2228).
(2) Back-badge: the Sphinx superscribed *Egypt* within a complete laurel-wreath. In light-bronze (Fig. 2229). Sealed 3rd May 1943.

The East Lancashire Regiment
The Sphinx superscribed *Egypt* and below this the Rose; the whole within a laurel-wreath surmounted by the Imperial crown. Resting on the lower portion of the wreath a scroll inscribed *East Lancashire.* In light-bronze (Fig. 2230). Sealed 29th April 1943.

The East Surrey Regiment
An eight-pointed star, the topmost-point displaced by an Imperial crown which rests on a shield bearing the Arms of Guildford. Below, a scroll inscribed *East Surrey.* In light bronze (Fig. 2231).

The Duke of Cornwall's Light Infantry
A bugle with strings. Resting on each end of the bugle a scroll inscribed *Cornwall.* Above the scroll a coronet. In silver-grey (Fig. 2232). Sealed 10th April 1943.

The Duke of Wellington's Regiment (West Riding)
The crest and motto of the Duke of Wellington above a scroll inscribed *The West Riding.* In light-bronze (Fig. 2233). Sealed 29th April 1943.

The Border Regiment
An eight-pointed star, the topmost-point displaced by an Imperial crown. On the star a cross, similar to that of the Order of the Bath, on the four arms of which are inscribed battle honours. The cross is superimposed on a laurel-wreath. In the centre of the cross a circlet inscribed *Arroyo dos Molinos 1811* and in the centre a Dragon superscribed *China* on a ground of one-third white (above) and two-thirds red (below). On the lower points of the star a scroll inscribed *The Border Regt.* In silver-grey (Fig. 2234). Sealed 3rd May 1943.

The Royal Sussex Regiment
The Star of the Order of the Garter over the Roussillon plume with a scroll below inscribed *The Royal Sussex Regt.* In silver-grey (Fig. 2235). Sealed 18th June 1943.

The Hampshire Regiment
The Hampshire Rose above which the Royal Tiger standing on an heraldic torse, the whole enclosed by a laurel-wreath. On the lower part of the wreath a scroll inscribed *Hampshire.* In light-bronze (Fig. 2236).

The South Staffordshire Regiment
The Stafford Knot surmounted by an Imperial crown. Below the Knot a scroll inscribed *South Staffordshire.* In silver-grey (Fig. 2237). Sealed 29th April 1943.

The Dorsetshire Regiment
The Castle and Key of Gibraltar. Above the Castle the Sphinx superscribed *Marabout.* Below, a scroll inscribed *Primus in Indis.* A laurel-wreath encloses the Castle and motto and is continued below the Castle by a scroll inscribed *Dorsetshire.* In light-bronze (Fig. 2238). Sealed 10th April 1943.

The South Lancashire Regiment (The Prince of Wales's Volunteers)
The Prince of Wales's plumes, coronet and motto. Below, the Sphinx superscribed *Egypt.* Above the plumes a scroll inscribed *South Lancashire* and below the Sphinx a scroll inscribed *Prince of Wales's Vols.* Branches of laurel connect the ends of the scrolls. In light-bronze (Fig. 2239).

The Welch Regiment
The Prince of Wales's plumes, coronet and motto. Below, a scroll inscribed *The Welch.* In light-bronze (Fig. 2240). Sealed 14th February 1943.

The Black Watch (Royal Highland Regiment)
The Star of the Order of the Thistle. On the Star a thistle-wreath. Within the wreath an oval inscribed *Nemo me impune lacessit* surmounted by an Imperial crown. Within the oval St. Andrew and Cross. Below the wreath the Sphinx. In silver-grey (Fig. 2241).

The Essex Regiment
The Castle and Key of Gibraltar. Above the Castle the Sphinx superscribed *Egypt.* The whole, except the Sphinx, enclosed in a wreath of oak. On the base of the wreath a scroll inscribed *The Essex Regt.* In chocolate-brown (Fig. 2242). Sealed 22nd February 1943.

2218 2219 2220 2221

2222 2223 2224 2225

2226 2227 2228 2229 2230

2231 2232 2233 2234

2235 2236 2237 2238

The Sherwood Foresters (Nottinghamshire and Derbyshire Regiment)
A Maltese cross surmounted by an Imperial crown. In the centre of the cross a wreath of oak and, within the wreath, a stag lodged. On the left arm of the cross and across the left branch of the wreath a half-scroll inscribed *Sherwood*, and on the right arm of the cross and across the right branch of the wreath a half-scroll inscribed *Foresters*. Below the cross a scroll inscribed *Notts & Derby*. In silver-grey (Fig. 2243).

The Loyal Regiment (North Lancashire)
The Royal Crest with the Imperial crown above the Rose of Lancaster. Below the Rose a scroll inscribed *The Loyal Regiment*. In light-bronze (Fig. 2244). Sealed 4th August 1943.

The Northamptonshire Regiment
The Castle and Key of Gibraltar within a laurel-wreath. Above the Castle a scroll inscribed *Gibraltar* and below the Castle a scroll inscribed *Talavera*. On the base of the wreath a scroll inscribed *Northamptonshire*. In light-bronze (Fig. 2245). Sealed 29th April 1943.

The Royal Marines
The Globe, showing the Eastern hemisphere, surmounted by the Royal Crest, within a laurel-wreath. In black (Fig. 2246). Sealed 12th September 1944.

The Queen's Own Royal West Kent Regiment
The White Horse of Kent on a scroll inscribed *Invicta* in Old English lettering. Below the motto-scroll another scroll inscribed *Royal West Kent*. In silver-grey (Fig. 2247). Sealed 3rd May 1943.

The King's Own Yorkshire Light Infantry
A French horn with the White Rose of York in the twist. In light-bronze (Fig. 2248). Sealed 9th July 1943.

The King's Shropshire Light Infantry
A strung bugle-horn, the strings tied in three bows. Within the bend of the bugle, and below the strings, within bars the letters *KSLI*. In light-bronze (Fig. 2249).

The Middlesex Regiment (The Duke of Cambridge's Own)
The Prince of Wales's plumes, coronet and motto. Below, the coronet and cypher of the Duke of Cambridge interlaced and reversed, all within a laurel-wreath. Across the base of the wreath a scroll inscribed *Albuhera*. Below the wreath a scroll inscribed *Middlesex Regt*. In chocolate-brown (Fig. 2250). Sealed 9th October 1942.

The King's Royal Rifle Corps
A Maltese cross. On the top arm a tablet inscribed *Celer et Audax* and above the tablet an Imperial crown. In the centre of the cross a circlet inscribed *The King's Royal Rifle Corps*. Within the circlet a bugle with strings. Battle honours on each arm of the cross. In black (Fig. 2251). Sealed 4th August 1943.

The Wiltshire Regiment (Duke of Edinburgh's)
A cross patée, lined, with burnished edges. On the cross a circular convex plate and thereon the cypher of the Duke of Edinburgh. Above the cross a coronet. Below, a scroll inscribed *The Wiltshire Regiment*. In light-bronze (Fig. 2252). Sealed 3rd May 1943.

2239 2240 2241 2242

2243 2244 2245 2246

2247 2248 2249 2250

2251 2252 2253 2254

2255 2256 2257 2258

The Manchester Regiment
A fleur-de-lys. In chocolate-brown (Fig. 2253). Sealed 4th December 1942.

The North Staffordshire Regiment (The Prince of Wales's)
The Stafford Knot with the Prince of Wales's plumes, coronet and motto above and a scroll inscribed *North Stafford* below. In light-bronze (Fig. 2254). Sealed 16th September 1943.

The York and Lancaster Regiment
The Royal Tiger with the Union Rose above and surmounted by a coronet. Below the Tiger a scroll inscribed *York and Lancaster* with laurel-sprays continuing the scroll to the coronet. In chocolate-brown (Fig. 2255). Sealed 15th January 1943.

The Durham Light Infantry
A Bugle with strings taken up into the base of an Imperial crown. Within the strings the letters *DLI.* In silver-grey (Fig. 2256).

The Highland Light Infantry (City of Glasgow Regiment)
The Star of the Order of the Thistle, thereon a bugle-horn. In the twist of the horn the monogram *HLI.* Above the horn an Imperial crown and below it the Elephant superscribed *Assaye* on a scroll. In silver-grey (Fig. 2257). Sealed 3rd March 1943.

The Queen's Own Cameron Highlanders
St. Andrew and Cross within a wreath of thistles. On the base of the wreath a scroll inscribed *Cameron.* In silver-grey (Fig. 2258). Sealed 4th April 1945.

The Royal Ulster Rifles
A Harp surmounted by an Imperial crown. Below the Harp a scroll inscribed *Quis Separabit,* In silver-grey (Fig. 2259). Sealed 3rd September 1943.

The Royal Irish Fusiliers (Princess Victoria's)
A fused grenade. On the ball a Harp surmounted by the Prince of Wales's plumes, coronet and motto. Above this, as a separate badge, a coronet. In chocolate-brown (Fig. 2260). Sealed 14th November 1943.

The Argyll and Sutherland Highlanders (Princess Louise's)
A circlet inscribed *Argyll and Sutherland.* Within the cirlet the letter *L*, cypher of the late Princess Louise, interlaced and reversed. Within the circlet and on the left of the cypher the Boar's Head and on the right of the cypher the Cat. Above the cypher and resting on the top part of the circlet the Princess's coronet. The whole within a wreath of thistles. In silver-grey (Fig. 2261).

The Rifle Brigade (Prince Consort's Own)
A cross based on that of the Order of the Bath and thereon a circlet inscribed *The Rifle Brigade* enclosing a bugle surmounted by an Imperial crown. The cross is surrounded by a wreath of laurel bearing fourteen battle-honour-scrolls and two further battle-honour-scrolls are below the cross. The upper-ends of the wreath are connected to a tablet inscribed *Waterloo* and surmounted by an Imperial crown. Battle honours are also inscribed on each arm of the cross. Across the base of the wreath a scroll inscribed *Prince Consort's Own.* In silver-grey (Fig. 2262).

The Parachute Regiment
Upon a spread of wings an open parachute. Above, the Royal Crest. In silver-grey (Fig. 2263). Sealed 5th February 1944.

Army Air Corps
An eagle, surmounted by an Imperial crown, alighting upon the uppermost of two bars inscribed with the letters *A.A.C.* and surrounded by a laurel-wreath. In light-bronze (Fig. 2264).

The Highland Regiment
A cross resembling St. Andrew's Cross, but sharpened at each point. On the cross a circular strap with the buckle on the left side level with the centre of the cross; on the opposite side, a thistle; the strap inscribed at the top *Highland* and at the bottom *Regiment.* On the arms of the cross, and within the strap, two claymores points-uppermost. In the centre of the cross a targe. In light-bronze (Fig. 2265).

The Cambridgeshire Regiment
A bridge (the crest of Cambridge City Council) on which is superimposed a shield bearing the arms of Ely. Beneath this a scroll inscribed *The Cambridgeshire Regt.* In light-bronze (Fig. 2266). Sealed 30th December 1942.

The Buckinghamshire Battalion
A Maltese cross surmounted by an Imperial crown. On this a circlet inscribed *Buckinghamshire Battalion.* In the centre a swan with a coronet round its neck. In black (Fig. 2267). Sealed 29th February 1944.

Royal Army Service Corps
An eight-pointed star, the topmost-point displaced by an Imperial crown; on the star a laurel-wreath bearing a scroll inscribed *Royal Army Service Corps*; within the wreath the Garter proper and, in the centre, the Royal Cypher of King George VI. In chocolate-brown (Fig. 2268).

Royal Army Medical Corps
The rod of Aesculapius, with a serpent twined round it, within a wreath of laurel surmounted by an Imperial crown. Beneath the wreath a scroll inscribed *Royal Army Medical Corps.* In chocolate-brown (Fig. 2269). Sealed 14th January 1942.

Royal Army Ordnance Corps
The Garter surmounted by an Imperial crown. Within the Garter a shield bearing the arms of the Board of Ordnance. Below the Garter a scroll inscribed *Royal Army Ordnance Corps.* In chocolate-brown (Fig. 2270).

Royal Electrical and Mechanical Engineers
Four shields, each bearing one of the initials of the Corps' title, placed on a laurel-wreath in the form of a cross with a pair of calipers in the centre. The whole ensigned with the Imperial crown. In chocolate-brown (Fig. 2271).

Corps of Military Police
The Royal Cypher of King George VI within a wreath of laurel and surmounted by an Imperial crown. Below the wreath a scroll inscribed *Military Police*. In chocolate-brown (Fig. 2272).

Army Educational Corps
An open book superimposed on crossed lances and rifles. Below, a scroll inscribed *Army Educational Corps*. In chocolate-brown (Fig. 2273).

Pioneer Corps
A "pile" consisting of a pick, placed centrally, with a rifle crossing it in front from the left and a shovel crossing it between the rifle and pick from the right; on the 'pile' a laurel-wreath pointing downwards; above the 'pile' an Imperial crown and, below, a scroll inscribed *Labor omnia vincit*. In chocolate-brown (Fig. 2274).

Intelligence Corps
A Rose, within two branches of laurel, surmounted by the Imperial crown. Below the laurel a scroll inscribed *Intelligence Corps*. In chocolate-brown (Fig. 2275). Sealed 9th May 1942.

Army Physical Training Corps
Crossed swords surmounted by an Imperial crown. In light-bronze (Fig. 2276).

Army Catering Corps
An ancient Grecian brazier within a circlet inscribed *Army Catering Corps* surmounted by an Imperial crown. In chocolate-brown (Fig. 2277).

General Service Corps
The Royal Arms. In chocolate-brown (Fig. 2278). Sealed 16th January 1943.

Auxiliary Territorial Service
The letters *ATS* within a laurel-wreath surmounted by an Imperial crown. In chocolate-brown (Fig. 2279).

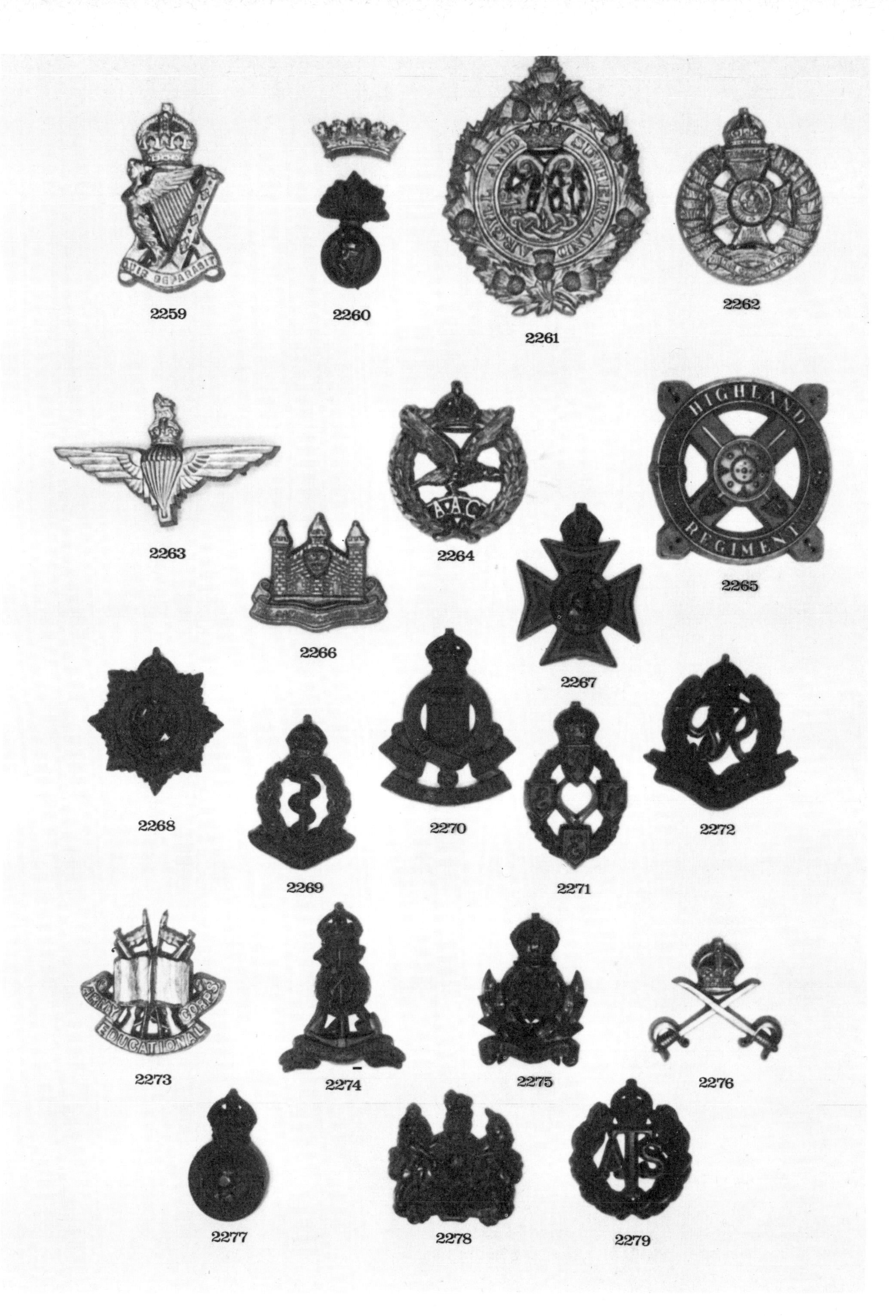

2259 2260 2261 2262 2263 2264 2265 2266 2267 2268 2269 2270 2271 2272 2273 2274 2275 2276 2277 2278 2279

CHAPTER 14

The Yeomanry

The Territorial Force, renamed The Territorial Army, was re-constituted in 1920. The Great War had shown that there was no longer a requirement for a large number of mounted cavalry and in the Yeomanry only the fourteen senior regiments retained their horses.

Of the remainder: twenty-six regiments adopted an artillery role; eight became Armoured Car Companies; one became a signal unit; another, part of an infantry battalion; while The Lincolnshire Yeomanry and The Welsh Horse were not re-raised.

Apart from some artillery units which changed over from Field to Anti-Tank regiments the Yeomanry continued in the same role up to the outbreak of the Second World War. In common with the rest of the Territorial Army they raised duplicate units in 1939 and, in so doing, certain previously-amalgamated units regained their individual designations and others reverted to their former titles.

The War saw the disappearance of horsed units which became either armoured regiments in the Royal Armoured Corps, artillery regiments or, in two instances, units of the Royal Corps of Signals.

In 1947 the Territorial Army again came into being and the Yeomanry regiments appeared mostly under their old titles as regiments of the Royal Armoured Corps, or of the Royal Artillery; the Middlesex Yeomanry still forming part of the Royal Corps of Signals.

This state of affairs did not last long; amalgamations soon commenced as Anti-Aircraft artillery units were no longer needed, and further amalgamations came with the disappearance of divisional organisations and reduction in the number of units required.

With the formation of the Territorial and Army Volunteer Reserve only the Royal Yeomanry Regiment (V), with five squadrons drawn from different regiments, survived of the previous Royal Armoured Corps regiments, while a few more existed only as batteries in the Royal Artillery.

The remainder in the Territorial-element of the Reserve were mostly in an infantry-role and were reduced eventually to cadres of eight of all ranks.

A Government decision to increase the Volunteer-element led to the formation of a number of new units and these were drawn from the Territorials; each regiment providing a squadron or equivalent battery or company. A number of changes were made in 1975 following the Majury Report on the T.A.V.R.

The various changes in nomenclature caused by amalgamation or change-of-role are summarised below:

The Royal Yeomanry Regiment

On the re-organisation of the Territorial Army into the Territorial Army and Volunteer Reserve, this regiment was formed as the sole volunteer regiment of the Royal Armoured Corps.

The squadrons comprising it were drawn from the following units:

H.Q. (Berkshire and Westminster Dragoons) Squadron
"A" (Royal Wiltshire Yeomanry) Squadron
"B" (Sherwood Rangers Yeomanry) Squadron
"C" (Kent and County of London Yeomanry) Squadron
"D" (North Irish Horse) Squadron

The regiment does not have a common cap-badge, each squadron wearing its own.

The Berkshire and Westminster Dragoons

The regiment was formed in May 1961 from the amalgamation of the Berkshire Yeomanry battery of 299th Field Regiment, R.A.(T.A.) and The Westminster Dragoons (2nd County of London Yeomanry).

A portcullis and chains on an heraldic wreath and between two sprays of leaves with a rose at the head, all surmounted by the White Horse of Berkshire. Below, a double-scroll inscribed *Berkshire and Westminster Dragoons*. In gold- and silver-anodised; the Horse and ground in silver, remainder in gold (Fig. 2280).

The Berkshire Yeomanry

On being re-formed after the Great War the regiment provided two batteries of the 99th (Buckinghamshire and Berkshire Yeomanry) Field Regiment, R.A.

On the doubling-up of the Territorial Army in March 1939 the duplicate unit was designated the 145th (Buckinghamshire and Berkshire Yeomanry) Field Regiment, R.A., but became in 1942 the 145th (Berkshire Yeomanry) Field Regiment, R.A.

When the Territorial Army was re-formed in 1947, it became the 345th (Berkshire Yeomanry) Medium Regiment, R.A., but, in 1950, was amalgamated to form the 299th (Royal Bucks Yeomanry, Berkshire Yeomanry and The Queen's Own Oxfordshire Hussars) Field Regiment, R.A.

In 1961 the Berkshire Yeomanry battery was withdrawn from this regiment and went to form The Berkshire and Westminster Dragoons.

On the formation of the T.A.V.R. in 1967 the Berkshire Yeomanry provided "A" Company of the Royal Berkshire Territorials which on the increase of the establishment of Volunteers, became "C" Company of the 2nd Wessex Regiment.

(1) The White Horse of Berkshire above a scroll inscribed *Berkshire*. All in gilding-metal (Fig. 1449). Also same size gold-anodised, sealed 8th May 1952, and same size silver-anodised.

(2) As (1) but smaller for wear on the beret. In gilding-metal (Fig. 2281). Also same size in gold-anodised, sealed 8th May 1952.

Westminster Dragoons (2nd County of London Yeomanry)

The regiment was re-formed after the Great War as the 22nd (London) Armoured Car Company (Westminster Dragoons) Royal Tank Corps but, in 1937, it was raised to battalion strength as the 22nd Battalion (Westminster Dragoons) Royal Tank Corps with the role of an officer-producing unit.

On the outbreak of the Second World War it became the 102nd Officer Cadet Training

Unit (Westminster Dragoons) but in November 1940 it was transferred to the Royal Armoured Corps as the 2nd County of London Yeomanry (Westminster Dragoons). It was re-raised in 1947 under the same title but in 1951 was re-styled The Westminster Dragoons (2nd County of London Yeomanry).

On 1st May 1961 it was amalgamated with "R" (Berkshire Yeomanry) Battery of 299th Field Regiment to form the Berkshire and Westminster Dragoons.

The arms of the City of Westminster. Below, a scroll inscribed *Westminster Dragoons T.Y.* In white-metal (Fig. 2282). Sealed 19th August 1929.

The Royal Wiltshire Yeomanry (Prince of Wales's Own)

The senior yeomanry regiment, it was one of the fourteen to retain their horses after the Great War. It was transferred to the Royal Armoured Corps in 1941 and was re-formed in 1947 under the same title.

On the formation of the T.A.V.R. it provided "A" (Royal Wiltshire Yeomanry) Squadron of the Royal Yeomanry Regiment and also "B" Company (Royal Wiltshire Yeomanry) of The Royal Wiltshire Territorials.

On the augmentation of the volunteers in 1971, besides retaining its commitment in the Royal Yeomanry Regiment, it also contributed "A" Squadron to The Wessex Yeomanry and "D" Company to the 1st Battalion, The Wessex Regiment.

(1) The Prince of Wales's plumes, coronet and motto. In bronze (Fig. 2283). Sealed 11th February 1916.
(2) As above but the coronet in gilding-metal, remainder in white-metal (Fig. 1407). Sealed 5th May 1948.
(3) As above but different shape to feathers and motto-scroll. In anodised-gold and silver (Fig. 2284). Also in gilding-metal and white-metal. Sealed 14th August 1951.

The Sherwood Rangers Yeomanry

Re-formed in 1920 as cavalry under the title of The Nottinghamshire Yeomanry (Sherwood Rangers). In 1947 it became a regiment of the Royal Armoured Corps and its title was changed in 1951 to The Sherwood Rangers Yeomanry.

When the T.A.V.R. was formed it provided "B" Squadron of the Royal Yeomanry Regiment and the Territorial-element was designated The Sherwood Rangers Yeomanry (T). With the increase in Volunteers in 1971 this latter unit became "A" Squadron, 3rd (Volunteer) Battalion, The Worcestershire and Sherwood Foresters Regiment.

(1) A bugle-horn strung. In gilding-metal (Fig. 1410).
(2) A strap inscribed *Notts Sherwood Rangers Yeomanry* surmounted by an Imperial crown. In a voided-centre a bugle-horn strung. In gilding-metal (Fig. 2285), and for senior N.C.Os in white-metal. Worn from 1936.
(3) As (2) but with St. Edward's crown. Also gold-anodised (Fig. 2286).
(4) As (3) but with circlet inscribed *The Sherwood Rangers Yeomanry*. In gold-anodised (Fig. 2287). Another version exists without 'The' in the title.

The Kent and County of London Yeomanry (Sharp Shooters)

The regiment was formed in 1961 by the amalgamation of the 3rd/4th County of London Yeomanry (Sharp Shooters) and the 297th (Kent Yeomanry) Light Anti-Aircraft Regiment, R.A.

2280 1449 2281 2282

2283 1407 2284 1410

2285 2286 2287 2288

1459 1438 1486 1487

2289 2290 2291 1503

Besides contributing a volunteer squadron to the Royal Yeomanry Regiment, it also provided two Territorial-elements in the T.A.V.R. These were "R" (Kent and County of London Yeomanry) Battery, London, and Kent Regiment, R.A., which latter regiment became "C" Battery of 6th (Volunteer) Battalion, The Queen's Regiment, and "B" (Kent and County of London Yeomanry) Company, 8th (Territorial) Battalion, The Queen's Regiment. In 1971 this battalion became "C" Company of the 7th (Volunteer) Battalion, The Queen's Regiment, and in 1975 "D" Company, 6th/7th (Volunteer) Battalion The Queen's Regiment.

A circlet inscribed *Kent & County of London Yeomanry* surmounted by St. Edward's crown. In a voided centre, superimposed on crossed rifles, the White Horse of Kent on a scroll inscribed *Invicta.* Below the circlet a scroll inscribed *Sharpshooters.* The White Horse of Kent and motto-scroll in silver-anodised, remainder in gold-anodised (Fig. 2288).

The West Kent Yeomanry (Queen's Own)
The Royal East Kent Yeomanry (The Duke of Connaught's Own Mounted Rifles)

After the Great War the two Kent Yeomanry regiments each provided two batteries to form the 97th (Kent Yeomanry) Army Field Regiment, R.A. In 1947 it was re-formed as the 297th (Kent Yeomanry) Light Anti-Aircraft Regiment, R.A., and, in May 1961, converted to Royal Armoured Corps and amalgamated with the 3rd/4th County of London Yeomanry (Sharp Shooters).

(1) The White Horse of Kent on a scroll inscribed *Invicta.* In white-metal (Fig. 1459).
(2) The Garter surmounted by the Imperial crown. In a voided centre the White Horse of Kent on a scroll inscribed *Invicta.* In bronzed-brass (Fig. 1438).

3rd County of London Yeomanry (Sharp Shooters)

Re-formed as the 23rd (London) Armoured Car Company (Sharp Shooters), Royal Tank Corps, it was transferred to the Royal Armoured Corps in 1939 as the 3rd County of London Yeomanry (Sharp Shooters) and raised a duplicate unit designated 4th County of London Yeomanry (Sharp Shooters) with which it was amalgamated in 1944.

Re-raised in 1947 as a unit of the Royal Armoured Corps and styled 3rd/4th County of London Yeomanry (Sharp Shooters), it was amalgamated in 1961 with the Kent Yeomanry to form the Kent and County of London Yeomanry (Sharp Shooters).

(1) A circlet inscribed *County of London Yeomanry* and surmounted by an Imperial crown. In the centre the numeral *3*, the whole superimposed on crossed rifles. Below, a scroll inscribed *South Africa, 1900–02.* In gilding-metal (Fig. 1486).
(2) A circlet inscribed *London Armoured Car Company* and surmounted by an Imperial crown. In the centre the Roman numerals *XXIII*, the whole superimposed on crossed rifles. Below, a scroll inscribed *Sharpshooters.* The numerals in white-metal, remainder in gilding-metal (Fig. 1487). Worn from 1922 to 1938.
(3) A circlet inscribed *23rd London Armoured Car Company* and surmounted by an Imperial crown. In the centre the letters *CLY*, the whole superimposed on crossed rifles. Below, a scroll inscribed *Sharpshooters.* The letters *CLY* in white-metal, remainder in gilding-metal (Fig. 2289). Sealed 19th August 1929.
(4) A circlet inscribed *County of London Yeomanry* and surmounted by an Imperial crown. In the centre the numeral *4*, the whole superimposed on crossed rifles. Below, a scroll inscribed *Sharpshooters.* The numeral in white-metal, remainder in gilding-metal (Fig. 2290).

(5) A circlet inscribed *County of London Yeomanry* and surmounted by an Imperial crown. In the centre the letters *CLY*, the whole superimposed on crossed rifles. Below, a scroll inscribed *Sharpshooters*. The letters *CLY* in white-metal, remainder in gilding-metal (Fig. 2291). Sealed 25th June 1940.

North Irish Horse

The regiment was not re-formed until 26th September 1939 and then as a regiment of the Royal Armoured Corps. It was re-formed again in 1947 and later contributed "D" Squadron to the Royal Yeomanry Regiment. It also provides 69 (North Irish Horse) Signal Squadron, 32nd (Scottish) Signal Regiment (Volunteers).

(1) The Irish Harp surmounted by an Imperial crown. Below, a scroll inscribed *North Irish Horse*. In gilding-metal (Fig. 1503). Also chromed, sealed 9th December 1952.

(2) As above but with St. Edward's crown. In silver-anodised (Fig. 2292). Also same design in white-metal, and chromed regimentally.

The Queen's Own Yeomanry

The augmentation of the T.A.V.R. in 1971 saw the formation of a second volunteer regiment in the Royal Armoured Corps. Its complement came from the cadres of the following territorial Yeomanry units.

"NH" Squadron—The Northumberland Hussars
"Y" Squadron—The Queen's Own Yorkshire Yeomanry
"A" Squadron—The Ayrshire (Earl of Carrick's Own) Yeomanry
"C" Squadron—The Cheshire Yeomanry (Earl of Chester's)

A running fox on a scroll inscribed *Queen's Own Yeomanry*. The fox gold-anodised, the scroll silver-anodised (Fig. 2293). Sealed 29th March 1972.

The Northumberland Hussars

Raised as cavalry after the Great War it was converted to an artillery-role in 1940 as the 102nd Light Anti-Aircraft/Anti-Tank Regiment, R.A. (Northumberland Hussars), the title being changed the following year to 102nd Anti-Tank Regiment, R.A. (Northumberland Hussars). Re-raised in 1947 as a regiment in the Royal Armoured Corps it became a Territorial unit in the T.A.V.R.

(1) A circlet inscribed *Northumberland Hussars* surmounted by an Imperial crown. In the centre the Norman castle from the arms of Newcastle-on-Tyne. Below the circlet a scroll inscribed *South Africa 1900–1902*. In gilding-metal (Fig. 1431), and in white-metal. Also anodised, sealed 17th September 1951.

(2) As above but with St. Edward's crown. In silver-anodised (Fig. 2294). Sealed in white-metal, 19th September 1956, and in silver-anodised, 13th March 1962.

The Queen's Own Yorkshire Yeomanry

This was the title given by Army Order 85 of 1957 to the amalgamated unit consisting of The Yorkshire Hussars, The Yorkshire Dragoons and The East Riding Yeomanry.
The White Rose of York superimposed on crossed lances and surmounted by St. Edward's crown. Across the butts of the lances a scroll inscribed *Forrard*. In white-metal (Fig. 2295). Also silver-anodised. Sealed in white-metal, 26th June 1957, and in silver-anodised, 20th April 1960.

The Yorkshire Hussars (Alexandra, Princess of Wales's Own)
Raised as cavalry after the Great War and transferred to the Royal Armoured Corps in 1941. Re-raised as a regiment of the Royal Armoured Corps in 1947 and amalgamated with the Yorkshire Dragoons and The East Riding Yeomany in 1956 to form The Queen's Own Yorkshire Yeomanry.
The White Rose of York surmounted by the Prince of Wales's plumes, coronet and motto. The coronet in gilding-metal, remainder in white-metal (Fig. 1409). There are small differences in manufacturers' designs.

The Queen's Own Yorkshire Dragoons
Raised as cavalry but transferred to the Royal Armoured Corps in 1939 becoming, in 1940, the 9th Battalion, The King's Own Yorkshire Light Infantry. Re-raised as a regiment in the Royal Armoured Corps in 1947 and amalgamated with the Yorkshire Hussars and The East Riding Yeomanry in 1956 to form The Queen's Own Yorkshire Yeomanry.
(1) The Yorkshire Rose surmounted by an Imperial crown. In brass (Fig. 1420), also in blackened-brass.
(2) As above but in white-metal (Fig. 2296). Sealed 11th October 1951. Also anodised.
(3) As above but with Rose in white-metal and Imperial crown in gilding-metal.

The East Riding Yeomanry
Formed in 1920 as the 26th (East Riding of Yorks Yeomanry) Armoured Car Company, Royal Tank Corps. Transferred to the Royal Armoured Corps in 1939 as the 1st East Riding Yeomanry. Re-raised in 1947 as The East Riding Yeomanry and amalgamated with The Yorkshire Hussars and The Yorkshire Dragoons in 1956 to form The Queen's Own Yorkshire Yeomanry.
The duplicate unit raised in 1939 as the 2nd East Riding Yeomanry became in 1940 the 10th (East Riding Yeomanry) Battalion, The Green Howards and, in 1943, the 12th (Yorkshire) Battalion, The Parachute Regiment. It was re-raised in 1947 with the same title.
A fox in full cry. Below, a scroll inscribed *Forrard.* The fox in gilding-metal, scroll in white-metal (Fig. 1496). Also anodised, sealed 11th March 1952.

The Ayrshire (Earl of Carrick's Own) Yeomanry
Formed as cavalry after the Great War, it was converted in 1940 to two regiments of artillery: 151st (Ayrshire Yeomanry) Field Regiment, R.A., and 152nd (Ayrshire Yeomanry) Field Regiment, R.A. Re-formed as a regiment of the Royal Armoured Corps in 1947 and in the T.A.V.R. it became The Ayrshire Yeomanry (Earl of Carrick's Own) (T).
(1) A lion's head and neck winged on an heraldic wreath. Below, a scroll inscribed *Earl of/Ayrshire Yeomanry/Carrick's.* In gilding-metal (Fig. 1416).
(2) As above but scroll inscribed *Ayrshire/Earl of Carrick's Own/Yeomanry.* In gilding-metal (Fig. 2297).
(3) As (2) but lion's-head in white-metal, remainder in gilding-metal (Fig. 2298).
(4) As (2) but word *of* smaller. In gilding-metal, sealed 5th December 1951, also in gold-anodised, sealed 30th April 1965.

The Cheshire Yeomanry (Earl of Chester's)
Formed in 1920 as a cavalry regiment, it was converted to Signals in 1940 as the 5th (later 17th) Line of Communications Signals, Royal Corps of Signals. In 1947 it became a

2292 2293 1431 2294

2295 1409 1420 2296

1496 1416 2297 2298

2299 2300 2301 1447

1454 2302 2303 2304

regiment of the Royal Armoured Corps and in the T.A.V.R. it was designated The Cheshire (Earl of Chester's) Territorials.

(1) The Prince of Wales's plumes, coronet and motto. Below, a scroll inscribed *Cheshire (Earl of Chester's) Yeomanry*. All in white-metal (Fig. 2300). Also in bronzed-brass.

(2) Similar to (1) but difference in the shape of the feathers and scroll. Coronet and title-scroll in gilding-metal, remainder in white-metal (Fig. 2301). Also anodised, sealed 19th February 1963.

The Wessex Yeomanry

On the increase of the Volunteer element of the T.A.V.R. in 1971 the above unit was formed but in an infantry role. The regiments comprising it were:

HQ Squadron, "A" Squadron, "C" Squadron } The Royal Gloucestershire Hussars
"B" Squadron – The Royal Wiltshire Yeomanry
"D" Squadron – Royal Devon Yeomanry/1st Rifle Volunteers

The Royal Gloucestershire Hussars

Re-formed in 1920 as the 21st (Royal Gloucestershire Hussars) Armoured Car Company, Royal Tank Corps. Transferred to the Royal Armoured Corps in 1939 as the 1st Royal Gloucestershire Hussars with the duplicate unit titled 2nd Royal Gloucestershire Hussars. Re-formed as a unit of the Royal Armoured Corps in 1947 as The Royal Gloucestershire Hussars and on the formation of the T.A.V.R. became "B" Squadron of The Royal Gloucestershire Hussars (T).

A portcullis with chains surmounted by a ducal coronet. Below, a scroll inscribed *Royal Gloucestershire Hussars*. In gilding-metal (Fig. 1447). Also gold-anodised.

Royal Devon Yeomanry/1st Rifle Volunteers

The Devonshire Territorials of the T.A.V.R. consisted of three squadrons:

"A" (Royal Devon Yeomanry) Squadron
"B" (Devon Fortress Engineers) Squadron
"C" (First Rifle Volunteers) Squadron

The Royal Devon Yeomanry is dealt with below but the First Rifle Volunteers were originally the 4th Battalion, The Devonshire Regiment: the senior Territorial Army infantry battalion which had the subsidiary title of '1st Rifle Volunteers".

The Royal Devon Yeomanry

The Royal 1st Devon Yeomanry and The Royal North Devon Yeomanry each formed two batteries of the 96th (Royal Devon Yeomanry) Field Regiment, R.A.

It formed a duplicate unit in 1939, the 142nd Field Regiment, R.A. (Royal Devon Yeomanry), and both regiments were re-raised after the Second World War as the 296th, and 342nd, Field Regiments (Royal Devon Yeomanry) R.A. respectively.

In 1950 these were amalgamated with the title of 296th (Royal Devon Yeomanry) Field Regiment, R.A., and later became "A" (Royal Devon Yeomanry) Squadron of The Devonshire Territorials.

(1) A circlet inscribed *Royal Devon Yeomanry R.F.A.* surmounted by the Royal Crest. In

the centre the crest of Lord Rolle. In gilding-metal (Fig. 1454). Worn only from 24th April to 18th December 1924.

(2) A circlet inscribed *Royal Devon Yeomanry Artillery* surmounted by the Royal Crest. In a voided-centre the crest of Lord Rolle. In gilding-metal (Fig. 2302). Worn from 18th December 1924. Found non-voided, and also in white-metal. Also anodised, sealed 21st February 1952.

(3) As (2) but with St. Edward's crown in the Royal Crest (Fig. 2303). Also gold-anodised. Sealed in gilding-metal, 22nd June 1956. Sealed in anodised, 22nd June 1956.

(4) As (3) but with circlet inscribed *Royal Devon Yeomanry* only. In silver-anodised (Fig. 2304).

The Queen's Own Mercian Yeomanry

This regiment was formed on the increase of the volunteer element of the T.A.V.R. in 1971 but in an infantry-role. It consists of:

"A" Squadron – The Queen's Own Warwickshire and Worcestershire Yeomanry
"B" Squadron – The Staffordshire Yeomanry (Queen's Own Royal Regiment)
"C" Squadron – The Shropshire Yeomanry

The regiment was granted the additional title of "The Queen's Own" on 25th May 1973. A strap inscribed *The Queen's Own Mercian Yeomanry* surmounted by St. Edward's crown. In a voided-centre a double-headed eagle displayed ensigned with a Saxon crown. The eagle silver-anodised, remainder gold-anodised (Fig. 2305).

The Queen's Own Warwickshire and Worcestershire Yeomanry

The Warwickshire Yeomanry and The Queen's Own Worcestershire Hussars were amalgamated on 1st October 1956 to form the above regiment.
The Bear and Ragged Staff within a wreath of pear-blossom. The Bear and Staff silver-anodised, the wreath gold-anodised (Fig. 2306).

The Warwickshire Yeomanry

Re-formed as cavalry in 1920 and transferred to the Royal Armoured Corps in April 1941. Re-formed in 1947 with same title and amalgamated with The Queen's Own Worcestershire Hussars in 1956 (A.O. 85/1957). On the formation of the T.A.V.R. it became "B" and "C" Squadrons of The Queens Own Warwickshire and Worcestershire Yeomanry.
The Bear and Ragged Staff. In gilding-metal (Fig. 1408). Also in bronzed-brass, white-metal, and anodised. Sealed in bronze, 29th February 1916 and in white-metal, 6th February 1952.

The Queen's Own Worcestershire Hussars

In 1922 became part of the 100th (Worcestershire and Oxfordshire Yeomanry) Army Field Brigade, R.A., which, in 1938, became the 53rd (Worcestershire and Oxfordshire Yeomanry) Anti-Tank Regiment, R.A. In 1943 it was the 53rd Air Landing Light Regiment, R.A. (Worcestershire and Oxfordshire Yeomanry).

Re-raised in 1947 as the 300th (Worcestershire Yeomanry) Anti-Tank Regiment, R.A., but transferred in 1950 to the Royal Armoured Corps as The Queen's Own Worcestershire Hussars and in 1956 amalgamated with The Warwickshire Yeomanry.

Within a laurel-wreath surmounted by an Imperial crown a spray of pear-blossom. Superimposed on the wreath a scroll inscribed *Queen's Own Worcestershire Hussars*. The pear-blossom in white-metal, remainder in gilding metal (Fig. 1458). Also in anodised, sealed 16th November 1951.

The Staffordshire Yeomanry (Queen's Own Royal Regiment)

Re-formed as cavalry after the Great War and transferred to the Royal Armoured Corps in 1941. Re-raised in 1947 as part of the Royal Armoured Corps. On the formation of the T.A.V.R. its title was The Staffordshire Yeomanry (Queen's Own Royal Regiment) (T).

(1) The Stafford Knot surmounted by an Imperial crown. In gilding-metal (Fig. 1413). Sealed 18th September 1916.

(2) The Garter surmounted by an Imperial crown. In the centre the Stafford Knot. Below, a scroll inscribed *Pro aris et focis*. In white-metal (Fig. 1414). Also anodised, sealed 8th August 1952.

(3) As (2) but with St. Edward's crown. In silver-anodised (Fig. 2307). Also in white-metal, sealed 26th June 1957.

The Shropshire Yeomanry

Re-formed as a cavalry regiment in 1920, it formed in 1940 the 75th and 76th Medium Regiments, R.A. (Shropshire Yeomanry). In 1947 it became a regiment of the Royal Armoured Corps and in the T.A.V.R. its title was The Shropshire Yeomanry (T).

(1) A circlet inscribed *Shropshire Yeomanry* surmounted by an Imperial crown. In the centre a shield charged with three loggerheads (leopards' faces) on a solid background. In gilding-metal (Fig. 1415).

(2) As (1) but with voided-centre and the loggerheads not on a shield. In gilding-metal (Fig. 2308). Also anodised, sealed 24th November 1950.

(3) As (2) but with St. Edward's crown. In gold-anodised (Fig. 2309). Sealed 8th April 1957.

The Duke of Lancaster's Own Yeomanry

A cavalry regiment in 1920, converted in 1940 to 77th and 78th Medium Regiments, R.A. (Duke of Lancaster's Own Yeomanry). In October 1945 became 78 Regiment, R.A. (Auxiliary Police) (Duke of Lancaster's Own Yeomanry).

Re-formed as a regiment in the Royal Armoured Corps in 1947, it amalgamated later with the 40/41st Royal Tank Regiment and, on formation of the T.A.V.R., became the Duke of Lancaster's Own Yeomanry (Royal Tank Regiment) (T). On the increase in the volunteer element in 1971 it became a regiment in an infantry-role. The suffix "Royal Tank Regiment" was omitted from the title in 1972.

(1) A rose within a wreath of laurel on left, oak on right. On the wreath, scrolls inscribed *Duke of Lancaster's Own*; the whole ensigned with the Duke's coronet. In gilding-metal (Fig. 1428).

(2) A strap inscribed *Duke of Lancaster's Own* surmounted by the Duke's coronet. In the centre a rose within a laurel-wreath. Rose and laurel-wreath in white-metal, remainder in gilding-metal (Fig. 2310). Also anodised, sealed 17th September 1951. There are two slighty different versions of this badge chiefly varying in the size of the coronet.

2305
2306
1408
1458
1413
1414
2307
1415
SHROPSHIRE YEOMANRY
2308
SHROPSHIRE YEOMANRY
2309
SHROPSHIRE YEOMANRY
1428
LANCASTERS
2310
DUKE OF LANCASTER'S OWN
2311
1430
LANARKSHIRE YEOMANRY
2312
1467
1470
1469
2313
2314

The Queen's Own Lowland Yeomanry

On 26th October 1956, The Lanarkshire Yeomanry, The Lothians and Border Horse and The Queen's Own Royal Glasgow Yeomanry were combined to form the above regiment.

Its present successor-unit is the 225th (Queen's Own Lowland Yeomanry) Field Tanker Squadron, 154 (Lowland) Regiment, Royal Corps of Transport (V).

The Scottish Royal Unicorn superimposed on a pair of crossed swords with blades uppermost. Below, a scroll inscribed *The Queen's Own Lowland Yeo.* Scroll in gold-anodised, remainder in silver-anodised (Fig. 2311).

The Lanarkshire Yeomanry

A cavalry regiment in 1920, it was converted in 1940 to the 155th and 156th Field Regiments, R.A. (Lanarkshire Yeomanry).

In 1947 became a regiment in the Royal Armoured Corps and in 1956 amalgamated with The Lothians and Border Horse and The Queen's Own Royal Glasgow Yeomanry to form The Queen's Own Lowland Yeomanry.

(1) A double-headed eagle grasping a bell in its right claw, the whole surmounted by an Imperial crown. Below, a scroll inscribed *Lanarkshire Yeomanry.* In gilding-metal (Fig. 1430). Sealed 1st October 1916.

(2) As above but without the title-scroll. In gilding-metal (Fig. 2312). Sealed 9th April 1953.

The Lothians and Border Horse

In 1922 became the 19th (Lothians and Border Horse) Armoured Car Company, Royal Tank Corps. Transferred to the Royal Armoured Corps in 1939 as the 1st Lothians and Border Horse, its duplicate unit being the 2nd Lothians and Border Horse.

Re-formed in 1947 as a regiment of the Royal Armoured Corps with the title 1st/2nd Lothians and Border Horse Yeomanry, it was amalgamated in 1956 with The Lanarkshire Yeomanry and The Queen's Own Royal Glasgow Yeomanry to form The Queen's Own Lowland Yeomanry.

A garb. In gilding-metal (Fig. 1467), also found in smaller size. Also anodised, sealed 11th January 1952.

The Queen's Own Royal Glasgow Yeomanry

Re-formed after the Great War as the 101st (Queen's Own Royal Glasgow Yeomanry) Army Field Brigade, R.A. In 1938 became the 54th (Queen's Own Glasgow Yeomanry) Anti-Tank Regiment, R.A.

Re-formed in 1947 as a regiment in the Royal Armoured Corps with the title The Queen's Own Royal Glasgow Yeomanry and in 1956 amalgamated with The Lanarkshire Yeomanry and The Lothians and Border Horse to form The Queen's Own Lowland Yeomanry.

(1) The Crest of Scotland over sprays of thistles. In gilding-metal (Fig. 1470).

(2) A strap inscribed *Queen's Own Royal Glasgow Yeomanry* surmounted by the Royal Crest. In the centre the Lion from the Crest of Scotland. In gilding-metal (Fig. 1469).

(3) Similar to (1) but different arrangement of thistle-sprays (Fig. 2313). Sealed 16th December 1948.

(4) As (3) but with St. Edward's crown (Fig. 2314). Sealed 7th February 1956. Also anodised.

The Highland Yeomanry

The above title was assumed by The Fife and Forfar Yeomanry/Scottish Horse in 1969. Its successor-unit is 239 (Highland Yeomanry) Squadron, 153 Highland Regiment, Royal Corps of Transport (V).

A knight in armour mounted on a horse caparisoned (the County badge known as the Thane of Fife) superimposed on St. Andrew's Cross. On the arms of the Cross a sprig of juniper (left) and bay (right), surmounted by St. Edward's crown. In white-metal, sealed 11th July 1957 (Fig. 2315). Also anodised, sealed 7th April 1960.

The Fife and Forfar Yeomanry

Re-formed in 1922 as 20th (Fife and Forfar Yeomanry) Armoured Car Company, Royal Tank Corps. Transferred to the Royal Armoured Corps in 1939 as 1st Fife and Forfar Yeomanry, its duplicate unit being 2nd Fife and Forfar Yeomanry.

In 1947 became part of the Royal Armoured Corps as The Fife and Forfar Yeomanry and amalgamated with The Scottish Horse in 1956 to form The Fife and Forfar Yeomanry/ Scottish Horse.

(1) The Thane of Fife in white-metal (Fig. 1474).
(2) As above but smaller for wear on the beret. In white-metal (Fig. 2316). Sealed 27th June 1951.

The Scottish Horse

Re-formed as Scouts in 1920 but transferred to the Royal Artillery in 1940 as 79th and 80th Medium Regiments, R.A. (Scottish Horse). In 1947 it became part of the Royal Armoured Corps as The Scottish Horse and amalgamated with The Fife and Forfar Yeomanry in 1956 to form The Fife and Forfar Yeomanry/Scottish Horse.

(1) An oval inscribed *Scottish Horse 1900* with scrolls below inscribed *South Africa 1900, 1901, 1902.* A wreath of juniper and bay encloses the oval. St Andrew's Cross is superimposed on the oval which is ensigned with a Scottish crown. In white-metal (Fig. 1501). Sealed 4th August 1916.
(2) As above but with Imperial crown. In white-metal (Fig. 1502). Also anodised, sealed 30th October 1951.

The Inns of Court and City Yeomanry

The regiment was formed in 1961 by the amalgamation of the Inns of Court Regiment and The City of London Yeomanry (Rough Riders).

When the T.A.V.R. was formed it became 'A' Company (Inns of Court and City Yeomanry) of The London Yeomanry and Territorials and its successor-unit is 68 (Inns of Court City Yeomanry) Signal Squadron, 71st (Yeomanry) Signal Regiment (Volunteers).

The arms of Lincoln's Inn, the Inner Temple, the Middle Temple and Gray's Inn conjoined in cross with, overall, the arms of the City of London, all within a laurel-wreath ensigned with St. Edward's crown. Below, a scroll inscribed *I.C. & C.Y.* The arms of the City of London silver-anodised, remainder gold-anodised (Fig. 2317).

The Inns of Court Regiment

After the Great War became the Inns of Court O.T.C. but expanded in 1932 to become The Inns of Court Regiment. Transferred to the Royal Armoured Corps in 1940. Re-raised in 1947 as a regiment in the Royal Armoured Corps and, in 1961, amalgamated with The City of London Yeomanry (Rough Riders) to form The Inns of Court and City Yeomanry.

(1) Within a laurel-wreath surmounted by an Imperial crown four shields placed in the form of a cross with the bottom points touching in the centre, each shield bearing the Arms of one of the following Inns, viz. Lincoln's Inn (a number of millrinds) top; Inner Temple (a Pegasus) right; Gray's Inn (a Griffin) bottom; Middle Temple (St. George's Cross with the Paschal Lamb in the centre) left. On the bottom of the wreath a scroll inscribed *Inns of Court Regt.* In gilding-metal (Fig. 2318).
(2) As above but with St. Edward's crown. In gold-anodised (Fig. 2319). Sealed 13th November 1958.

The City of London Yeomanry (Rough Riders)
Re-formed as 'C' Battery of the 11th (Honourable Artillery Company and City of London Yeomanry) Brigade, R.H.A., it was expanded in 1939 to form the 11th (City of London Yeomanry) Light Anti-Aircraft Brigade, R.A.

Re-raised as a regiment in the Royal Armoured Corps in 1947 as The City of London Yeomanry (Rough Riders). In 1956 became an infantry battalion in The Rifle Brigade without change of title and in 1961 amalgamated with The Inns of Court Regiment to form The Inns of Court and City Yeomanry.

(1) Within a laurel-wreath a circlet inscribed *The City of London Yeomanry* and surmounted by an Imperial crown. In the centre the arms of the City of London. Below the circlet, two scrolls, the top inscribed *Rough Riders* and the bottom *South Africa 1900–02.* The arms in white-metal, remainder in gilding-metal (Fig. 1484).
(2) A spur with rowel to the right entwined with the letters *RR.* Worn on the Field-service cap. Spur in white-metal, letters in gilding-metal (Fig. 2320).
(3) A circlet inscribed *The City of London Yeomanry* surmounted by an Imperial crown. In the centre the arms of the City of London. Below, a scroll inscribed *Rough Riders.* The arms and scroll in white-metal, remainder in gilding-metal (Fig. 2321). Sealed 16th January 1949.
(4) As (3) but with St. Edward's crown. In gold- and silver-anodised (Fig. 2322). Sealed 3rd April 1959.

The Sussex Yeomanry
In 1922 formed two batteries of 98th (Surrey and Sussex Yeomanry, Queen Mary's) Army Field Regiment, R.A. In 1939 the duplicate unit was the 144th (Surrey and Sussex Yeomanry, Queen Mary's) Field Regiment. On re-construction after the Second World War it became the 344th (Sussex Yeomanry) Light Anti-Aircraft/Searchlight Regiment, R.A.

In 1955 it amalgamated with 258 Light Anti-Aircraft Regiment, R.A., 313 Heavy Anti-Aircraft Regiment, R.A., and 614 (Mixed) Heavy Anti-Aircraft Regiment, R.A., to form 258 (Sussex Yeomanry) Light Anti-Aircraft Regiment, R.A.

It was amalgamated further in 1961 with 257 (County of Sussex) Field Regiment, R.A., to form 257 (Sussex Yeomanry) Field Regiment, R.A.

On the formation of the T.A.V.R. it became 200th (Sussex Yeomanry) Medium Battery of 100th (Eastern) Medium Regiment, R.A.(V).

(1) On a shield six martlets, the whole on an ornamental ground surmounted by an Imperial crown. Below, a scroll inscribed *Sussex Yeomanry.* In gilding-metal (Fig. 1480). Also gold-anodised, sealed 5th May 1952.
(2) As above but with St. Edward's crown. In gold-anodised (Fig. 2323). Sealed 8th January 1957.

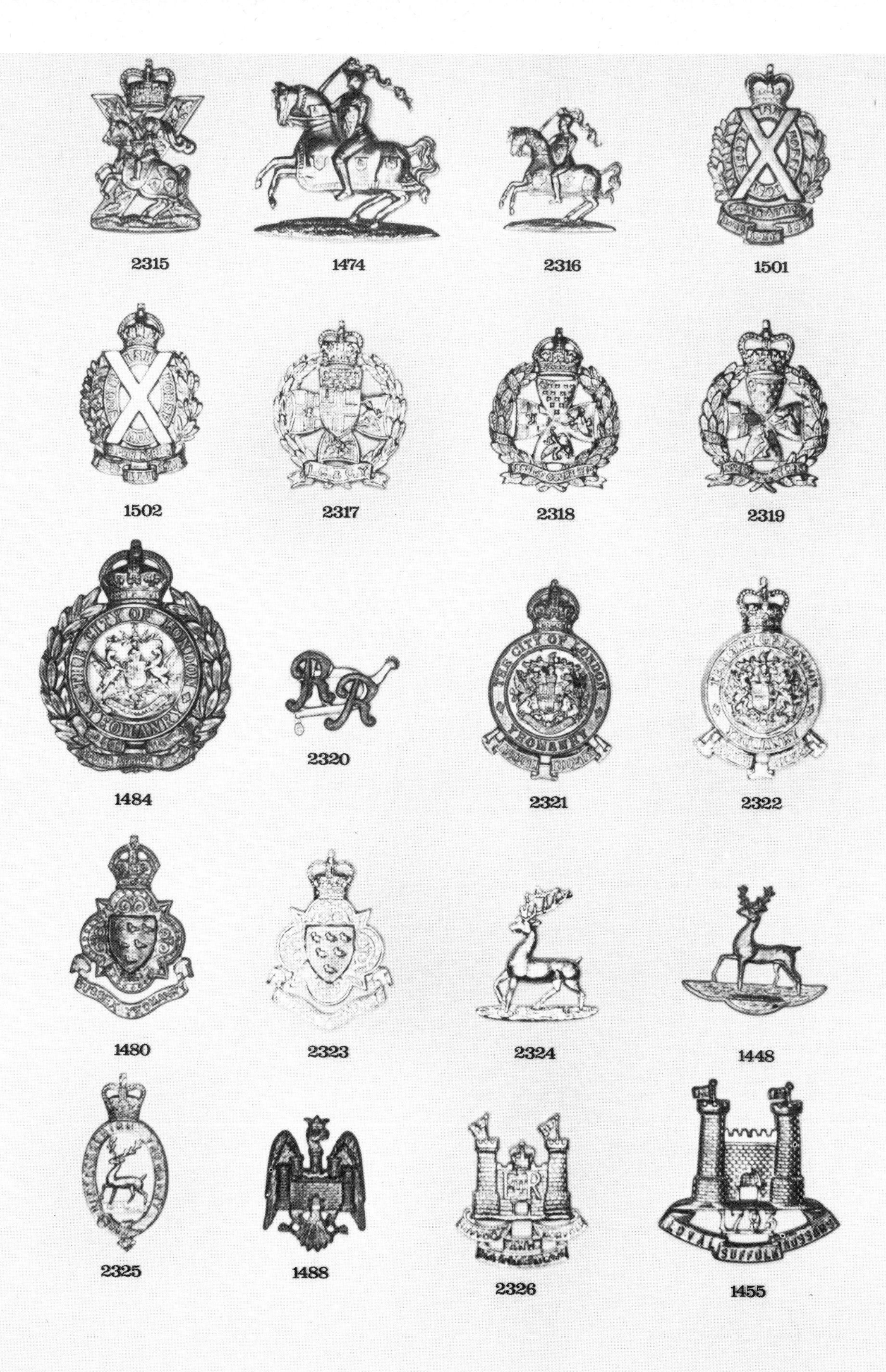

2315 1474 2316 1501

1502 2317 2318 2319

1484 2320 2321 2322

1480 2323 2324 1448

2325 1488 2326 1455

The Hertfordshire and Bedfordshire Yeomanry

The 286th (Hertfordshire and Bedfordshire Yeomanry) Regiment, R.A., was formed in 1961 from the amalgamation of the 286th (Hertfordshire Yeomanry) Field Regiment, R.A., and the 305th (Bedfordshire Yeomanry) Light Regiment, R.A.

On the formation of the T.A.V.R. it became the 201st (Hertfordshire and Bedfordshire Yeomanry) Medium Battery of 100th (Eastern) Medium Regiment, R.A. (V).

It also provided No. 2 (Hertfordshire Yeomanry) Company and No. 3 (Bedfordshire Yeomanry) Company of The Bedfordshire and Hertfordshire Regiment (T). In 1971 this regiment became 'B' Company of 6th (Volunteer) Battalion, The Royal Anglian Regiment.
A Hart in gold-anodised (Fig. 2324). Also in white-metal, and silver-anodised.

Hertfordshire Yeomanry

In 1920 formed the 86th (East Anglian) (Herts Yeomanry) Field Regiment, R.A., which, in 1947, became the 286th (Hertfordshire Yeomanry) Field Regiment, R.A. In 1961 amalgamated with 305th (Bedfordshire Yeomanry) Light Regiment, R.A., to form the 286th (Hertfordshire and Bedfordshire Yeomanry) Regiment, R.A.

(1) A Hart trippant on a ford (the County crest of Hertfordshire). In gilding-metal (Fig. 1448).

(2) A strap inscribed *Hertfordshire Yeomanry* surmounted by St. Edward's crown. In white-metal. Sealed 18th July 1952 (Fig. 2325). Also anodised, sealed 21st May 1955.

Bedfordshire Yeomanry

Re-organised in 1922 as the 105th (Bedfordshire Yeomanry) Army Field Regiment, R.A., and in 1939 became the 52nd Heavy Regiment (Bedfordshire Yeomanry). Re-formed in 1947 as 305th Medium Regiment, R.A. (Bedfordshire Yeomanry); style changed to 'Light' in 1956. In 1961 amalgamated with 286th (Hertfordshire Yeomanry) Field Regiment, R.A., to form the 286th (Hertfordshire and Bedfordshire Yeomanry) Regiment, R.A.
An eagle, on which is superimposed a castle, surmounted by a coronet. In gilding-metal (Fig. 1488). Sealed 29th February 1916.

The Suffolk and Norfolk Yeomanry

The 284th (The King's Own Royal Regiment, Norfolk Yeomanry) Light Anti-Aircraft Regiment, R.A., and the 358th (Suffolk Yeomanry) Field Regiment, R.A., were amalgamated in 1961 to form the 308th (Suffolk and Norfolk Yeomanry) Regiment, R.A.

On the formation of the T.A.V.R. it became the 202nd (Suffolk and Norfolk Yeomanry) Medium Battery of 100 (Eastern) Medium Regiment, R.A.(V).

It also provided 'A' and 'D' (Suffolk and Norfolk Yeomanry) Companies of The Suffolk and Cambridgshire Regiment (T). This regiment became in 1971 'D' Company, 6th (Volunteer) Battalion, The Royal Anglian Regiment.
A castle with two turrets, St. George's flag flying to the left from each turret; superimposed above the gate is the Royal Cypher ensigned with St. Edward's crown. Below, a double scroll inscribed *Suffolk and Norfolk Yeomanry*. The castle including the flags in gold-anodised, the Royal cypher, crown and scrolls in silver-anodised (Fig. 2326).

The Duke of York's Own Loyal Suffolk Hussars

In 1920 formed part of 108th (Suffolk and Norfolk Yeomanry) Army Field Brigade, R.A., which in 1938 became the 55th (Suffolk and Norfolk Yeomanry) Anti-Tank Regiment, R.A.

Following the doubling-up of the Territorial Army in 1939 the regiment was re-named in 1942 the 55th (Suffolk Yeomanry) Anti-Tank Regiment, R.A.

Re-formed in 1947 as the 308th (Suffolk Yeomanry) Anti-Tank Regiment, R.A., it amalgamated in 1950 with 358 (Suffolk) Medium Regiment, R.A., to form 358 (Suffolk Yeomanry) Medium Regiment, R.A.

It was amalgamated further in 1956 with 419 (Suffolk) Coast Regiment, R.A., to form 358 (Suffolk Yeomanry) Field Regiment, R.A., and in 1961 amalgamated with 284 (King's Own Royal Regiment, Norfolk Yeomanry) Light Anti-Aircraft Regiment, R.A., to form 308 (Suffolk and Norfolk Yeomanry) Field Regiment, R.A.

(1) A castle, below which the date *1793*, and a scroll inscribed *Loyal Suffolk Hussars*. The castle and date in gilding-metal, the scroll in white-metal (Fig. 1455).

(2) As above but smaller for wear on the beret. All in gilding-metal (Fig. 2327). Also gold-anodised, sealed 14th September 1953.

The Norfolk Yeomanry (The King's Own Royal Regiment)

In 1921 provided two batteries of the 108th (Suffolk and Norfolk Yeomanry) Army Field Brigade, R.A., and in 1938 the title was changed to 55th (Suffolk and Norfolk Yeomanry) Anti-Tank Regiment, R.A. In 1939 it took the title of the duplicate unit as 65th (Norfolk Yeomanry) Anti-Tank Regiment, R.A.

Re-formed in 1947 as the 389th Light Anti-Aircraft Regiment, R.A., and amalgamated in 1955 with 284th (1st East Anglian) (Mixed) Heavy Anti-Aircraft Regiment, R.A., to form 284th (King's Own Royal Regiment, Norfolk Yeomanry) Light Anti-Aircraft Regiment, R.A.

In 1961 it amalgamated with 358th (Suffolk Yeomanry) Field Regiment, R.A., to form the 308th (Suffolk and Norfolk Yeomanry) Field Regiment, R.A.

(1) The Royal cypher of King George v. In gilding-metal (Fig. 1477).

(2) The Royal cypher of King George vi. In gilding-metal (Fig. 2328). Sealed 15th February 1937.

(3) The Royal cypher of Queen Elizabeth ii. In gilding-metal (Fig. 2329). Also anodised. Both patterns sealed 17th October 1953.

The Glamorgan Yeomanry

On the re-forming of the Territorial Army after the Great War this Regiment became the 324th (Glamorgan Yeomanry) Battery of 81st (Welsh) Field Regiment, R.A.

Re-formed in 1947 as the 281st (Welsh) Field Regiment, R.A., its title changed in 1953 to 281st (Glamorgan Yeomanry) Field Regiment, R.A., and in 1961 it was reduced to 'P' (Glamorgan Yeomanry) Battery of 282nd (Glamorgan and Monmouthshire) Field Regiment.

On formation of the T.A.V.R. it became 'E' (Glamorgan Yeomanry) Troop, 211 (South Wales) Light Air Defence Battery, R.A. (V), of 104 Light Air Defence Regiment, R.A.(V).

The Prince of Wales's plumes and coronet, but the scrolls normally carrying the motto left blank. Below, a scroll inscribed *Glamorgan Yeomanry* with a dot, diamond and dot where the word *Imperial* had been engraved. Coronet and scroll in gilding-metal, remainder in white-metal (Fig. 2330). Pattern re-sealed 19th March 1922.

The Essex Yeomanry

In 1921 it was the 104th (Essex Yeomanry) Army Field Brigade, R.A., but its title was changed in 1939 to 104th (Essex Yeomanry) Regiment, R.H.A. In 1947 re-formed as the

304th (Essex Yeomanry) Regiment R.H.A. and became a Territorial regiment as The Essex Yeomanry (R.H.A.) R.A. (T), in the T.A.V.R. Its successor-unit is 70 (Essex Yeomanry) Signal Squadron, 71st (Yeomanry) Signal Regiment (Volunteers).

(1) A circlet inscribed *Essex Yeomanry* surmounted by an Imperial crown. In the centre a shield bearing the Essex County arms. Below, a scroll inscribed *Decus et tutamen.* In gilding-metal (Fig. 1493). Sealed 4th August 1916.

(2) A circlet inscribed *Decus et tutamen* surmounted by an Imperial crown. In the centre a shield bearing the Essex County arms. In gilding-metal (Fig. 1491).

(3) As (1) but smaller for wear on the beret. In gilding-metal (Fig. 2331). Also gold-anodised, sealed 17th June 1952.

(4) As (3) but with St. Edward's crown. In gold-anodised (Fig. 2332). Sealed 30th August 1957.

(5) As (4) but larger. In gold-anodised (Fig. 2333).

The Lancashire Hussars

In 1922 the 106th (Lancashire Yeomanry) Army Field Brigade, R.A. Changed in 1938 to 106th (Lancashire Yeomanry) Regiment, R.H.A., and in 1941 to 106th Light Anti-Aircraft Regiment, R.H.A. (Lancashire Yeomanry). Later that year it was amalgamated with its duplicate unit as the 149th Anti-Tank Regiment, R.A. (Lancashire Yeomanry).

Re-constituted in 1947 as 306th (Lancashire Hussars) Heavy Anti-Aircraft Regiment, R.A., and changed to Medium in 1954. In 1956 became 'P' (Lancashire Hussars) Battery of 287th (1st West Lancs) Medium Regiment, R.A. Title changed to 'Field' in 1961.

On formation of the T.A.V.R. became 'A' Troop (The Lancashire Hussars) of 'P' Battery (1st West Lancashire) R.A.(V) of the West Lancashire Regiment, R.A.(V). This regiment was absorbed into 208 (3rd West Lancashire) Light Air Defence Battery, R.A.(V).

The Red Rose of Lancashire. Below, a scroll inscribed *Lancashire Hussars.* In gilding-metal (Fig. 1472).

1st County of London Yeomanry (Middlesex, Duke of Cambridge's Hussars)

In 1920 formed 2nd Cavalry Divisional Signals (Middlesex Yeomanry) Royal Corps of Signals. Mobile Divisional Signals in 1938 and 1st Cavalry Divisional Signals in 1939. In 1940 was 9th Armoured Brigade Signals of 10th Armoured Divisional Signals.

Re-formed in 1947 as 16th Airborne Divisional Signals (Middlesex Yeomanry). Re-titled Middlesex Yeomanry Signal Regiment in 1950, it amalgamated with 47th (London) Signal Regiment.

In the T.A.V.R. it is the 47th (Middlesex Yeomanry) Signal Squadron (V) of the 31st (Greater London) Signal Regiment (V).

(1) An eight-pointed star on which a circlet inscribed *Pro aris et focis: Middlesex Yeomanry.* In the centre the cypher of King George v. In white-metal (Fig. 1451).

(2) As above but with the cypher of King George vi. In white-metal (Fig. 2334).

(3) An eight-pointed star, the topmost-point displaced by St. Edward's crown. On this a circlet inscribed *Pro aris et focis: M.D.C.H.* In the centre the cypher of Queen Elizabeth ii. Star and crown in white-metal, remainder in gilding-metal (Fig. 2335). Also anodised.

The Lovat Scouts

The 1st and 2nd Lovat Scouts were amalgamated in 1920 to form The Lovat Scouts. Transferred to the Royal Armoured Corps in 1939 as 1st Lovat Scouts; duplicate unit, 2nd Lovat Scouts.

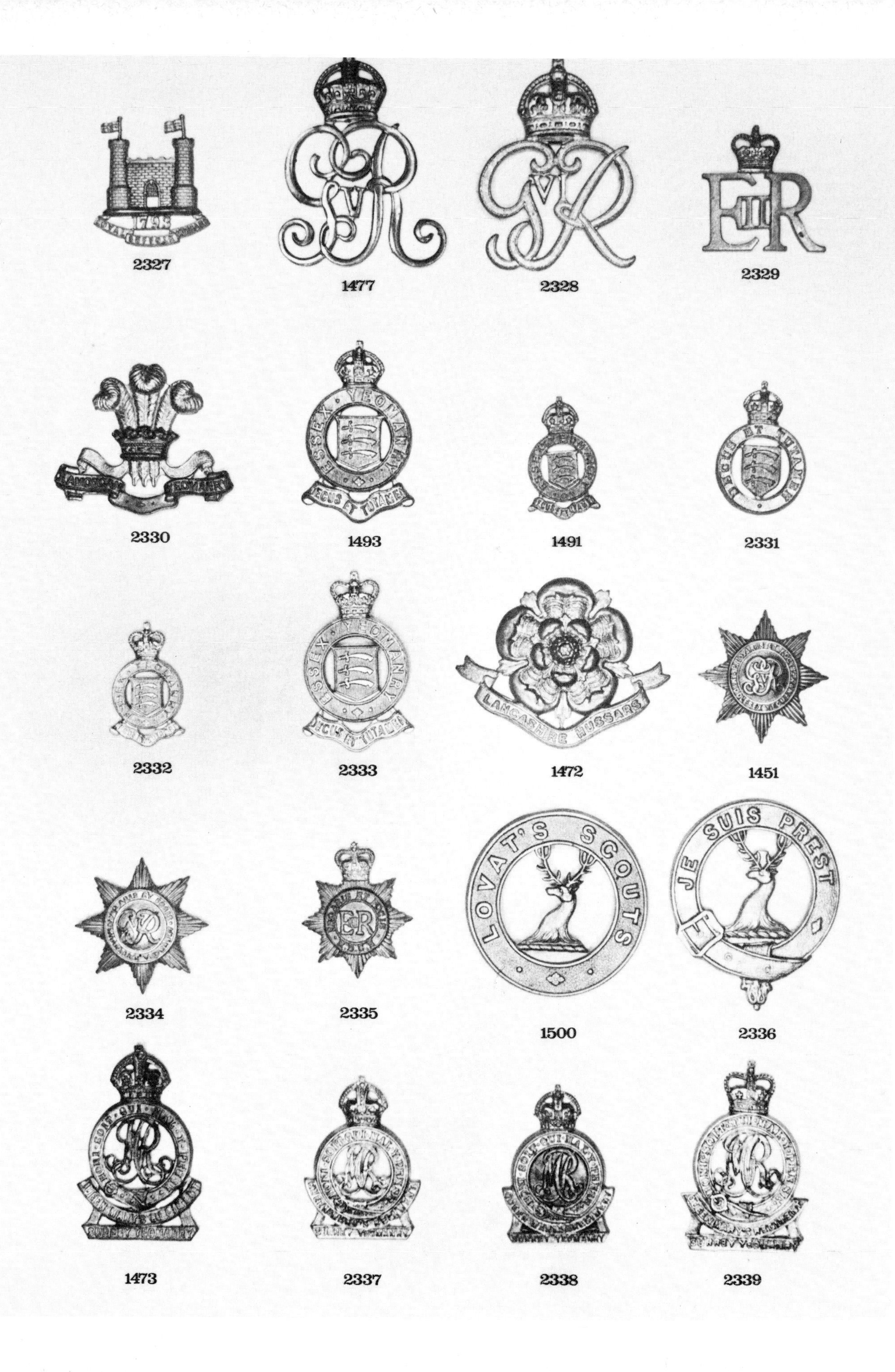
2327
1477
2328
2329
2330
ESSEX YEOMANRY
DECUS ET TUTAMEN
1493
1491
2331
2332
ESSEX YEOMANRY
DECUS ET TUTAMEN
2333
LANCASHIRE HUSSARS
1472
1451
2334
2335
LOVAT'S SCOUTS
1500
JE SUIS PREST
2336
1473
2337
2338
2339

Re-formed in 1947 as a squadron of The Scottish Horse but, soon after, became the 850 Mountain Battery, R.A. (Lovat Scouts), and expanded in 1949 to 677 Mountain Regiment, R.A. (Lovat Scouts).

Amalgamated in 1950 with 532 and 540 Light Anti-Aircraft Regiments to form 532 Light Anti-Aircraft Regiment (Lovat Scouts) which was renumbered 540 in 1954.

In the T.A.V.R. they formed the Orkney and Zetland (Lovat Scouts) Battery of The Highland Regiment, R.A.(T) which has since been disbanded.

They also formed 'A' (Lovat Scouts) Company of the 3rd (Territorial) Battalion, Queen's Own Highlanders (Seaforth and Camerons). In the re-organisation of the 51st Highland Volunteers in 1975 they formed 'A' (The Lovat Scouts) Company of the 2nd Battalion.

(1) A circlet inscribed *Lovat's Scouts*. In the centre a stag's head on an heraldic wreath. In white-metal (Fig. 1500).

(2) A strap inscribed *Je suis prest*. In the centre a stag's head on an heraldic wreath. In white-metal (Fig. 2336). Also anodised. With 'square' lettering to motto sealed in both white-metal and anodised, 10th January 1951. Slightly different pattern with 'tall' lettering sealed in both white-metal and anodised 21st September 1965.

The Surrey Yeomanry (Queen Mary's Regiment)

In 1922 formed two batteries of the 98th (Surrey and Sussex Yeomanry, Queen Mary's) Army Field Regiment, R.A. Re-constituted in 1947 as the 298th Field Regiment, R.A. (Surrey Yeomanry, Queen Mary's). In 1961 it was amalgamated with 291 (4th London) Field Regiment, R.A., 263 (6th London) Light Regiment, R.A., and 381 (East Surrey) Light Regiment, R.A., to form 263 (Surrey Yeomanry, Queen Mary's) Field Regiment, R.A.

On the formation of the T.A.V.R. in 1967 they became The Surrey Yeomanry (Queen Mary's Regiment) (T) and on the augmentation of the volunteers in 1971 'D' Battery, 6th (Volunteer) Battalion, The Queen's Regiment.

(1) Within the Garter surmounted by an Imperial crown the cypher of Queen Mary. Below, a scroll inscribed *Queen Mary's Regiment Surrey Yeomanry*. In gilding-metal (Fig. 1473). Also in white-metal.

(2) As above but smaller. In white-metal (Fig. 2337).

(3) As (2) but in gilding-metal with red-enamel centre (Fig. 2338).

(4) As (1) but with St. Edward's crown. In white-metal (Fig. 2339). Sealed in anodised, 24th January, 1958.

(5) As (2) but with St. Edward's crown. In white-metal, sealed 9th June 1952 (Fig. 2340). Also anodised, sealed 28th January 1958.

The Leicestershire and Derbyshire (Prince Albert's Own) Yeomanry

This regiment was formed in 1956 by the amalgamation of The Leicestershire (Prince Albert's Own) Yeomanry and The Derbyshire Yeomanry.

It formed a Territorial unit in the T.A.V.R. and in 1971, on the increase in the volunteer-element, became a company in the 7th (Volunteer) Battalion, The Royal Anglian Regiment. A rose surmounted by St. Edward's crown. Superimposed on the rose the crest of the Prince Consort and, below, a scroll inscribed *The Leicestershire & Derbyshire Yeomanry*. The Prince Consort's crest in white-metal, remainder in gilding-metal (Fig. 2341). Also anodised, sealed 14th March 1957.

The Leicestershire (Prince Albert's Own) Yeomanry

Formed as a cavalry regiment in 1920 and transferred to the Royal Artillery in 1940 as 153rd and 154th Field Regiment, R.A. (Leicestershire Yeomanry).

Re-formed in 1947 as a regiment of the Royal Armoured Corps and amalgamated with The Derbyshire Yeomanry to form The Leicestershire and Derbyshire (Prince Albert's Own) Yeomanry (A.O.85/1957).
The crest of the Prince Consort with a scroll above inscribed *Leicestershire* and a scroll below inscribed *Prince Albert's Own Yeo.* Below this another scroll inscribed *South Africa 1900–02.* In gilding-metal, sealed 24th April 1952 (Fig. 1424). Also in white-metal, sealed 9th May 1952, and in gold-anodised.

The Derbyshire Yeomanry

After the Great War it became the 24th (Derbyshire Yeomanry) Armoured Car Company, Royal Tank Corps. Transferred to the Royal Armoured Corps in 1939 as 1st Derbyshire Yeomanry, its duplicate unit being 2nd Derbyshire Yeomanry.

Re-formed in 1947 as The Derbyshire Yeomanry, a regiment in the Royal Armoured Corps, it was amalgamated in 1957 with The Leicestershire (Prince Albert's Own) Yeomanry to form The Leicestershire and Derbyshire (Prince Albert's Own) Yeomanry.

(1) A rose within a laurel-wreath surmounted by an Imperial crown. On the wreath, scrolls inscribed *South Africa 1900, 1901.* Below, a scroll inscribed *Derbyshire Yeomanry* with a blank space between the two words replacing the former word *Imperial.* In gilding-metal (Fig. 1443).
(2) As above but with a laurel-spray replacing the blank space. In white-metal (Fig. 2342). Sealed 22nd February 1940.
(3) As (1) but smaller and with St. Edward's crown. Laurel-wreath in white-metal, remainder in gilding-metal (Fig. 2343).

The Northamptonshire Yeomanry

Re-formed after the Great War as the 25th (Northamptonshire Yeomanry) Armoured Car Company, Royal Tank Corps. Transferred to the Royal Armoured Corps in 1939 as the 1st Northamptonshire Yeomanry with duplicate unit, 2nd Northamptonshire Yeomanry.

In 1947 became a regiment of the Royal Armoured Corps as The Northamptonshire Yeomanry, but in 1956 formed 'D' (Northamptonshire Yeomanry) Squadron of The Inns of Court Regiment. Converted in 1961 to become the 250 (Northamptonshire Yeomanry) Field Squadron, Royal Engineers.

When the T.A.V.R. was formed they became 'A' Company of The Northamptonshire Regiment (T). In 1971 this regiment provided 'C' and 'D' Companies of 7th (Volunteer) Battalion, The Royal Anglian Regiment.

(1) The White Horse of Hanover. In white-metal (Fig. 1494).
(2) Within an oval inscribed *Northamptonshire Yeomanry* the White Horse of Hanover. In white-metal (Fig. 2344). Sealed 20th March 1940 and worn by the 2nd Northamptonshire Yeomanry only during the Second World War.

The Hampshire Carabiniers Yeomanry

In 1923 it was a battery in the 95th (Hampshire) Field Regiment, R.A., and in 1939 became 72nd Heavy Anti-Aircraft Regiment, R.A. (Hampshire).

Re-formed in 1947 as 295th (Hampshire Carabiniers Yeomanry) Heavy Anti-Aircraft Regiment, R.A., and in 1963 amalgamated with 457 (Wessex) Regiment, R.A., to form 457 (Wessex) Heavy Air Defence Regiment, R.A. (Hampshire Carabiniers Yeomanry).

In the T.A.V.R. this regiment became 'C' Company (Wessex R.A., Princess Beatrice's) The Hampshire and Isle of Wight Territorials which, in 1971, became 'C' Company, 2nd Battalion, The Wessex Regiment.

(1) The Hampshire Rose within an oval inscribed *Hampshire Yeomanry* superimposed on crossed carbines and surmounted by an Imperial crown. Below, a scroll inscribed *Carabiniers*. In gilding-metal (Fig. 1440). Sealed 25th May 1916.
(2) As above but rose and scroll in white-metal, remainder in gilding-metal (Fig. 2345). Sealed 27th September 1951. Also anodised.

The Royal Buckinghamshire Hussars

In 1921 formed two batteries of 99th (Buckinghamshire and Berkshire Yeomanry) Army Field Regiment, R.A. Following the doubling-up of the T.A. its title was changed in 1942 to 99th (Buckinghamshire Yeomanry) Field Regiment, R.A.

Re-constituted in 1947 as 299th (Buckinghamshire Yeomanry) Field Regiment, R.A., and amalgamated in 1950 to form 299th (Royal Bucks Yeomanry and Queen's Own Oxfordshire Hussars) Field Regiment, R.A.

In 1956 amalgamated with 345th (Berkshire Yeomanry) Field Regiment, R.A., to form 299th (Royal Bucks Yeomanry, Berkshire Yeomanry and The Queen's Own Oxfordshire Hussars) Field Regiment, R.A. With further amalgamation in 1961 the title became 299th (Royal Bucks Yeomanry, Queen's Own Oxfordshire Hussars and Berkshire) Field Regiment, R.A.

On the formation of the T.A.V.R. it became 'P' Battery (Royal Bucks Yeomanry) The Buckinghamshire Regiment, R.A. (T), which, in 1971, became 'B' Company, 2nd Battalion, The Wessex Regiment.

(1) A circlet inscribed *Yeomen of Bucks Strike Home*. Within the circlet a swan with a coronet round its neck. The circlet surmounted by an Imperial crown. Below, a scroll inscribed *Royal Bucks Hussars*. In gilding-metal (Fig. 1441). Also in white-metal.
(2) As above but with St. Edward's crown. In silver-anodised (Fig. 2346). Sealed 22nd February 1952.
(3) A circlet inscribed *The Buckinghamshire Regiment* surmounted by St. Edward's crown. In the centre a swan with a coronet round its neck. In silver-anodised (Fig. 2347).

The Queen's Own Dorset and West Somerset Yeomanry

In 1961, the 255th (West Somerset Yeomanry) Medium Regiment, R.A., and 294th (Queen's Own Dorset Yeomanry) Field Regiment, R.A., were amalgamated to form 250th (Queen's Own Dorset and West Somerset Yeomanry) Regiment, R.A.

In front of a sword and rifle in saltire, point and muzzle upwards, a dragon rampant within the Garter, the whole ensigned with St. Edward's crown. Below, two scrolls inscribed *Queen's Own Dorset*, *West Somerset Yeomanry* with *and* between the two scrolls. The dragon in gold and remainder, silver-anodised (Fig. 2348).

The Queen's Own Dorset Yeomanry

Formed in 1920 as 94th (Somerset and Dorset Yeomanry) Army Field Brigade, R.A. Title changed in 1929 to 94th (Queen's Own Dorset Yeomanry) Field Regiment, R.A., and, in 1938, to 94th (Dorset and Hampshire) Field Regiment, R.A.

Re-formed in 1947 as 294th (Queen's Own Dorset Yeomanry) Field Regiment, R.A., and amalgamated with 255th (West Somerset Yeomanry) Medium Regiment, R.A., to form 250th (Queen's Own Dorset and West Somerset Yeomanry) Regiment, R.A.

On the formation of the T.A.V.R. it formed 'A' Company (Queen's Own Dorset Yeomanry) of The Dorset Territorials which, in 1971, became 'D' Company, 2nd Battalion, The Wessex Regiment.

2340 2341 1424 1443

2342 2343 1494 2344

1440 2345 1441 2346

2347 2348 1446 2349

1460 1465 1433 2350

(1) The Garter surmounted by an Imperial crown. Within the Garter *Q.O. Dorset Y.*, the word *Dorset* being borne on a scroll; the whole within a laurel-wreath. On the wreath scrolls inscribed *South Africa 1900, 1901* and across the base of the wreath a further scroll inscribed *The Great War*. In white-metal (Fig. 1446). Also in bronze, sealed 2nd October 1935.
(2) As above but with St. Edward's crown. In white-metal (Fig. 2349). Sealed 6th May 1953.

The West Somerset Yeomanry

In 1922 it was the 94th (Somerset and Dorset Yeomanry) Army Field Brigade, R.A., but, in 1929, it became two batteries of 55th (Wessex) Army Field Regiment, R.A.

Re-constituted in 1947 as 255th (Wessex) Medium Regiment, R.A. Amalgamated in 1956 with 421st (Dorset) Coast Regiment, R.A., to form 255th (West Somerset Yeomanry and Dorset Garrison) Medium Regiment, R.A. Amalgamated in 1961 with 294th (Queen's Own Dorset Yeomanry) Field Regiment, R.A., to form 250th (Queen's Own Dorset and West Somerset Yeomanry) Medium Regiment, R.A.

In the T.A.V.R. it was 'B' Company (West Somerset Yeomanry) The Somerset Yeomanry and Light Infantry (T) and, in 1971, became 'B' Company, 6th Battalion, The Light Infantry (Volunteers).

An oval inscribed *West Somerset Yeomanry*. In the centre a wyvern. Below, a scroll inscribed *S. Africa 1900–01*. In gilding-metal (Fig. 1460). Also in white-metal.

Montgomeryshire Yeomanry

After the Great War it provided two companies of the 7th (Montgomeryshire) Battalion, The Royal Welch Fusiliers. In 1947 it was re-formed as 636th (Royal Welch) Light Anti-Aircraft Regiment, R.A., and in 1955 amalgamated with 635th Light Anti-Aircraft Regiment, R.A., to form 446th (Royal Welch) Light Anti-Aircraft Regiment, R.A. In 1956 it became part of 6th/7th Battalion, The Royal Welch Fusiliers.

This battalion became a Territorial battalion in the T.A.V.R. and, in 1971, provided 'D' Company, 3rd (Volunteer) Battalion, The Royal Welch Fusiliers.

The Welsh Dragon. Below, a scroll inscribed *MY*. In white-metal (Fig. 1465).

Denbighshire Yeomanry

In 1921 it provided two batteries of the 61st (Carnarvon and Denbigh Yeomanry) Medium Regiment, R.A.

Re-formed in 1947 as 361st (Caernarvon and Denbigh Yeomanry) Medium Regiment, R.A., and amalgamated in 1956 with 384th Light Regiment, R.A. (5th Royal Welch Fusiliers) to form 372nd (Flintshire and Denbighshire Yeomanry) Light Regiment, R.A. Changed to 'Field' regiment in 1961.

On the formation of the T.A.V.R. it became The Flintshire and Denbighshire Yeomanry R.A.(T), which, in 1971, became 'B' Company, 3rd (Volunteer) Battalion, The Royal Welch Fusiliers.

(1) The Prince of Wales's plumes, coronet and motto. In bronzed brass (Fig. 1433).
(2) The Prince of Wales's plumes, coronet and motto. Below, a scroll inscribed *Caernarvon & Denbigh Yeo.* Coronet and scroll in gilding-metal, remainder in white-metal. Sealed 5th April 1948 (Fig. 2350). Also anodised, sealed 28th January, 1952.
(3) As (2) but scroll inscribed *Flint and Denbigh Yeo.* Coronet and scroll in gilding-metal, remainder in white-metal (Fig. 2351). Also anodised, sealed 28th January 1958.

Pembroke Yeomanry (Castlemartin)

In 1920 it formed 102nd (Pembroke and Cardiganshire) Army Field Regiment, R.A.

In 1947 it became 302nd (Pembroke Yeomanry) Field Regiment, R.A., but, in 1961, was transferred to the Royal Armoured Corps as The Pembroke Yeomanry (Castlemartin).

In the T.A.V.R. it provided 'A' Company (Pembroke Yeomanry) 4th (Territorial) Battalion, The Welch Regiment, which, in 1971, became 4th (Volunteer) Battalion, The Royal Regiment of Wales.

(1) The Prince of Wales's plumes, coronet and motto. Below, a scroll inscribed *Fishguard.* The coronet in gilding-metal, remainder in white-metal (Fig. 1437).

(2) As above but both coronet and scroll in gilding-metal, remainder in white-metal. Sealed 18th July 1952 (Fig. 2352). Also anodised.

(3) As (2) but smaller size for wear on the beret (Fig. 2353). Also anodised.
There are several versions of these badges including an all-white-metal pattern.

The South Nottinghamshire Hussars

In 1922 it formed two batteries of 107th (The South Nottinghamshire Hussars Yeomanry) Army Field Brigade, R.A. Title changed later to 107th (The South Nottinghamshire Hussars Yeomanry) Regiment, R.H.A. Re-formed in 1947 as 307th Field Regiment, R.A. (South Notts Hussars Yeomanry); title changed in 1956 to 307th (R.H.A.) (South Nottinghamshire Yeomanry) Field Regiment, R.A.

In the T.A.V.R. it became The South Nottinghamshire Hussars Yeomanry (R.H.A.), R.A.(T), and is now 307 (South Nottinghamshire Hussars Yeomanry Royal Horse Artillery) Observation Post Battery, Royal Artillery (Volunteers).

In 1939 the regiment raised a duplicate unit: the 150th Regiment, R.H.A. (South Nottinghamshire Hussars Yeomanry). This regiment was re-formed after the war as 350th (South Nottinghamshire Hussars Yeomanry) Heavy Regiment, R.A. In 1955 it amalgamated with 528 Light Anti-Aircraft Regiment, R.A., and 577th Light Anti-Aircraft/Searchlight Regiment, R.A., to form 350th (The Robin Hood Foresters) Heavy Regiment, R.A., which, in 1961, became 350th (The Robin Hood Foresters) Field Squadron, R.E.

On the formation of the T.A.V.R. it was The Robin Hood (Territorial) Battalion, The Sherwood Foresters (Nottinghamshire and Derbyshire Regiment). With the volunteer-augmentation in 1971 it became 'B' Battery, 3rd (Volunteer) Battalion, The Worcestershire and Sherwood Foresters Regiment.

A slip of oak with acorn. In gilding-metal (Fig. 1432). Also in white-metal, chromed, and anodised, sealed 14th February 1952.

The North Somerset Yeomanry

Re-formed as a horsed regiment in 1920, it was transferred to the Royal Armoured Corps in 1941. In 1943 it became 4 Air Formation Signals (North Somerset Yeomanry) Royal Corps of Signals. Re-constituted in 1947 as a regiment of the Royal Armoured Corps it was amalgamated in 1956 with 44th/50th Royal Tank Regiment with the title North Somerset Yeomanry/44th Royal Tank Regiment which was changed, in 1965, to The North Somerset and Bristol Yeomanry.

On the formation of the T.A.V.R. it became 'A' Company (North Somerset and Bristol Yeomanry) The Somerset Yeomanry and Light Infantry (T) and, in 1971, became 'A' Company, 6th (Volunteer) Battalion, The Light Infantry.

(1) A ten-pointed star the topmost-point displaced by an Imperial crown. In the centre a circlet inscribed *Arma pacis fulcra*. Within the circlet the cypher of King George v. In white-metal (Fig. 1426).
(2) As above but with the cypher of King George vi. In white-metal (Fig. 2354). Sealed 25th February 1937.
(3) A ten-pointed star the topmost-point displaced by St. Edward's crown and surrounded by a wreath of laurel. On the star a circlet inscribed *Arma pacis fulcra* and in the centre a tank. Below the circlet a scroll inscribed *Fear Naught*. In silver-anodised (Fig. 2355). Sealed 18th November 1958.

Westmorland and Cumberland Yeomanry

Re-formed after the Great War as two batteries of 51st (Westmorland and Cumberland) Field Regiment, R.A. Re-raised in 1947 as 251st (Westmorland and Cumberland) Field Regiment, R.A.

When the T.A.V.R. was formed it became 'B' (Westmorland and Cumberland) Company, 4th (Territorial) Battalion, The Border Regiment which, in 1971, provided 'B' Company, The Northumbrian Volunteers, and which in 1975 became 'B' Company, 4th (Volunteer) Battalion, The King's Own Royal Border Regiment.

(1) An oval within a laurel-wreath inscribed *Westmorland & Cumberland Y.* surmounted by an Imperial crown. In the centre three sprigs of heather. In gilding-metal (Fig. 1435).
(2) A circlet inscribed *Westmorland & Cumberland Yeo.* surmounted by St. Edward's crown, In the centre three sprigs of heather. In silver-anodised (Fig. 2356).

The Queen's Own Oxfordshire Hussars

After the Great War it became part of 100th (Worcestershire and Oxfordshire Yeomanry) Army Field Brigade, R.A., which, in 1938, became 53rd (Worcestershire and Oxfordshire Yeomanry) Anti-Tank Regiment, R.A. Re-formed in 1947 as 387th (Queen's own Oxfordshire Hussars) Field Regiment, R.A.

In 1950 it amagamated with The Royal Buckinghamshire Hussars to form 299th (Royal Bucks Yeomanry and Queen's Own Oxfordshire Hussars) Field Regiment, R.A.

When the T.A.V.R. was formed it constituted "A" (Queen's Own Oxfordshire Hussars) Company, The Oxfordshire Territorials.

Its successor-unit is 5 (The Queen's Own Oxfordshire Hussars) Signal Squadron (Volunteers) of the 39th (City of London) Signal Regiment (Volunteers).

(1) The cypher *AR* of Queen Adelaide surmounted by her crown. Below, a scroll inscribed *Queen's Own Oxfordshire Hussars*. In bronze (Fig. 1461). Also in white-metal, and in brass.
(2) As above but with different shape of crown. In white-metal (Fig. 1462).
(3) As above but with Imperial crown. In white-metal (Fig. 1463). Also in bronze. Sealed in white-metal and also anodised, 9th May 1952.

FISHGUARD
2351
1437
2352
FISHGUARD
2353
1432
1426
2354
WESTMORLAND & CUMBERLAND
2355
1435
2356
1461
1462
1463

CHAPTER 15

Territorial Army Infantry: 1920 to 1947

The Territorial Force, re-named The Territorial Army, was re-constituted in 1920; the majority of infantry battalions reverting to their original role although no cyclist battalions were reformed.

Very little change took place until shortly before the Second World War when a number of battalions adopted an anti-aircraft- or anti-tank-role.

The Royal Scots (The Royal Regiment)
4th and 5th Battalions

The Star of the Order of the Thistle with an Imperial crown above the motto and a bugle-horn below. In white-metal (Fig. 1697). Officers': in silver-plate with gilt crown and bugle, and gilt-centre with green-enamel backing.

These battalions, reformed in 1920, were amalgamated on 31st December 1921 to form the 4th/5th Battalion (Queen's Edinburgh). In 1938 they were converted to the 52nd Searchlight Regiment.

The King's Regiment (Liverpool)
5th Battalion

(1) The White Horse of Hanover on a scroll inscribed *The King's*. In blackened-brass (Fig. 1701).
(2) The White Horse of Hanover on a scroll inscribed *King's* in Old English lettering. In blackened-brass (Fig. 2357). Sealed 4th May 1927.

6th (Rifle) Battalion

A bugle-horn surmounted by the Rose of Lancaster. In blackened-brass (Fig. 1702). Sealed on 25th September 1916 and worn until 1936 when the battalion was converted to the 38th Searchlight Regiment. Officers wore a blackened-silver bugle-horn on a black-cord boss.

7th Battalion

(1) The White Horse of Hanover on ground above a scroll inscribed *The King's*. All in white-metal (Fig. 1703). Worn until 1927.
(2) The White Horse of Hanover on ground above a scroll inscribed *King's* in Old English lettering. All in white-metal (Fig. 2358). Worn until 1938 when the battalion was converted to the 40th Battalion, Royal Tank Corps.

8th (Irish) Battalion
The Irish Harp surmounted by an Imperial crown and resting on a wreath of shamrocks. Below, a scroll inscribed *8th (Irish) Bn The King's Regiment L'pool.* In white-metal on a green-cloth patch (Fig. 2359). Sealed 23rd November 1939.
Re-formed in 1939 as duplicate of 5th Battalion.

10th (Liverpool Scottish) Battalion
Superimposed on St. Andrew's Cross the White Horse of Hanover on ground and below this a scroll inscribed *The King's* and below this two thistle-sprays, joining the tops of which a scroll inscribed *Liverpool Scottish.* Struck in one piece in white-metal (Fig. 1706). Also in silver. Worn until 1937 when the battalion was transferred as The Liverpool Scottish, The Queen's Own Cameron Highlanders. Also worn by Sergeants with the Horse mounted on the badge.

The Lincolnshire Regiment
4th and 5th Battalions
The Sphinx resting on a blank tablet above a scroll inscribed *Lincolnshire.* The scroll in gilding-metal, remainder in white-metal (Fig. 1708).
The 5th battalion was converted to 46th A.A. Battalion, R.E., in 1936. The Regiment received the 'Royal' title on 28th November 1946.

The Devonshire Regiment
4th Battalion
An eight-pointed star, the topmost-point displaced by an Imperial crown. On this a circlet inscribed *The Devonshire Regiment.* In the centre the Castle of Exeter. In blackened-brass.

5th (Prince of Wales's) Battalion
As 4th Battalion but all in white-metal (Fig. 1709).

The Suffolk Regiment
4th Battalion
Within a wreath of oak a plain circlet surmounted by an Imperial crown. In the centre a castle and, below, a scroll inscribed *The Suffolk Regt.* The scroll in gilding-metal, remainder in white-metal (Fig. 1710). Also found in bronze and in all-brass.
The 4th and 5th Battalions were re-constituted in 1920 but were amalgamated on 26th August 1921 to form the 4th Battalion.

The Somerset Light Infantry (Prince Albert's)
4th and 5th Battalions
A bugle with strings surmounted by a mural crown. Above this a scroll inscribed *South Africa 1900–01.* The letters *PA* within the strings of the bugle. In white-metal (Fig. 1711). Officers': in hall-marked silver, also in bronze.

The West Yorkshire Regiment (The Prince of Wales's Own)
7th and 8th Battalions (Leeds Rifles)
(1) A cross based on that of the Order of the Bath surmounted by an Imperial crown. In the centre of the cross a circlet inscribed *Leeds Rifles* and, within this, a bugle with

strings surmounted by a crown. The whole surrounded by a laurel-wreath. Across the base of the wreath a scroll inscribed *7*, (or *8*), *Bn PWO West Yorkshire Regt.* In blackened-metal (Fig. 1712). Also in white-metal, and in all-brass. Officers': in hall-marked silver.

(2) A cross based on that of the Order of the Bath surmounted by an Imperial crown. On the arms of the cross the following battle honours are inscribed: (top) *Namur 1695, Tournay, Corunna, Java, Waterloo*; (left) *South Africa 1899–02, Armentieres 1914, Neuve Chapelle, Somme 1916, '18, Ypres 1917, '18*; (right) *Cambrai 1917, '18, Villers Bretonneux, Lys, Piave, Suvla*; (bottom) *Bhurtpore, Sevastopol, New Zealand, Afghanistan 1879–80, Relief of Ladysmith.* Below the cross a scroll inscribed *Tardenois.* In the centre of the cross a circlet inscribed *Leeds Rifles* and within this a bugle-horn with strings surmounted by a crown. The whole surrounded by a laurel-wreath. On the left branch of the wreath a scroll inscribed *7th 8th Bns* and on the right, a scroll inscribed *P.W.O.* Across the base of the wreath a scroll inscribed *West Yorkshire Regt* (Fig. 2360). In white-metal. Officers': in hall-marked silver.

The 7th Battalion became the 45th Battalion, Royal Tank Corps, in 1938 and the 8th Battalion, the 66th A.A. Brigade, R.A., in 1936.

The Leicestershire Regiment
4th and 5th Battalions

The Tiger on ground. Below this a scroll inscribed *Leicestershire.* The scroll in white-metal, remainder in gilding-metal (Fig. 1714). Also in bronze for officers' service-dress.
In 1936 the 4th Battalion was converted to the 44th A.A. Battalion, R.E.

The Lancashire Fusiliers
5th, 6th, 7th and 8th Battalions

A fused grenade with, on the ball within a laurel-wreath, the Sphinx resting on a blank tablet. Below, a scroll inscribed *The Lancashire Fusiliers.* The scroll in white-metal, remainder in gilding-metal (Fig. 1716). Officers': in gilt-and-silver, also in bronze.
The 7th Battalion became the 39th A.A. Battalion, R.E., in 1936.

The South Wales Borderers
The Brecknockshire Battalion

(1) The Welsh Dragon on a scroll inscribed *Brecknockshire.* In gilding-metal (Fig. 1717). Also in silver, white-metal and bronze. Sealed in brass 3rd February 1916.

(2) As above but with longer scroll (Fig. 1718). In same metals as above.

This battalion was amalgamated in 1922 with the 3rd Battalion, The Monmouthshire Regiment.

The Cameronians (Scottish Rifles)
5th Battalion

Within a complete wreath of thistles a bugle with strings surmounted by a mullet. The numeral *5* within the strings of the bugle. In white-metal (Fig. 1719).
This battalion was amalgamated with the 8th Battalion in 1921 and designated the 5th/8th Battalion. The above badge then ceased to be worn.

1697 1701 2357 1702

1703 2358 2359 1706

1708 1709 1710 1711

1712 2360 1714 1716

1717 1768 1719 1720

The Gloucestershire Regiment
5th and 6th Battalions
The Sphinx resting on a blank tablet above two sprigs of laurel. Below, a scroll inscribed *Gloucestershire* (Fig. 1720). In white-metal, also in bronze.
In 1938 the 6th Battalion became the 44th Battalion, Royal Tank Corps.

4th Battalion
The above badge in blackened-brass.
Converted in 1938 to the 66th Searchlight Regiment.

The East Lancashire Regiment
4th and 5th Battalions
Within a laurel-wreath surmounted by an Imperial crown the Sphinx resting on a blank tablet and beneath this a rose. On the base of the wreath a scroll inscribed *East Lancashire.* All in white-metal except the rose which is in gilding-metal (Fig. 1722).
Re-constituted on 7th February 1920, these two battalions were amalgamated on 26th August 1921 to form the 4th/5th Battalion.

The East Surrey Regiment
6th Battalion
(1) A Maltese cross, the edge of the top arm inscribed *South Africa* and the edge of the bottom arm *1900–1902.* In the centre a circlet inscribed *The East Surrey Regt 6th Battalion.* In the centre an eight-pointed star with, in its centre, the arms of Guildford. In blackened-brass (Fig. 1723). Officers': in blackened-silver with raised parts polished. This badge was approved on 11th July 1921 and declared obsolete on 15th January 1927.
(2) An eight-pointed star, the topmost-point displaced by an Imperial crown. In the centre a shield bearing the arms of Guildford. Below, a scroll inscribed *East Surrey.* In blackened-brass (Fig. 1724).

The Border Regiment
4th Battalion
On an eight-pointed star, the topmost-point displaced by an Imperial crown, a Maltese cross. On this a circlet inscribed *South Africa* 1900–02 with, in the centre, *4th.* At the base a scroll inscribed *Border Cumberland & Westmorland Regiment* (Fig. 1725). In white-metal, also in bronze.

5th Battalion
Same design as above but honour is *South Africa 1901–02,* in the centre *5th* and the scroll at the base reads *Border Cumberland Regiment* (Fig. 1726). In white-metal, also in bronze.

The Royal Sussex Regiment
5th (Cinque Ports) Battalion
A Maltese cross behind which the Roussillon plume. In the centre, on a circular background, a shield bearing the arms of the Cinque Ports. Below the cross a scroll inscribed *Cinque Ports.* In gilding-metal (Fig. 1728). Also in bronze.
There was also an officers' version in bronze with red- and blue-enamel in the centre.

1722 1723 1724 1725

1726 1728 1729 1730

1731 1732 1733 1734

1736 1735 2361

1737 1738 1740 2362

The Hampshire Regiment
6th (Duke of Connaught's Own) Battalion

(1) Within a laurel-wreath a strap inscribed *Duke of Connaught's Own* surmounted by a ducal coronet. In the centre the Hampshire Rose (Fig. 1729). Officers' pattern in silver with blue-enamel behind lettering and the Rose in red- and white-enamel.
(2) Same design as above but with the addition of a scroll inscribed *Hampshire* at the base (Fig. 1730). Other-ranks' pattern; the Rose and bottom-scroll in gilding-metal, remainder in white-metal.

7th Battalion

(1) Within a laurel-wreath surmounted by an Imperial crown a dog-gauge. Below, a scroll inscribed *7th Bn Hampshire Regt* (Fig. 1731). Officers' pattern in bronze, also in gilt.
(2) As above but without the crown (Fig. 1732). Other-ranks' pattern in gilding-metal, also in white-metal.

8th (Isle of Wight Rifles, Princess Beatrice's) Battalion

Within a laurel-wreath a circlet inscribed *Isle of Wight Rifles* and in the centre the Tower of Carisbrooke Castle. Above the circlet a scroll inscribed *South Africa 1900–01* and above this the Imperial crown. Below the circlet a scroll inscribed *Princess Beatrice's* (Fig. 1733). In chromed-metal, also found in black, white-metal and silver.

The Dorsetshire Regiment
4th Battalion

The Castle and Key of Gibraltar with, above, the Sphinx resting on a blank tablet. Below the Castle a scroll inscribed *Primus in Indis.* A laurel-wreath encloses the Castle and motto and is continued below the motto by a scroll inscribed *Dorsetshire.* The wreath and title-scroll in gilding-metal, remainder in white-metal (Fig. 1734).

The South Lancashire Regiment (The Prince of Wales's Volunteers)
4th Battalion

The Prince of Wales's plumes, coronet and motto. Below, a Sphinx resting on a blank tablet. Above the plumes a scroll inscribed *South Lancashire* and below the Sphinx a scroll inscribed *Prince of Wales's Vols.* Branches of laurel connect the ends of the scroll. The plumes, motto and Sphinx in white-metal, remainder in gilding-metal (Fig. 1735).

5th Battalion

As above but in blackened-brass.
This battalion became the 61st Searchlight Regiment in 1938.

The Black Watch (Royal Highland Regiment)
4th/5th and 6th/7th Battalions

The Star of the Order of the Thistle. On the Star a thistle-wreath enclosing an oval inscribed *Nemo me impune lacessit* and surmounted by an Imperial crown. Within the oval St. Andrew and Cross. Across the top of the wreath a scroll inscribed *Royal Highlanders* and, across the bottom, a two-part scroll inscribed *Black Watch.* In white-metal (Fig. 1736). The badge is found with the spellings *lacessit* and *lacesset.* In May 1925 instructions were given that

when existing stocks had been exhausted the spelling should be changed from *lacesset* to *lacessit.*
The 4th and 5th Battalions, re-formed in 1920, were amalgamated in 1921 to form the 4th/5th Battalion. The 6th and 7th Battalions, also re-formed in 1920, were amalgamated at the same time to form the 6th/7th Battalion. The sub-title was changed from 'Royal Highlanders' to 'Royal Highland Regiment' in 1935.

The Tyneside Scottish
Within a thistle-wreath St. Andrew's Cross. Across the base of the Cross a tablet inscribed *Tyneside Scottish.* Superimposed on the Cross a tower. Above this, with one paw on the top of the tower, a lion holding a forked-pennon inscribed *X*. In white-metal (Fig. 2361). Also for officers in hall-marked silver. Sealed 19th April 1940.
Formed in 1939 as 12th (Tyneside Scottish) Battalion, The Durham Light Infantry, it was transferred later that year as 1st Battalion The Tyneside Scottish, The Black Watch (Royal Highland Regiment).

The Oxfordshire and Buckinghamshire Light Infantry
The Buckinghamshire Battalion
A Maltese cross surmounted by an Imperial crown. On this a circlet inscribed *Buckinghamshire Battalion.* In the centre a swan with a coronet round its neck. In white-metal (Fig. 1737). Also in silver, bronze, and black.

The Essex Regiment
4th, 5th, 6th and 7th Battalions
The Castle and Key of Gibraltar. Above the Castle the Sphinx resting on a blank tablet. The whole, except the Sphinx, enclosed in a wreath of oak. On the base of the wreath a scroll inscribed *The Essex Regt* and below this a further scroll inscribed *South Africa 1900–02.* The title-scroll and Sphinx in white-metal, remainder in gilding-metal (Fig. 1738).
The 6th Battalion became the 64th Searchlight Regiment in 1939 and the 7th Battalion, the 59th A.A. Brigade, R.A., in 1935.

The Sherwood Foresters (Nottinghamshire and Derbyshire Regiment)
7th (Robin Hood) Battalion
A laurel-wreath surmounted by an Imperial crown. Within this a cross based on that of the Order of the Bath. On the arms of the cross: (left) *South*; (right) *Africa*; (bottom) *1900–02.* In the centre of the cross a circlet inscribed *The Robin Hoods* and in the centre a bugle with strings surmounted by a crown (Fig. 1740). In white-metal, also in black. Officers': in silver, also in blackened-white-metal with high points polished to show white (Fig. 2362)
This battalion was converted in 1936 to 42nd A.A. Battalion, R.E.

The Northamptonshire Regiment
4th Battalion
(1) The Castle and Key of Gibraltar within a laurel-wreath. Above the Castle a scroll inscribed *4th Battalion* and below the Castle a scroll inscribed *South Africa 1900–02.* On the base of the wreath a scroll inscribed *Northamptonshire* (Fig. 1741). The title-scroll in gilding-metal, remainder in white-metal. Also in bronze.
(2) As above but with blank scrolls above and below the Castle (Fig. 1742). Title-scroll in gilding-metal, remainder in white-metal.

The Middlesex Regiment (Duke of Cambridge's Own)
7th, 8th and 9th Battalions
The Prince of Wales's plumes, coronet and motto. Below the coronet the cypher *G* of the Duke of Cambridge, interlaced and reversed, all within a laurel-wreath. Across the base of the wreath a scroll inscribed *South Africa 1900–02.* Below the wreath a scroll inscribed *Middlesex Regt.* The plumes, motto and title-scroll in white-metal, remainder in gilding-metal (Fig. 1743). Also in bronze, and silver, for officers.
In 1938 the 9th Battalion became the 60th Searchlight Regiment.

The Wiltshire Regiment (Duke of Edinburgh's)
4th Battalion
A cross patée, lined, with burnished edges. On the cross a circular convex plate and thereon the cypher of the Duke of Edinburgh. Above the cross a coronet. Below, a scroll inscribed *The Wiltshire Regiment.* All in black-metal. Sealed 7th April 1916 (Fig. 1745).

The Manchester Regiment
7th Battalion
A floriated fleur-de-lys (Fig. 1746). In bronze.

8th (Ardwick) and 9th Battalion
These battalions wore the ordinary-pattern fleur-de-lys (as Fig. 2014, Chapter 5) but, in 1959, both had their cap- and collar-badges chromed for the presentation of new Colours.

The Durham Light Infantry
6th Battalion
A Maltese cross with a blank tablet above the cross and on this an Imperial crown. In the centre a circlet inscribed *6th Battn The Durham Light Infantry* with, in the centre, a bugle with strings (Fig. 1747). In blackened-brass for officers. Other-ranks wore the bugle surmounted by the Imperial crown with the letters *DLI* within the strings in blackened-brass.

5th, 7th, 8th and 9th Battalions
A bugle with strings surmounted by an Imperial crown and the letters *DLI* within the strings. Underneath the bugle a scroll inscribed *South Africa 1900–02.* For officers, in bronze, also in silver (Fig. 1748).
In 1936 the 7th Battalion became the 47th A.A. Battalion, R.E., and in 1938 the 5th Battalion became the 54th Searchlight Regiment.

The Highland Light Infantry (City of Glasgow Regiment)
5th, 6th and 7th Battalions
The Star of the Order of the Thistle and thereon a bugle-horn. In the twist of the horn the monogram *HLI.* Above the horn an Imperial crown and below it a scroll inscribed *South Africa 1900–02* and beneath this the Elephant. In white-metal (Fig. 1750).
7th Battalion converted to 83rd A.A. Regiment, R.A., in 1938.

9th (Glasgow Highland) Battalion
(1) The Star of the Order of the Thistle. On the Star a thistle-wreath enclosing an oval inscribed *Nemo me impune lacessit* and surmounted by an Imperial crown. Within the

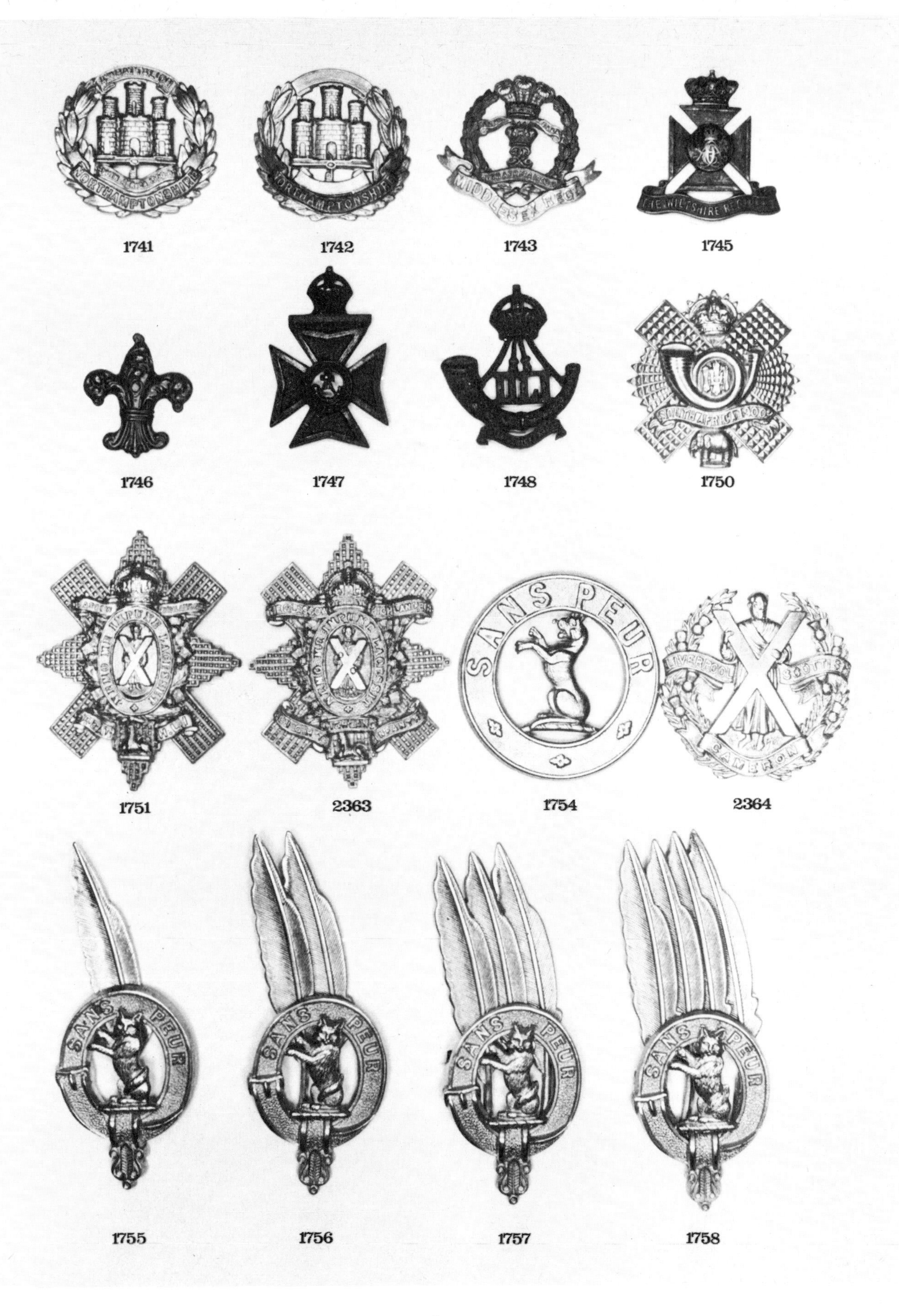

1741 1742 1743 1745

1746 1747 1748 1750

1751 2363 1754 2364

1755 1756 1757 1758

oval St. Andrew and Cross. Across the top of the wreath a two-part scroll inscribed *Glasgow Highlanders* and a similar scroll at the base inscribed *9th Batt. H.L.I.* with, beneath the two parts, the Sphinx on a blank tablet (Fig. 1751). In white-metal, also in silver-plate.

(2) Similar to above but with longer scrolls, the top one inscribed *The Glasgow Highlanders* and the bottom one a tri-part scroll inscribed *Highland Light Infantry*. In white-metal (Fig. 2363). Sealed 2nd December 1939. For officers': St. Andrew and Cross and the title-scrolls in silver, remainder in gilt.

The battalion was re-designated 1st Battalion, The Glasgow Highlanders in 1939.

Seaforth Highlanders (Ross-shire Buffs, The Duke of Albany's)
5th (The Sutherland and Caithness Highland) Battalion

Within a circlet inscribed *Sans Peur* a cat-a-mountain. In white-metal (Fig. 1754). Sealed 29th April 1916.

Officers' badges

Subalterns: within a strap inscribed *Sans Peur* a cat-a-mountain with one silver feather behind the strap (Fig. 1755).
Captains: as above but with two silver feathers (Fig. 1756).
Majors: as above but with three silver feathers (Fig. 1757).
Lieutenant-Colonels and the Colonel of the Regiment: } as above but with four silver feathers (Fig. 1758).

The battalion was re-formed in 1920 but, in the following year, it was amalgamated with the 4th (Ross Highland) Battalion.

The Queen's Own Cameron Highlanders
The Liverpool Scottish

Within a wreath of thistles St. Andrew with Cross. Mid-centre left a scroll inscribed *Liverpool* and right, *Scottish*. At the base a further scroll inscribed *Cameron*. In white-metal (Fig. 2364). Sealed 28th March 1938.

The Honourable Artillery Company
Artillery

(1) Officers': a gun with a scroll above inscribed *HAC* surmounted by an Imperial crown. Below the gun a scroll inscribed *Arma pacis fulcra*. In gilt, with a mounted wheel on the gun (Fig. 1761). Also in bronze. Sealed 10th October 1923.
(2) Officers': as above but smaller for wear on the beret. In gilt (Fig. 2365).
(3) Other-ranks': same design as for officers (1) but all in gilding-metal (Fig. 1762). Sealed 10th October 1923.

Infantry

(1) Officers': a fused grenade. On the ball the letters *HAC*. All in gilt (Fig. 1763). Sealed 13th July 1916. Also in bronze, in bronze with silver lettering, and also in all-bronze but with letters two-thirds the size.
(2) Warrant Officers' and Sergeants': same design as above but with the grenade in gilding-metal and the letters in white-metal (Fig. 1764).
(3) Other-ranks': same design as above but all in gilding-metal (Fig. 1765). Also anodised, sealed 28th November 1952.

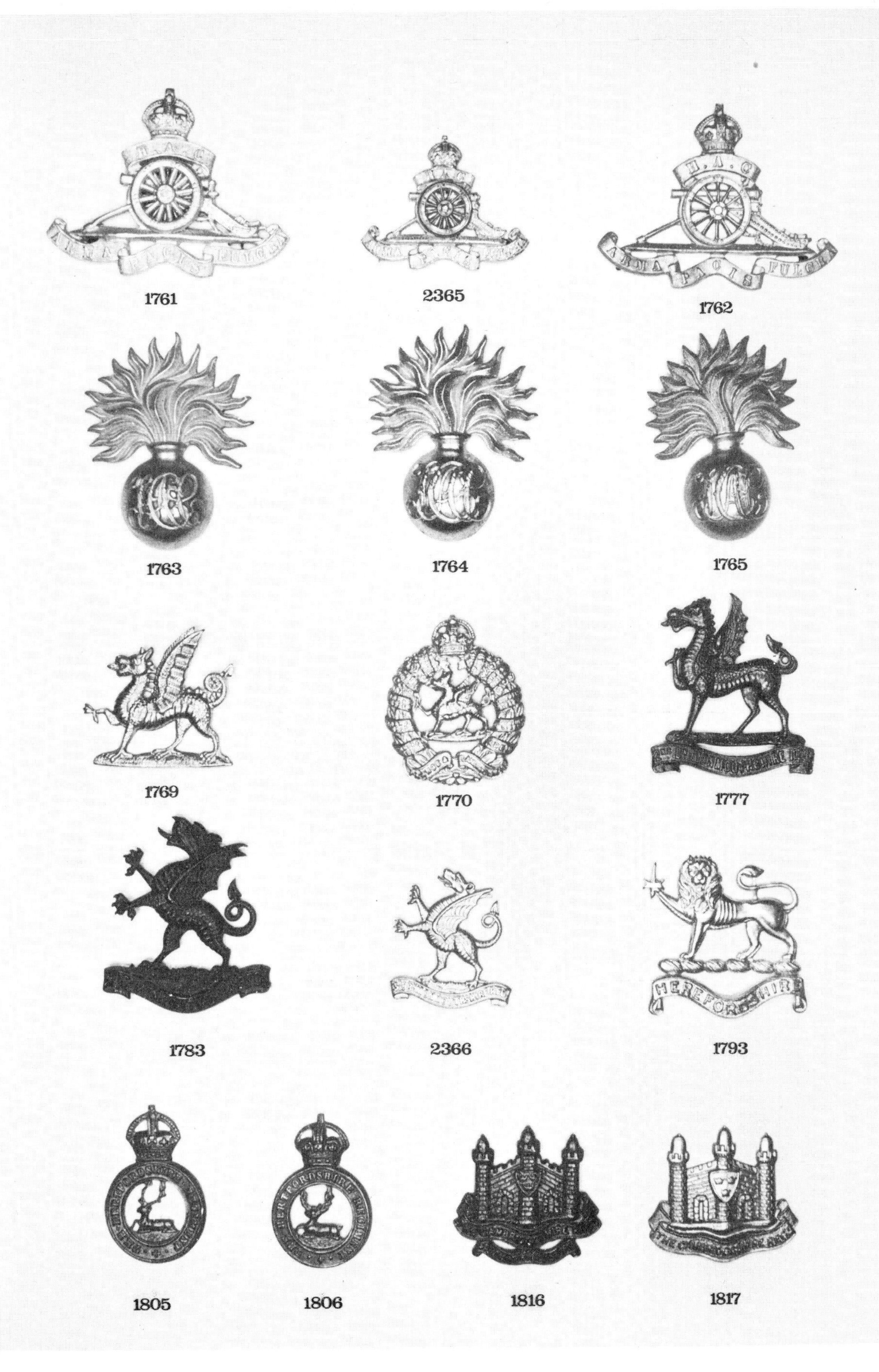

1761 2365 1762

1763 1764 1765

1769 1770 1777

1783 2366 1793

1805 1806 1816 1817

The Monmouthshire Regiment
1st Battalion

(1) The Welsh Dragon standing on ground. In white-metal (Fig. 1769). Worn until 1925.
(2) A laurel-wreath surmounted by an Imperial crown. On the wreath are battle-honour scrolls inscribed as follows: (left) *South Africa, 1900–02, Ypres 1915, '17, '18, Somme 1916, Scarpe 1917, Cambrai 1917, '18*; (right) *St. Julien, Arras 1917, Langemarck 1917, Hindenburg Line, Aden.* Across the base of the wreath a scroll inscribed *France & Flanders 1914–18.* In the centre the Welsh Dragon standing on ground. In white-metal. Officers' in silver, also in bronze (Fig. 1770). Also in all-brass. Sealed 25th May 1925.

In 1938 the battalion became the 68th Searchlight Regiment.

2nd Battalion

(1) Officers': the Welsh Dragon on ground. Below, a scroll inscribed *2nd Bn Monmouthshire Regt.* In silver-plate, also in bronze (Fig. 1777).
(2) Other-ranks': the same badge as shown in Fig. 1769 but in gilding-metal.

3rd Battalion

(1) Officers': the Welsh Dragon rampant above a scroll inscribed *3rd Bn Monmouthshire Regt.* In silver, also in bronze (Fig. 1783).
(2) As above but smaller. In silver-plate (Fig. 2366).

The Herefordshire Regiment

The lion from the crest of the City of Hereford. Below, a scroll inscribed *Herefordshire.* The lion in white-metal, scroll in gilding-metal. Also in bronze (Fig. 1793). Officers also wore the lion on a torse, without the title-scroll, in silver.

The Hertfordshire Regiment

(1) A circlet inscribed *The Hertfordshire Regiment* surmounted by an Imperial crown. In the centre a hart lodged. In gilding-metal (Fig. 1805). Officers' in silver-plate, gilt, or bronze.
(2) As above but with wider antlers on the hart (Fig. 1806). In same metals.

The Cambridgeshire Regiment

(1) Officers': a bridge (the crest of Cambridge City Council) on which is superimposed a shield bearing the arms of Ely. Beneath this a scroll inscribed *The Cambridgeshire Regt.* and beneath this a further scroll inscribed *South Africa 1900–01.* In silver-plate, also in bronze (Fig. 1816).
(2) Other-ranks': same design as for officers but without the honour scroll. The title in gilding-metal, remainder in white-metal (Fig. 1817). Sealed 25th May 1916. Officers' in silver. Also found in bronze.

CHAPTER 16

Territorial Army Infantry from 1947, and the Territorial Army Volunteer Reserve

---

The Territorial Army was re-constituted in 1947 and the regiments re-formed; the majority in the role in which they had ended the war. It was not long, however, before the changing needs of National Defence caused amalgamations of units which were surplus to requirements, and this was a continuing process until 1967 when the whole force was restructured and the Territorial Army Volunteer Reserve came into being.

This consisted of Territorial Army Volunteer Reserve I and II (Volunteers) and Territorial Army Volunteer Reserve III (Territorials) but a year later, as an economy measure, it was decided to place the Territorial element on a care-and-maintenance basis; subsequently amended to reducing the regiments to small cadres.

With a change of Government a decision was reached to increase the Volunteer element with recruiting to start as from the 1st April 1971.

In most instances this was achieved by expanding the cadres to company strength and then grouping them to form additional battalions to the existing Volunteer units. This was further revised following the Majory Report in 1975.

It is not intended here to give all the various changes in nomenclature the regiments have experienced since they were re-formed, but merely to depict and describe those special badges worn by Territorial infantry units which have been authorised in the period covered by this volume.

For convenience the H.A.C. Battery, R.H.A. (Volunteers), has been included in this chapter.

Honourable Artillery Company
The Honourable Artillery Battery, Royal Horse Artillery (Volunteers)

(1) Officers': a gun with a scroll above inscribed *HAC* surmounted by St. Edward's crown. Below the gun a scroll inscribed *Arma pacis fulcra.* In gilt with a mounted wheel on the gun (Fig. 2367). Also in bronze.
(2) As above but smaller for wear on the beret (Fig. 2368).
(3) Other-ranks': same design as for officers but all in gilding-metal (Fig. 2369).
(4) Same design as (3) but smaller for wear on the beret. In gilding-metal (Fig. 2370). Sealed 8th November 1954.

The Honourable Artillery Company Infantry Company (Volunteers)

(1) Officers' beret-badge: the crest from the arms of the H.A.C., viz. a man's right arm,

armoured, the hand grasping a staff with an ornamental head; on each side of the arm a wing, each bearing St. George's Cross; the whole on a torse. In white-metal (Fig. 2371).

(2) Officers': a fused grenade. On the ball the letters *HAC*. In bronze with silver lettering (Fig. 2372).

(3) As (2) but all-bronze (Fig. 2373).

(4) Warrant Officers' and Sergeants': same design as for officers but with the grenade in white-metal and the letters in gilding-metal (Fig. 2374). Sealed 9th March 1954.

(5) Other-ranks': same design but all anodised-silver (Fig. 2375).

Different sizes of the initials on all patterns can be found.

The Queen's Royal Surrey Regiment

On an eight-pointed star, the topmost-point displaced by St. Edward's crown, the Paschal Lamb. The Lamb silver- and the star, gold-anodised (Fig. 2376).

The Queen's Royal Regiment (West Surrey) and The East Surrey Regiment were amalgamated on 14th October 1959. This badge was worn by the Territorial element as, at that time, the regular battalion was wearing the badge of the Home Counties Brigade.

The King's Regiment (Liverpool)
8th (Irish) Battalion

The Irish Harp, surmounted by St. Edward's crown, resting on a wreath of shamrocks. Below, a scroll inscribed *8th (Irish) Bn The King's Regiment L'pool*. In silver-anodised (Fig. 2377).

Re-formed in 1947 as 626 H.A.A. Regiment, R.A. (Liverpool Irish).

The Devonshire Territorials

Within the Garter surrounded by a laurel-wreath a castle. Above, the Royal Crest; below, a scroll inscribed *Devonshire Territorials*. The castle and laurel-wreath gold-anodised, remainder silver-anodised (Fig. 2378).

This regiment consisted of 'A' (Royal Devon Yeomanry) Squadron, 'B' (Devon Fortress Engineers) Squadron and 'C' (1st Rifle Volunteers) Squadron.

The Cambridgeshire Regiment

A bridge (the crest of Cambridge City Council) on which is superimposed a shield bearing the arms of Ely. Beneath this a scroll inscribed *The Cambridgeshire Regt*. In white-metal (Fig. 1817). Sealed 24th October 1952.

The Suffolk and Cambridgeshire Regiment

The Castle and Key of Gibraltar surmounted by St. Edward's crown. Superimposed on the castle-wall, beneath the centre-turret, a shield bearing the arms of Ely. Below, a scroll inscribed *Suffolk and Cambridgeshire*. Gold-anodised except the castle, which is silver-anodised (Fig. 2379).

4th Battalion, The Suffolk Regiment and 1st Battalion, The Cambridgeshire Regiment were amalgamated in 1961.

The Somerset Yeomanry and Light Infantry

A bugle stringed, thereon a circlet inscribed *Arma pacis fulcra*; within the circlet a wyvern, the whole surmounted by St. Edward's crown. The wyvern in gold-, remainder in silver-

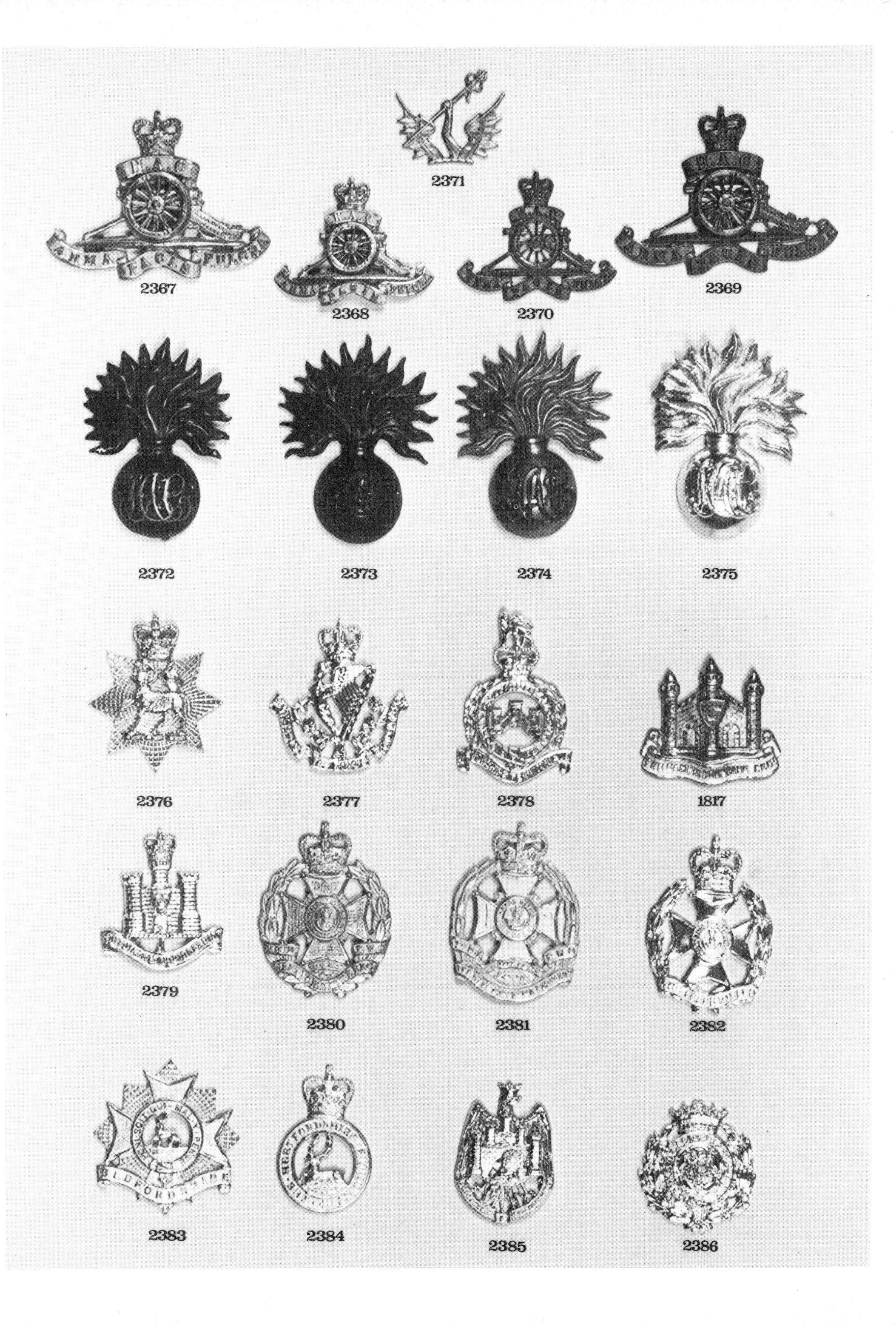

2371

2367 2368 2370 2369

2372 2373 2374 2375

2376 2377 2378 1817

2379 2380 2381 2382

2383 2384 2385 2386

anodised. Although authorised this badge was not manufactured as the regiment was reduced to a cadre soon after formation.
The regiment consisted of 'A' Company (North Somerset and Bristol Yeomanry), 'B' Company (West Somerset Yeomanry) and 'C' Company (Somerset Light Infantry), and later became 'A' and 'B' companies of the 6th (Volunteer) Battalion, The Light Infantry.

The Prince of Wales's Own Regiment of Yorkshire
The Leeds Rifles

(1) A cross based on that of the Order of the Bath surmounted by St. Edward's crown. On the arms of the cross the following battle honours are inscribed: (top) *Namur 1695, Tournay, Corunna, Java, Waterloo*; (left) *South Africa 1899–02, Armentieres 1914, Neuve Chapelle, Somme 1916, '18, Ypres 1917, '18*; (right) *Cambrai 1917, '18, Villers Bretonneux, Lys, Piave, Suvla*; (bottom) *Bhurtpore, Sevastopol, New Zealand, Afghanistan 1879–80, Relief of Ladysmith*. Below the cross a scroll inscribed *Tardenois*. In the centre of the cross a circlet inscribed *Leeds Rifles* and within this a bugle-horn with strings surmounted by a crown. The whole surrounded by a laurel-wreath. On the left branch of the wreath a scroll inscribed *7th 8th Bns* and on the right a scroll inscribed *P.W.O.* Across the base of the wreath a scroll inscribed *West Yorkshire Regt* (Fig. 2380). In white-metal. Officers': in silver-plate.

(2) Officers': a cross based on that of the Order of the Bath surmounted by St. Edward's crown. Below the cross a scroll inscribed *N. Africa 1942–43 R.T.R.* and below this a reproduction of a tank. In the centre of the cross a circlet inscribed *Leeds Rifles* and within this a bugle-horn with strings surmounted by a crown. The whole surrounded by a laurel-wreath. On the left branch of the wreath a scroll inscribed *7th Bn* and on the right, a scroll inscribed *P.W.O.* Across the base of the wreath a scroll inscribed *The West Yorkshire Regiment* (Fig. 2381). In silver-plate.

(3) A cross based on that of the Order of the Bath surmounted by St. Edward's crown. In the centre a circlet inscribed *The Prince of Wales's Own* and within this a bugle-horn with strings surmounted by a crown. The whole surrounded by a laurel-wreath. Across the base of the wreath a scroll inscribed *The Leeds Rifles* (Fig. 2382). In silver-plate for officers and silver-anodised for other-ranks.

In 1947 the 7th Battalion was known as the 45th/51st (Leeds Rifles) Royal Tank Regiment. It was converted to infantry in 1956 but amalgamated with the 8th Battalion, then the 466 (Leeds Rifles) L.A.A. Regiment in 1961.

The Bedfordshire Regiment

A Maltese cross superimposed on an eight-pointed star. On this the Garter proper and in the centre a Hart crossing a ford. Below, a scroll inscribed *Bedfordshire* (Fig. 2383). In silver-plate for officers and silver-anodised for other-ranks. Sealed 1st January 1960.
The 5th Battalion resumed this title in 1958 when the regular battalion, The Bedfordshire and Hertfordshire Regiment, was amalgamated with The Essex Regiment to form the 3rd East Anglian Regiment.

The Hertfordshire Regiment

A circlet inscribed *The Hertfordshire Regiment* surmounted by St. Edward's crown. In the centre a Hart lodged (Fig. 2384). In gilding-metal. Sealed 9th January 1957. Officers': in silver-plate.

The Bedfordshire and Hertfordshire Regiment
An eagle displayed, head to the right and ducally crowned, and across its body and wings a triple-tiered castle. In front of the legs and castle a Hart lodged on water. Below, a scroll inscribed *Bedfordshire & Hertfordshire* (Fig. 2385). The castle silver-anodised, remainder gold-anodised.
In April 1961 the 5th Battalion, The Bedfordshire Regiment was amalgamated with the 1st Battalion, The Hertfordshire Regiment to form The Bedfordshire and Hertfordshire Regiment.

The Royal Hampshire Regiment
Duke of Connaught's 6th Royal Hampshire R.A.
Within a laurel-wreath a strap inscribed *Duke of Connaught's Own* surmounted by a ducal coronet. In the centre the Hampshire Rose. In white-metal (Fig. 2386). In anodised-silver, sealed 6th August 1952.

The Hampshire and Isle of Wight Territorials
The Hampshire Rose surmounted by St. Edward's crown in gold-anodised. Laurel-sprays either side and a scroll below inscribed *Hampshire & Isle of Wight* in silver-anodised (Fig. 2387).
The unit consisted of 'A' Company (4th/5th Royal Hampshire), 'B' Company (Duke of Connaught's 6th Royal Hampshire R.A.), 'C' Company (Wessex Royal Artillery Princess Beatrice's), 'D' Company (Hampshire Fortress Royal Engineers) and 'E' Company (7th Royal Hampshire).

The Staffordshire Regiment (The Prince of Wales's)
5th/6th (Territorial) Battalion
The Stafford Knot in gold-anodised (Fig. 2388).

The Dorset Territorials
On a shield a castle with a scroll below inscribed *Who's a-fear'd?* In silver-anodised (Fig. 2389). Worn with a grass-green backing.

The Oxfordshire Territorials
The cypher *AR*, of Queen Adelaide, surmounted by St. Edward's crown. Below, a bugle (Fig. 2390). All in silver-anodised.

The Buckinghamshire Battalion
A Maltese cross surmounted by St. Edward's crown. On this a circlet inscribed *Buckinghamshire Battalion*. In the centre a swan with a coronet round its neck. In black-metal (Fig. 2391). Officers': in silver-plate.

The Sherwood Foresters (Nottinghamshire and Derbyshire Regiment)
The Robin Hood (Territorial) Battalion
A cross based on that of the Order of the Bath surmounted by St. Edward's crown. On the arms of the cross is inscribed: (left) *South*, (right) *Africa*, (bottom) *1900–2*. In the centre of the cross a circlet inscribed *The Robin Hoods*. Within this a bugle-horn surmounted by a crown. The whole enclosed within a laurel-wreath (Fig. 2392). In silver-plate or silver-anodised. Sealed 21st September 1951.

The Royal Berkshire Territorials

The White Horse of Berkshire on a scroll inscribed *Berkshire*. In silver-anodised (Fig. 2393). The regiment consisted of 'A' Company (Berkshire Yeomanry), 'B' Company (Berkshire Artillery) and 'C' Company (Royal Berkshire).

The Herefordshire Light Infantry

The lion from the crest of the City of Hereford standing on a tablet inscribed *Manu forti* superimposed on a strung bugle-horn. Officers': in silver-plate. Other-ranks': in white-metal, also silver-anodised (Fig. 2394). Sealed 9th December 1949.

The Royal Wiltshire Territorials

A cross patée, lined and with burnished edges, surmounted by St. Edward's crown. In the centre the Prince of Wales's plumes, coronet and motto. Cross and crown gold-anodised, remainder silver-anodised (Fig. 2395).
The regiment consisted of 'A' Company (The Wiltshire Regiment) and 'B' Company (Royal Wiltshire Yeomanry).

The Durham Light Infantry
5th, 7th, 8th and 9th Battalions

(1) A bugle with strings surmounted by St. Edward's crown and the letters *DLI* within the strings. Underneath the bugle a scroll inscribed *South Africa 1900–2*. For officers' in silver-plate (Fig. 2396).
(2) A bugle with strings surmounted by St. Edward's crown and the letters *DLI* within the strings. In blackened-brass (Fig. 2397).
There was also a version with the Imperial crown in this size which was sealed 14th August 1951.

The Highland Light Infantry (City of Glasgow Regiment)
The Glasgow Highlanders

(1) The Star of the Order of the Thistle. On the Star a thistle-wreath enclosing an oval inscribed *Nemo me impune lacessit* and surmounted by an Imperial crown. Within the oval St. Andrew and Cross. Across the top of the wreath a two-part scroll inscribed *The Glasgow Highlanders* and at the base a three-part scroll inscribed *Highland Light Infantry*. Below this the Sphinx on a blank tablet. In white-metal (Fig. 2398). Sealed 13th April 1952.
Officers': St. Andrew and Cross and the title-scrolls in silver, remainder in gilt.
(2) Similar to above but slightly different arrangement of scrolls and shape of Star. In same metals (Fig. 2399). Sealed 13th April 1953.
(3) Similar to (2) but with St. Edward's crown and in anodised-silver (Fig. 2400). Sealed 19th February 1957.

The London Yeomanry and Territorials

A laurel-wreath surmounted by St. Edward's crown imposed on St. Andrew's Cross. In the centre a shield bearing the arms of the City of London. In silver-anodised (Fig. 2401). The regiment consisted of 'A' Company (Inns of Court and City Yeomanry), 'B' Company (1st London Engineers) and 'C' Company (The London Scottish).

2387
2388
2389
2390
2391
2392
2393
MANU FORTI
2394
2395
DLI
2396
2397
2398
2399
2400
2401
WESSEX
2402
2403

The Wessex Regiment

The Wessex Wyvern on a plinth inscribed *Wessex*. Officers' in silver-plate, other-ranks' in gold-anodised (Fig. 2402).

1st Battalion The Wessex Regiment (Rifle Volunteers) consists of 'H.Q.' Company (Devon), 'A' Company (Gloucester), 'B' Company (Hampshire), 'C' Company (Dorset) and 'D' Company (Wiltshire). 2nd Battalion The Wessex Regiment consists of 'A' Company formed from The Hampshire and Isle of Wight Territorials, 'B' Company formed from The Buckinghamshire Regiment, R.A., 'C' Company formed from The Royal Berkshire Territorials and 'D' Company from The Dorset Territorials.

The Ulster Defence Regiment

The Irish Harp surmounted by St. Edward's crown. Officers' in gilt, other-ranks' gold-anodised (Fig. 2403). The regiment was formed in January 1970.

CHAPTER 17

The London Regiments

In 1920, all the old battalions of The London Regiment were re-formed with the exception of the 25th (Cyclist), which became part of the 47th (2nd London) Divisional Signals.

By 1922, most battalions had formed new, or revived old, links with line regiments and, during that year, they were designated themselves as 'regiments' so that, for instance, the old 12th (County of London) Battalion, The London Regiment, lost both the 'County' and 'Battalion' designations and became simply the 12th London Regiment (The Rangers).

During the same year the 7th and 8th Battalions amalgamated to form the 7th City of London Regiment (Post Office Rifles) and the new Regiment retained the cap-badge of the old 7th Battalion but took into wear as collar-badges miniatures of the cap-badge of the old 8th.

The 15th and 16th Battalions also amalgamated in 1922 to form the 16th London Regiment (Queen's Westminster and Civil Service Rifles) and their new badge combined elements of both badges of the old Battalions.

In 1929, the 10th London Regiment (Hackney) was transferred to The Royal Berkshire Regiment (Princess Charlotte of Wales's Own) and the 28th London Regiment (Artists Rifles) became part of The Rifle Brigade (Prince Consort's Own).

In 1935, seven regiments were converted to anti-aircraft-roles: the 4th and 11th as Royal Artillery; the 6th, 7th, 19th, 20th and 21st as searchlight battalions of the Royal Engineers.

By 1937 all titular connections with The London Regiment vanished as each of the remaining sixteen regiments was re-designated as a battalion of its parent infantry regiment and this was reflected particularly in two changes of badge: that of the 12th, now The Rangers, The King's Royal Rifle Corps: and that of the 17th, now the Tower Hamlet Rifles, The Rifle Brigade (Prince Consort's Own).

The following year, the 10th Battalion, The Royal Fusiliers (the old 3rd London Regiment) was converted to a searchlight-role and the 7th Battalion, The East Surrey Regiment (the old 23rd London Regiment) became the 42nd Battalion, Royal Tank Corps.

After the Second World War, the regiments were re-formed mostly in the same role as their war-service, but this did not last for long as amalgamations and changes followed swiftly one after the other. Two of particular interest are: The Rangers who, in 1947, were transferred from The King's Royal Rifle Corps to The Rifle Brigade – and that change is reflected in the last pattern of cap-badge (Fig. 2418) – and The Artists Rifles which became a Special Air Service Regiment.

In 1950, the London Rifle Brigade amalgamated with The Rangers to form the London Rifle Brigade Rangers and in 1956 they adopted the badge previously worn by The Rifle

Brigade (Fig. 2020). That same year, the old 23rd reverted to its original infantry-role, taking up an updated version of its original badge.

In 1955 the old 10th London Regiment (Hackney), which had become the 648th H.A.A. Regiment R.A. (Royal Berks), was disbanded.

The next few years saw numerous minor amalgamations and changes and, in 1961, The Queen Victoria's Rifles and The Queen's Westminsters amalgamated to form the Queen's Royal Rifles whose new badge incorporated insignia drawn from all three of its illustrious ancestors.

The changes that followed the formation of the Territorial and Army Volunteer Reserve in 1967, and the subsequent re-organisations of 1971 and 1975, are too numerous and complex to detail in this work but, by the time they were completed, the old London volunteers were scarcely recognisable. Of the twenty-five battalions we started with in 1920: thirteen had disappeared into volunteer battalions of The Queen's Regiment; five made-up the 4th (Volunteer) Battalion of The Royal Green Jackets; two became a company of the 5th (Volunteer) Battalion of The Royal Regiment of Fusiliers; one joined its one-time companion, the old 25th (Cyclist), in what had become the 31st (Greater London) Signal Regiment (Volunteers); the London Irish Rifles and the London Scottish became respectively D Coy 4th (Volunteer) Battalion, The Royal Irish Rangers, and G Coy 1st Battalion 51st Highland Volunteers; the 10th had been disbanded back in 1955, leaving only the 21st Special Air Service Regiment (Artists) (Volunteers) as the sole battalion to survive in its own right.

1st to 4th City of London Regiments (Royal Fusiliers)

(1) A fused grenade with, on the ball, the Garter ensigned with an Imperial crown and within the Garter a rose. In gilding-metal (Fig. 1818). Also anodised. Officers': in bronze.

(2) As above but with St. Edward's crown (Fig. 2404). In same metals.

5th City of London Regiment (London Rifle Brigade)

(1) Within an oak-wreath a circlet inscribed *London Rifle Brigade South Africa 1900–02* and surmounted by an Imperial crown. In the centre a shield bearing the Royal Arms. Behind the circlet are crossed the City Mace and Sword. At the base of the wreath a scroll inscribed *Primus in Urbe* and, below this, a small shield bearing the arms of the City of London. In white-metal with the centre voided (Fig. 1819). Officers': silver-plated.

(2) As above but with non-voided-centre (Fig. 1820).

(3) As (1) but with the Great War honours added as follows: below the crown *France & Flanders 1914–18*; between the circlet and motto *Ypres 1915, '17*; on the left branch of the wreath *Somme 1916, '18, Albert 1918, Arras 1917, '18, Scarpe 1917, '18*; on the right-hand wreath *Bullecourt, Menin Road, Cambrai 1917, Canal du Nord.* In white-metal (Fig. 1821). Officers': in silver, also in bronze.

(4) As (3) but much smaller. In white-metal (Fig. 2405). Officers': in silver-plate.

6th City of London Regiment (City of London Rifles)

A Maltese cross with the top arm inscribed *South Africa 1900–02* and, above this, a tablet inscribed *Domine dirige nos* surmounted by an Imperial crown. In the centre a circlet inscribed *6th Battn. City of London Regt.* and within this a bugle-horn with strings. In black-metal (Fig. 1824). Sealed in blackened-brass 9th June 1916.

7th City of London Regiment (Post Office Rifles)

(1) A fused grenade with the numeral *7* on the ball. The grenade in gilding-metal, numeral in white-metal (Fig. 1826).

(2) Officers': similar design to (1) but in imitation embroidery. In gilt (Fig. 2406). Also in bronze. Worn on a red-cloth backing.

9th London Regiment (Queen Victoria's Rifles)

(1) A Maltese cross. Above this a tablet inscribed *South Africa 1900–02* surmounted by an Imperial crown. In the centre of the cross a circlet inscribed *Queen Victoria's* with, in the centre, St. George and the Dragon (Fig. 1828). In blackened-brass and also in white-metal. Found in different sizes and some with the centre voided. Sealed 19th May 1916.

(2) Officers': same design as (1) but much smaller for wear on the red-cord-boss (Fig. 2407). In blackened-brass and also in silver-plate.

(3) As (2) but with St. Edward's crown (Fig. 2408).

(4) A Maltese cross. Above this a tablet inscribed *South Africa 1900–02*. On the arms of the cross the following battle honours are inscribed: (top) *France & Flanders 1914–1918, Hill 60*; (left) *Amiens, Arras 1917, Ypres 1915, '17*; (right) *Hindenburg Line, Somme 1916, '18*; (bottom) *Scarpe 1917, Cambrai 1917, Villers Bretonneux*. In the centre of the cross a circlet inscribed *Queen Victoria's Rifles* and within this St. George and the Dragon. In blackened-brass with high points polished (Fig. 2409).

(5) St George and the Dragon surmounted by an Imperial crown. In silver (Fig. 2410). Worn by officers on a small cord-boss.

(6) As (5) but with St. Edward's crown (Fig. 2411). In silver-plate.

(7) As (1) but with St. Edward's crown. Sealed in black-plastic 22nd May 1959.

10th London Regiment (Hackney)

(1) Within a laurel-wreath an eight-pointed star, the topmost-point displaced by an Imperial crown. On the star a circlet inscribed *Justitia turris nostra* and within this a tower on ground. Below the star a three-part scroll inscribed *Tenth London Hackney* (Fig. 1832). In brass, also in bronze. Officers': silver star and scroll; gilt circlet, centre and crown.

(2) Similar to (1) but with more ground behind the tower and without the gap between the star and the wreath (Fig. 1833).

11th London Regiment (Finsbury Rifles)

(1) A Maltese cross above which a tablet inscribed *South Africa 1900–02* surmounted by an Imperial crown. On the four arms of the cross the motto *Pro aris et focis*. On the cross a circlet inscribed *Finsbury Rifles* with, in the centre, a strung bugle (Fig. 1834). In gilding-metal, also in blackened-brass, sealed 27th June 1916. Both types with, and without, voided-centres.

(2) Officers': as above but larger and without the crown which was worn separately on a cord-boss (Fig. 2412). In blackened-silver with high points polished.

12th London Regiment (The Rangers)

(1) A Maltese cross with, on the top arm, *South Africa 1900–02* and above this a tablet inscribed *Excel* surmounted by an Imperial crown. On the cross a circlet inscribed *12th County of London* with, in the centre, a bugle with strings. Below the cross a scroll inscribed *The Rangers* (Fig. 1835). In blackened-brass. Officers wore the same pattern

in blackened white-metal, with the high points polished to show white, but without the crown which was worn separately on a cord-boss.

(2) As above but smaller for wear on the side-hat (Fig. 2413).

(3) Officers': a Maltese cross surmounted by an Imperial crown. On the arms of the cross the following battle honours are inscribed: (top) *South Africa 1900–02, St. Julien*; (left) *Albert 1916, '18, Cambrai 1917, Epehy*; (right) *Somme 1916, '18, Scarpe 1917, Cinchy*; (bottom) *Amiens, Frezenberg, Ypres 1915, '17.* On the cross a circlet inscribed *Excel 12th London Regt* and within this a bugle with strings. Below the cross a scroll inscribed *Rangers* (Fig. 2414). In white-metal.

(4) Other-ranks': similar to (3) but larger and with the addition of a tablet inscribed *Excel* between the top of the cross and the crown and the wording on the circlet now reads *12th London Regiment* (Fig. 2415). In blackened-brass.

(5) Officers': similar to (3) but with circlet inscribed *The King's Royal Rifle Corps* and the title-scroll *The Rangers* (Fig. 2416). In hall-marked silver.

(6) Other-ranks': as (5) but larger (Fig. 2417). In blackened-brass. Sealed 22nd August 1938.

(7) Officers': a Maltese cross surmounted by an Imperial crown. In the centre a circlet inscribed *The Rifle Brigade* with, in the centre, a strung bugle. Below the cross a scroll inscribed *The Rangers* (Fig. 2418). In silver-plate.

13th London Regiment (Princess Louise's Kensington Regiment)

On an eight-pointed star the arms of the Royal Borough of Kensington, viz. a shield with red and gold quarters within a border quartered gold and black. In the first quarter a celestial crown above a gold fleur-de-lys and in the dexter chief point a five-pointed silver star. In the second a black cross flory and four black martlets. In the third a red cross bottony and four red roses with stems and leaves in natural colours and in the fourth a gold mitre (Fig. 1839). In gilding-metal, also in white-metal. Officers': in silver-plate and in bronze. Also anodised, sealed 13th March 1953.

14th London Regiment (London Scottish)

(1) St. Andrew's Cross on which is superimposed the Lion of Scotland, the whole upon a circlet inscribed *Strike Sure* with, on the lower part of the circlet, *S. Africa 1900–02.* Across the top of the Cross a scroll inscribed *London* and on the bottom a scroll inscribed *Scottish.* The whole surrounded by a wreath of thistles. In white-metal (Fig. 1840). Sealed in white-metal 16th May 1916 and in anodised-silver 27th June 1964.

(2) Same design as above but of superior construction in separate parts and mounted. For officers, in silver-plate (Fig. 1841).

16th London Regiment (Queen's Westminster and Civil Service Rifles)

(1) A Maltese cross surmounted by an Imperial crown. On the arms of the cross the following battle honours are inscribed: (top) *South Africa 1900–02, Hooge 1915*; (left) *Somme 1916, '18, Flers-Courcelette, Arras 1917, '18*; (right) *Messines 1917, Ypres 1917, '18, Cambrai 1917*; (bottom) *France and Flanders 1914–18, Jerusalem, Jericho.* In the centre of the cross two oval escutcheons surmounted by an Imperial crown; the left bearing the portcullis and ducal coronet (from the Queen's Westminsters) and the right, the Prince of Wales's plumes, coronet and motto (from the Civil Service Rifles). In white-metal (Fig. 1846). Also in blackened-brass, sealed 16th March 1925. Officers': in silver, and in bronze.

1818
2404
1819
1820
1821
2405
1824
1826
2406
1828
SOUTH AFRICA 1900-2
FRANCE & FLANDERS 1914-1918 HILL 60
QUEEN VICTORIAS RIFLES
AMIENS ARRAS 1917
YPRES 1915-17
SOMME 1916-18
HINDENBURG LINE
SCARPE CAMBRAI 1917 1917
VILLERS BRETONNEUX
2410
2411
2409
2407
2408
SOUTH AFRICA 1900-02
ARIS
PRO
ET
FINSBURY RIFLES
FOCIS
THE RANGERS
1832
1833
2412
1834
1835
2415
2413
2414
2418
2416

(2) Two oval escutcheons surmounted by an Imperial crown, the left bearing a portcullis and ducal coronet, the right the Prince of Wales's plumes, coronet and motto. In silver-plate. Worn by officers on a red-cord-boss (Fig. 2419).

In 1961 the Regiment was amalgamated with the former Queen Victoria's Rifles to form the Queen's Royal Rifles.

(3) A Maltese cross, above which a tablet inscribed *Celer et Audax* surmounted by St. Edward's crown. On the arms of the cross the following battle honours are inscribed: (top) *South Africa 1900 1902*; (left) *France–Flanders 1914–18, Hill 60, Somme, Ypres*; (right) *N.W. Europe 1944–45, Jerusalem, Calais*; (bottom) *Athens, Italy 1943–44, El Alamein.* Superimposed on the cross and surmounted by the Prince of Wales's plumes, coronet and motto two oval escutcheons, the left bearing St. George and the Dragon and the right, a portcullis and ducal coronet. In blackened-brass (Fig. 2420).

17th London Regiment (Poplar and Stepney Rifles)

(1) Within a laurel-wreath a Maltese cross. On the arms of the cross the following is inscribed: (top) *South*, (bottom) *Africa*, (left) *1899*, (right) *1902.* Above the cross a blank tablet surmounted by an Imperial crown. On the cross a circlet inscribed *Rifle Brigade* and in the centre a bugle with strings surmounted by an Imperial crown (Fig. 1847). In gilding-metal, white-metal and blackened-brass. Officers': in silver, and in bronze.

In 1926 the designation was changed to Tower Hamlets Rifles and, in 1937, to Tower Hamlet Rifles, The Rifle Brigade (Prince Consort's Own).

(2) A cross based on that of the Order of the Bath. On the arms of the cross the following battle honours are inscribed: (top) *Festubert 1915, Loos, Somme 1916, '18, Messines 1917;* (left) *Ypres 1917, '18, Cambrai 1917, Doiran 1917*; (right) *Jerusalem, Jordan, Gaza*; (bottom) *Macedonia 1916–17, Palestine 1917–18, France & Flanders 1915–18.* In the centre of the cross a circlet inscribed *Tower Hamlets Rifles The Rifle Brigade* with, in the centre, a bugle with strings surmounted by a crown. Above the cross a tablet inscribed *South Africa 1900–02* surmounted by an Imperial crown. The whole enclosed by a laurel-wreath. On the left branch of the wreath the following battle honours are inscribed: *Aubers, Flers-Courcelette, Morval, Le Transloy, Langemarck, St. Quentin, Bapaume 1918.* On the right branch: *Ancre 1918, Albert 1918, Courtrai, El Mughar, Nebi Samwil, Jericho, Tel'Asur.* Across the base of the wreath a scroll inscribed *Prince Consort's Own.* In white-metal (Fig. 2421). Officers': in hall-marked silver and in silver-plate.

(3) Field-service cap: as (2) but half-size (Fig. 2422).

18th London Regiment (London Irish Rifles)

(1) The Irish Harp surmounted by an Imperial crown (Fig. 1848). In blackened-brass, also in white-metal and gilding-metal. Officers': silver-plated.

(2) The Irish Harp surmounted by an Imperial crown (Fig. 2423). In white-metal, silver-plated for officers. Worn from 1937 by officers and Warrant Officers.

(3) As (2) but with St. Edward's crown (Fig. 2424). Worn by all ranks. Sealed in white-metal and in anodised-silver, 6th March 1957. Silver-plated for officers.

19th London Regiment (St. Pancras)

Within a laurel-wreath a cross as in the Order of the Bath surmounted by an Imperial crown. On the top arm of the cross *South Africa* and on the bottom arm *1900–02.* On the cross a circlet inscribed *County of London St. Pancras* with, in the centre, the Roman numerals *XIX*

2417 1840 1841 1839

1846 2419 2420 1847 2421

2422 2423 1848 2424 1851

1852 1853 1854 1855

2425 2426 1858

(Fig. 1851). In blackened-brass, white-metal, and gilding-metal. Sealed 27th June 1916. Officers': in silver-plate and in bronze. All types are found with the incorrect date of *1899*.

20th London Regiment (The Queen's Own)
The White Horse of Kent standing on a scroll inscribed in old English lettering *Invicta*. Below this another scroll inscribed *20th Batt The London Regt* (Fig. 1852). In white-metal, sealed 15th May 1917. Officers': Horse and motto in silver-plate, title-scroll in gilt; or Horse only in silver and both scrolls in gilt, or in bronze.

21st London Regiment (First Surrey Rifles)
A cross, as in the Order of the Bath, on the top arm of which is inscribed *South Africa 1900–02* and on the bottom arm, the date *1803* (this being the date of the formation of the first Surrey Volunteers). Above the cross a scroll inscribed *Concordia Victrix* surmounted by an Imperial crown. On the cross a circlet inscribed *First Surrey Rifles* with, in the centre, a strung bugle. Below the cross a scroll inscribed *21st County of London* (Fig. 1853). In blackened-brass. Officers': in silver-plate or blackened white-metal with the high points polished. Sealed in black-metal, 25th August 1916. Specimens can be found with the incorrect date of *1903*.

22nd and 24th London Regiments (The Queen's)
The Paschal Lamb with swallow-tail flag on a scroll inscribed *The Queens*. The Lamb in gilding-metal and scroll in white-metal (Fig. 1854).

23rd London Regiment
(1) An eight-pointed star the topmost-point displaced by an Imperial crown. On this a circlet inscribed *South Africa 1900–2* with, in the centre, a shield bearing the arms of Guildford. Below the star a scroll inscribed *23rd Bn The London Regt* (Fig. 1855). The ground of the shield, the crown and the scroll in gilding-metal, remainder in white-metal. Officers': in gilt-and-silver, also in bronze. Sealed 27th June 1916. All versions are found with the date *1900–02* instead of *1900–2*.
(2) Same design as above but with St. Edward's crown and the scroll inscribed *The 23rd London Regt* (Fig. 2425). In gold-and-silver-anodised, sealed 28th January 1958. Officers': in silver-and-gilt.

28th London Regiment (Artists Rifles)
(1) The heads of Mars and Minerva with a scroll below inscribed *Artists Rifles* (Fig. 1858). In blackened-brass, gilding-metal and white-metal. Officers': in silver-plate, and in bronze.
(2) As above but with the scroll inscribed *Artists* only (Fig. 2426). Sealed in white-metal, 14th April 1938.

CHAPTER 18

The Home Guard

The Local Defence Volunteers were raised in May 1940 and re-named the following month as The Home Guard. It was stood-down in December 1944, as the possibility of invasion for which it had been raised had long since receded, but revived on a smaller scale in December 1951 and finally disbanded in July 1957.

The vast majority of units wore the same badge as their County regiment but there were a few which did not have a County affiliation and consequently had their own special badges:

Huntingdonshire
A stag springing on ground, below which a scroll inscribed *Huntingdonshire* (Fig. 1870). In gilding-metal. This is the same as the badge previously worn by The Huntingdonshire Cyclist Battalion (1914 to 1918). Re-sealed 14th July 1953.

Ulster
The Harp surmounted by an Imperial crown. In blackened-brass (Fig. 2427).
This was the badge worn by the Royal Ulster Constabulary. When the Home Guard was re-raised in 1951 the Ulster battalions wore the badges of the three Northern Ireland regiments: i.e. The Royal Inniskilling Fusiliers, The Royal Ulster Rifles or The Royal Irish Fusiliers.

Isle of Man
(1) A strap inscribed *Quocunque jeceris stabit* surmounted by an Imperial crown. In the centre the arms of the Isle of Man. In gilding-metal (Fig. 2428).
(2) A circlet inscribed *Quocunque jeceris stabit* surmounted by St. Edward's crown. In the centre the arms of the Isle of Man. Below the circlet a scroll inscribed *Home Guard.* In white-metal (Fig. 2429). Sealed 30th July 1953.

Upper Thames Patrol
Two overlapping escutcheons: that on the left bearing the arms of the City of London with the Sword and Mace crossed behind it; that on the right, the arms of the Thames Conservancy with a fouled anchor behind it. Above the escutcheons an Imperial crown and below them a tablet with the letters *U T P.* In gilding-metal (Fig. 2430).

Rutland
A horse-shoe inscribed *Rutland.* In gilding-metal (Fig. 2431). During the second phase of the Force this unit wore the badge of The Northamptonshire Regiment.

1st American Squadron

An eagle bearing in its left claw thunderbolts, and in its right, an olive-branch. On its breast a shield. Above its head two scrolls inscribed *epluribus* and *unum*. In gilding-metal (Fig. 2432). This badge is the same as the American Army officer's cap-badge but without the constellation above the eagle's head. The unit was authorised by a special Order in Council signed by King George VI in September 1940 to permit it to be incorporated in the British Armed Forces. It was composed of Americans living in London and was attached to H.Q. London District.

Palace of Westminster

A portcullis with chains surmounted by a flat-topped crown and resting on a tablet inscribed *Home Guard*. Below, a scroll inscribed *Palace of Westminster*. In chromed-silver (Fig. 2433). This was a phase-II unit only.

Radnor

(1) A Maltese cross with lions between each arm. On this a circlet inscribed *Radnor* with, in the centre, the Prince of Wales's plumes and coronet. A laurel-wreath surrounds the cross with, at the top, a plain bar on which rests a crown. In gilding-metal, also in bronze (Fig. 2434).

(2) A Maltese cross with lions between each arm. On this a circlet inscribed *Radnor H.G.* with, in the centre, the Prince of Wales's plumes and coronet. A laurel-wreath surrounds the cross and is surmounted by St. Edward's crown. In gilding-metal (Fig. 2435). Sealed 29th July 1953.

The badge is based on the 1852-pattern shako-plate of the Royal Radnor Rifles Militia.

Caithness and Sutherland

(1) Within a circlet inscribed *Sans peur* a cat-a-mountain. In white-metal (Fig. 1754).

(2) Within a strap inscribed *Sans peur* a cat-a-mountain with one silver feather behind the strap (Fig. 1755). Worn by Subalterns.

(3) As above but with two silver feathers (Fig. 1756). Worn by Captains.

(4) As above but with three silver feathers (Fig. 1757). Worn by field officers.

(5) As above but with four silver feathers (Fig. 1758). Worn by the Colonel.

These badges are identical to those previously worn by the 5th (The Sutherland and Caithness Highland) Battalion, Seaforth Highlanders.

The Windsor Castle Company

As a Berkshire unit it should have worn the badge of The Royal Berkshire Regiment but permission was granted for it to wear the badge of the Grenadier Guards.

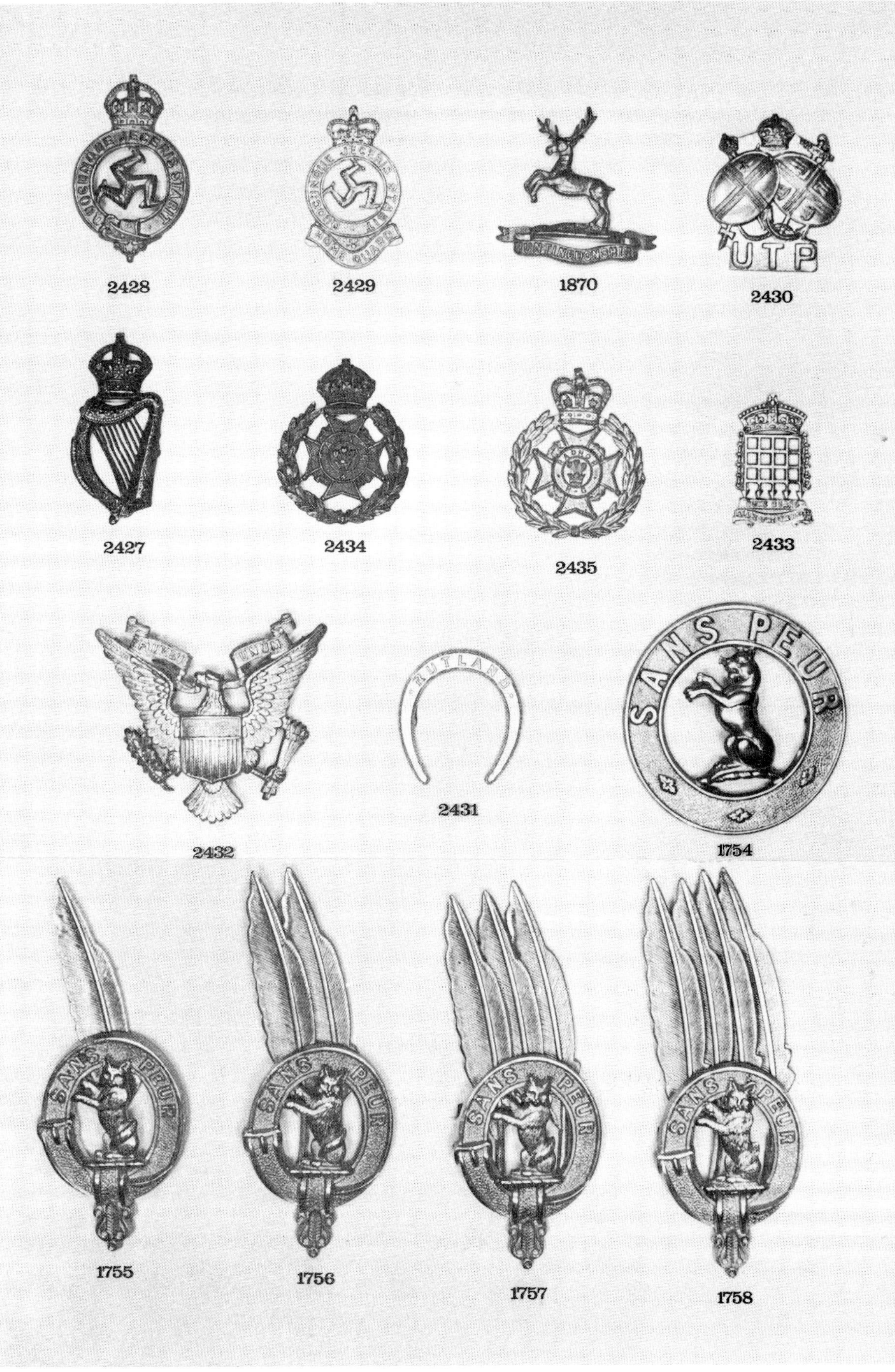
2428
HOME GUARD
2429
HUNTINGDONSHIRE
1870
UTP
2430
2427
2434
2435
2433
RUTLAND
2431
2432
SANS PEUR
1754
SANS PEUR
1755
SANS PEUR
1756
SANS PEUR
1757
SANS PEUR
1758

CHAPTER 19

The Officers Training Corps

The Officers Training Corps traces its true beginnings back to the volunteer-revival of 1859 and 1860 during which both of the senior universities raised volunteer units.

First in the field was the 1st Oxfordshire (Oxford University) Rifle Volunteer Corps, formed in August 1859, which became the 1st Volunteer Battalion of The Oxfordshire Light Infantry in 1887.

The 3rd Cambridgeshire (Cambridge University) Rifle Volunteer Corps followed hard on its heels and was formed in 1860, being re-numbered 2nd in 1880. Seven years later, in 1887, it became the 4th Volunteer Battalion of The Suffolk Regiment.

Colleges and schools throughout the country followed suit and by the end of the century numerous cadet-corps had been raised and were serving in various arms of the Army by attachment to local volunteer units.

Under the Haldane re-organisation of 1908, all volunteers became part of the new Territorial Force and what had been cadet contingents became the new Officers Training Corps with the specific task of making good the deficiency of suitable officers, of which Mr. Haldane had said: 'There is no more serious problem to be solved.'

It was divided into two sections: the Senior Division to accommodate the university-battalions, and the Junior Division for all the college- and school-contingents.

Under Army Order No. 164 of 19th September 1940, the Senior Division received the new designation of Senior, or University, Training Corps but, in 1948, it was re-designated University Training Corps, Territorial Army. However, by 1955 it had reverted to its original title of Officers Training Corps.

Under the same Army Order of 1940, the Junior Division became the Junior Training Corps and, in 1948, it combined with cadets of other services to form the new Combined Cadet Force.

Even though it was decided not to include badges of the cadets worn prior to 1908, there are still many hundreds of different head-dress badges worn by all the units that existed in the period from 1908, and the selection which follows has been chosen with the intention of showing the widest variety in design and subject.

Some units, especially more recently, simply wear the badge of their parent- or affiliated-unit, a regular County or Corps badge, for example. These have been excluded.

SENIOR DIVISION

Aberdeen University O.T.C.

(1) A shield bearing the arms of the University. Below, a scroll inscribed *Aberdeen University*

O.T.C. In white-metal (Fig. 2436). Also in gilding-metal. Another pattern exists in white-metal but with *O.T.C.* erased from the centre of the scroll which is left blank.
(2) A wild boar's head within a circlet, displaced on the right, inscribed with the motto *Non confundar.* In white-metal (Fig. 2437). Sealed 26th January 1951.

Belfast (Queen's University O.T.C.)
(1) An ornamental escutcheon bearing the arms of the University, surmounted by a flattened crown, and with a scroll below inscribed *Queen's.* In gilding-metal (Fig. 2438). Also in bronzed-brass. Sealed 24th August 1950.
(2) As above, but with St. Edward's crown. In white-metal, sealed 11th February 1957 (Fig. 2439). Also in gold-anodised, and silver-anodised for pipers.

Birmingham University O.T.C.
(1) An ornamental escutcheon bearing the arms of the University. Below, a scroll inscribed *Birmingham University O.T.C.* The scroll in gilding-metal, remainder in white-metal (Fig. 2440). Also in all-brass and in bronzed-brass.
(2) As (1), but with the scroll altered to read *Birmingham University U.T.C.* In gilding-metal (Fig. 2441).
(3) As (2), but with the scroll reading *Birmingham University* only. In silver-anodised (Fig. 2442). Sealed 24th August 1950.

Bristol University O.T.C.
(1) A shield bearing the arms of the University. Below, a scroll inscribed *Bristol University O.T.C.* In gilding-metal (Fig. 2443).
(2) As above but without the scroll. In gold-anodised (Fig. 2444). Was worn first in brass or bronze.

Cambridge University O.T.C.
All units of the Contingent wore the following cap-badges but were differentiated by their collar-badges.
(1) The arms of the University, granted in 1573, within a strap inscribed *Cambridge University OTC.* The whole surmounted by an Imperial crown and, below, a scroll inscribed *Discendo duceo.* In white-metal (Fig. 2445).
(2) General design as above but smaller. In white-metal (Fig. 2446). Also in bronze.
(3) As (2) but strap inscribed *Cambridge University T.C.* In white-metal. Sealed 26th January 1951.
(4) As (2) but with St. Edward's crown. In silver-anodised (Fig. 2447).

Cardiff University O.T.C.
The same badge as The Royal Regiment of Wales (Fig. 2046).

Dublin University O.T.C.
(1) A shield bearing the arms of the University and surmounted by an Imperial crown. A continuous scroll surrounding the shield inscribed left: *Tam marti,* base: *D.U.O.T.C.*, right: *Quam minervae.* In gilding-metal (Fig. 2448). Also in white-metal.
(2) A shield bearing the arms of the University and surmounted by an Imperial crown. Below, a scroll inscribed *Tam marti quam minervae* and, beneath this, a further scroll

inscribed *Dublin University Officers Training Corps.* In bronze (Fig. 2449). Also in white-metal.

(3) The arms of the University on a shield within a circlet inscribed *Coll sangtae individvae trinitatis reg elizab ivxta Dublin* and surmounted by an Imperial crown. Below, a scroll inscribed *Dublin University O.T.C.* In bronze (Fig. 2450).

Durham University O.T.C.

Now Northumbrian Universities O.T.C.

A cross patée quadrate. In bronze, sealed 18th July 1950 (Fig. 2451). Also in gold-anodised, and silver-anodised.

Edinburgh University O.T.C.

Now Edinburgh and Heriot-Watt Universities O.T.C.

(1) A shield bearing the arms of the University and surmounted by an Imperial crown. Below, a scroll inscribed *Edinburgh University O.T.C.* In gilding-metal (Fig. 2452). Also in white-metal.

(2) As (1) but larger and scroll inscribed *Edinburgh University Training Corps* (*T.A.*). In white-metal (Fig. 2453). Sealed 5th February 1951.

(3) As (2) but with St. Edward's crown and scroll inscribed *Edinburgh University Officers Training Corps.* In silver-anodised (Fig. 2454).

(4) On St. Andrew's Cross an open book surmounted by St. Edward's crown. Cross in silver-anodised, remainder in gold-anodised (Fig. 2455).

Exeter University College O.T.C.

An ornamental escutcheon bearing the arms of the University and, superimposed, the letters *O.T.C.* Below, a scroll inscribed *Univ. Coll. Exeter.* In gilding-metal (Fig. 2456).

The contingent was suspended on 30th November 1947.

Glasgow University O.T.C.

Now Glasgow and Strathclyde Universities O.T.C.

(1) A shield bearing the arms of the University: the University mace surmounted by an open book and in base a salmon with a ring in its mouth; to the dexter a robin-redbreast perched on a tree and to the sinister a bell. Below, a scroll inscribed *Glasgow University O.T.C.* In blackened-brass (Fig. 2457).

(2) St. Mungo (or Kentigern: the Patron Saint of Glasgow) within a diamond-shaped scroll inscribed *Glasgow University O.T.C.* The whole on St. Andrew's cross with a leaved-thistle at top, bottom and both sides. In gilding-metal (Fig. 2458). Also chromed.

(3) As above but scroll inscribed *Glasgow University T.C.* (*T.A.*). In gilding-metal. Sealed 27th March 1951 (Fig. 2459). Also chromed.

(4) As above but scroll inscribed *Glasgow and Strathclyde U.O.T.C.* In gold-anodised (Fig. 2460).

Leeds University O.T.C.

(1) Within a circlet inscribed *Training Corps* a shield bearing the arms of the University. Resting on the shield a winged Sphinx sejant on a torse. Below the shield a scroll inscribed *Leeds University.* In blackened-brass (Fig. 2461). Sealed 18th July 1950.

(2) A winged Sphinx resting on a torse. In gilding-metal (Fig. 2462).

NON
CONFUND
QUEENS
QUEENS
2436
2437
2438
2439
2440
2441
2442
BRISTOL
UNIVERSITY
O.T.C
2443
2444
DISCENDO DVCES
2445
DISCENDO DVCES
2446
2447
2448
2449
2450
2451
EDINBURGH
UNIVERSITY
2453
2452
2455
2454

(3) A winged Sphinx with a scroll below inscribed *Officers Training Corps*. In gold-anodised (Fig. 2463).

Liverpool University O.T.C.

The White Horse of Hanover on a torse. Below, a wavy scroll inscribed *King's* in Old English characters. The White Horse and torse in white-metal, remainder in gilding-metal (Fig. 2464). Also anodised.

University of London O.T.C.

(1) On an eight-pointed star, the topmost-point displaced by an Imperial crown, a shield bearing the arms of the University. In gilding-metal (Fig. 2465). Sealed 18th July 1950. Also in bronzed-brass.

(2) As above but with St. Edward's crown and with a scroll below inscribed *University of London O.T.C.* In silver-anodised (Fig. 2466). Also gold-anodised.

Manchester University O.T.C.

Now Manchester and Salford Universities O.T.C.

A lion rampant, from the arms of the University. In gilding-metal (Fig. 2467). Also anodised, sealed 18th July 1950.

Nottingham University O.T.C.

Now The East Midlands Universities O.T.C.

(1) A Maltese cross surmounted by an Imperial crown. In the centre of the cross a wreath of oak and within the wreath a stag lodged. On the left arm of the cross and across the left branch of the wreath a half-scroll inscribed *University*. On the right arm of the cross and across the right branch of the wreath a half-scroll inscribed *College*. Below the cross a scroll inscribed *Nottingham O.T.C.* All in white-metal except the bottom scroll which is in gilding-metal (Fig. 2468).

(2) As (1) but the right half-scroll inscribed *T.C.*(*T.A.*) and the bottom scroll *Nottingham*. Metals as above (Fig. 2469). Sealed 27th March 1951.

(3) As (2) but the right half-scroll inscribed *O.T.C.* and the cross surmounted by St. Edward's crown. Metals as above (Fig. 2470).

(4) As (3) but bottom scroll inscribed *East Midlands*. In same metals.

Oxford University O.T.C.

(1) An escutcheon bearing the arms of the University: between three open crowns an open book bearing on the dexter side seven seals and inscribed with the words *Dominus illuminatio mea*, all within a strap inscribed *Oxford University O.T.C.* and surmounted by an Imperial crown. Below, a scroll inscribed *Militia nobis studium*. In white-metal (Fig. 2471).

(2) As (1) but strap inscribed *Oxford University S.T.C.* (Fig. 2472).

(3) As (1) but strap inscribed *Oxford University U.T.C.* (Fig. 2473). Sealed 24th September 1950.

(4) **Cavalry.** In the centre a trumpet with crossed sabre and scabbard passing through it at the point of intersection. Above, a scroll inscribed *Oxford University*. Below, a scroll inscribed *O.T.C.* In gilding-metal (Fig. 2434).

(5) **Artillery.** A gun surmounted by a scroll bearing a laurel-spray above which an Imperial crown. Below the gun a scroll inscribed *Oxford University O.T.C.* In gilding-metal (Fig. 2475).

2456 2457 2458 2459

2460 2461 2462 2463

2464 2465 2466 2467

2468 2469 2470 2471

2472 2473 2474 2475

(6) **Engineers.** A laurel-wreath surmounted by an Imperial crown. Within this the Garter and in the centre the cypher of King George v. Across the base of the wreath a scroll inscribed *Oxford University O.T.C.* In gilding-metal (Fig. 2476).

(7) **Signals.** An oval inscribed *O.U.O.T.C. Signals* with, in the bottom-centre, the Globe with a sprig of laurel either side and a further spray in the top-centre. The oval surmounted by an Imperial crown. In the centre the figure of Mercury holding a caduceus in his left hand, his right hand held aloft, poised on the Globe with his left foot. Oval and crown in gilding-metal, remainder in white-metal (Fig. 2477).

(8) **Infantry.** A bugle stringed. Within the strings the letters *O.T.C.* In white-metal (Fig. 2478).

(9) As (1) but with St. Edward's crown. In silver-anodised (Fig. 2479). Also in white-metal.

Reading University O.T.C.

(1) A shield bearing the arms of the University. Below, a scroll inscribed *University College Reading O.T.C.* In gilding-metal (Fig. 2480). Also in bronzed-brass.

(2) As above but scroll inscribed *Reading University U.T.C.* In gilding-metal (Fig. 2481). Also in bronzed-brass.

Royal Agricultural College O.T.C.

A roundel containing a wreath of wheat joined at the head by the letters *R.A.C.* Superimposed on the base of the wreath the letters *O.T.C.* In a voided-centre the Phoenix, arising from the flames, resting on a tablet inscribed *Cirencester.* In gilding-metal (Fig. 2482).

Royal College of Surgeons O.T.C. (Ireland)

(1) A shield charged with St. Patrick's Cross on which is superimposed the Red Hand of Ulster. On a chief of ermine the Irish Harp surmounted by an Imperial crown with, on either side, a fleam. The shield surmounted by an Imperial crown and with two stags as supporters. Below, a scroll inscribed *Consilio/R.C.S.I.O.T.C./Manuque.* In bronze.

(2) A shield bearing the arms of the college. Below the shield the letters *O.T.C.* and, below this, a scroll inscribed *Royal College of Surgeons.* In bronze (Fig. 2483).

Royal Dick Veterinary College O.T.C.

A laurel-wreath surmounted by an Imperial crown. On the wreath a scroll inscribed *Royal Dick Veterinary College.* In a voided-centre the monogram *OTC.* In gilding-metal (Fig. 2484). Also known non-voided.

Royal Veterinary College of Ireland O.T.C.

A circlet inscribed *Royal Veterinary College of Ireland* with a shamrock in the bottom-centre and surmounted by an Imperial crown. In the centre, on a shamrock-leaf, four shields bearing the arms of Ulster, Leinster, Connaught and Munster, all surmounted by a horse. Below the circlet a scroll inscribed *Officers Training Corps.* In bronze (Fig. 2485).

St. Andrew's University O.T.C.

Now Tayforth Universities O.T.C. *q.v.*

(1) A circlet inscribed *St. Andrew's University O.T.C.* with, in a voided-centre, St. Andrew's Cross. In white-metal (Fig. 2486).

2476 2477 2478 2479

2480 2481 2482 2483

2484 2485 2486 2487

2488 2489 2490 2491

2492 2493 2494 2495

(2) A shield bearing the arms of the University surmounted by an Imperial crown. Below, a scroll inscribed *St. Andrew's University U.T.C.* In gilding-metal (Fig. 2487). Also in white-metal. Sealed 25th January 1951. Also anodised, sealed 26th January 1951.
(3) As (2) but scroll inscribed *St. Andrew's University O.T.C.* In gilding-metal (Fig. 2488). Also in white-metal.

Sheffield University O.T.C.
(1) A shield bearing the arms of the University. Below, a scroll inscribed *Sheffield University O.T.C.* In gilding-metal (Fig. 2489), also anodised.
(2) As above but scroll inscribed *Sheffield University U.T.C.* In gilding-metal (Fig. 2490). Sealed 18th July 1950. Also anodised.

Southampton University O.T.C.
(1) A shield with in the first quarter, the arms of Hampshire County Council, a rose with a crown above between two sprays of laurel; second, four bars; third, three lions passant guardant; and four, a tower. The shield surmounted by the crest of Southampton County Borough Council consisting of on a mount a tower of two tiers from which rises the figure of Justice holding in her right hand a sword and in her left a balance. Below the shield a scroll inscribed *Strenus ardua cedunt.* In blackened-brass (Fig. 2491).
(2) On a shield the arms of the University. Above the shield a helm with mantling and the crest on a torse consisting of a dragon rampant supporting a staff bearing a banner charged with three roses. Below the shield a scroll inscribed *Strenus ardua cedunt.* In gilding-metal (Fig. 2492). Sealed 26th January 1951.

The contingent was suspended on 15th April 1951.

Tayforth Universities O.T.C.
St. Andrew's, Dundee and Stirling
St. Andrew's Cross superimposed on a laurel-wreath. Behind the Cross a sword, point downwards, with a cinquefoil on the lower portion. In the centre, behind the Cross a lined background with a fleur-de-lys on either side of the Cross. Below, a scroll inscribed *Tayforth U.O.T.C.* In silver-anodised (Fig. 2493). Also with wreath in gilding-metal and remainder in white-metal.

University of Wales O.T.C.
This contingent comprised Aberystwyth University College O.T.C. (suspended 31st October 1952) and Bangor University College O.T.C. (suspended 31st March 1948).
(1) The Welsh Dragon on a plinth inscribed *Aberystwyth* within a wreath of daffodils joined at the head by the letters *U.C.W.* Across the base of the wreath the letters *O.T.C.* In bronze (Fig. 2494).
(2) As above, but with the letters *U.T.C.* on the base of the wreath. In gilding-metal (Fig. 2495). Also anodised, sealed 24th August 1950.

JUNIOR DIVISION

Abingdon School, Berks
A griffin, from the school arms, on a triple-scroll inscribed *School/Abingdon/O.T.C.* In gilding-metal (Fig. 2496).

Adam's Grammar School, Newport
On a shield of ermine, three leopards passant guardant. Below a scroll inscribed *Serve & Obey*. In gilding-metal (Fig. 249).

Alderham School, Elstree, Herts
(1) A trellised shield with helm, mantling and the crest of a demi-lion holding between the paws a ball. A scroll under inscribed *In God is all our trust*. In white-metal (Fig. 2498).
(2) As above but smaller and without a scroll. In gilding-metal, also bronze.

Alleyn's School, London, S.E.22
The school arms: a chevron between three cinquefoils; on a chief ermine a cinquefoil. A scroll below inscribed *God's Gift*. In gilding-metal (Fig. 2499). Also an earlier pattern in blackened-brass.

All Hallows School, Rousdon
An eight-pointed star, the topmost-point displaced by an Imperial crown. On the star a circlet inscribed *All Hallows School O.T.C.* In a voided-centre the castle of Exeter above a scroll inscribed *Semper fidelis*. In bronze (Fig. 2500).

Ampleforth College, York
(1) A grid-iron within a palm-wreath on the base of which is inscribed the letters *O.T.C.* Below, a scroll inscribed *Ampleforth*. In bronze (Fig. 2501).
(2) As above, but wreath inscribed *J.T.C.* In bronzed-brass.
(3) As above, but wreath inscribed *C.C.F.* In bronzed-brass.

Ardingly College, Sussex
(1) The Star of the Order of the Garter superimposed on the Roussillon plume. Below, a scroll inscribed *Ardingly O.T.C.* In gilding-metal (Fig. 2502). Also in bronzed-brass.
(2) As above, but scroll inscribed *Ardingly C.C.F.* The scroll in gilding-metal, remainder in white-metal.

Army School, Maidenhead
On a shield three interlaced loops. Below, a scroll inscribed *Army School O.T.C.* In gilding-metal (Fig. 2503).

Bancroft's School, Woodford Green
A shield charged with three triple-crowns each issuing from a cloud shedding rays of sun. In gilding-metal (Fig. 2504).

Barnard Castle School
Two shields side-by-side: the left charged with an orle; the right, a saltire charged with a cinquefoil between four eagles. In gilding-metal (Fig. 2505).

Batley Grammar School
A circlet inscribed *Batley Grammar School C.C.F.* In the solid centre a shield charged with three antique crowns. In bronze (Fig. 2506).

Beaumont College, Windsor

(1) An eight-pointed star with the topmost-point displaced by a wing and arrow. On the star a shield charged with a horse-shoe and three crosses fitchy. Below, a scroll inscribed *Beaumont O.T.C.* In blackened-brass (Fig. 2507).

(2) As above, but without scroll, worn in blackened-brass and, later, by the C.C.F. in gilding-metal on a circular red-plastic disc.

Birkenhead School

(1) The school arms. Below, a scroll inscribed *Birkenhead School O.T.C.* In brass (Fig. 2508).

(2) As above, but scroll inscribed *Birkenhead School C.C.F.* In gilding-metal.

Bloxham School, Oxon

A shield charged with a chevron between three pheons. Below, a scroll inscribed *Justoram semita lux splendens.* In gilding-metal (Fig. 2509). Officers' also in gilt.

Blundell's School, Tiverton

On a shield paly a squirrel proper. Below, a scroll inscribed *Pro Patria Populoque.* In white-metal (Fig. 2510). Also in bronze.

Bournemouth School

The arms, helm, crest and mantling of Bournemouth County Borough Council. Below the shield a scroll inscribed *Bournemouth School.* In gilding-metal (Fig. 2511).

Bradfield College, Berks

The China Dragon on a torse. Below, a scroll inscribed *Bradfield College O.T.C.* In bronze (Fig. 2512).

Brentwood School, Essex

(1) A shield bearing the arms of the school. Below, a scroll inscribed *Brentwood School O.T.C.* In gilding-metal (Fig. 2513).

(2) As above, but scroll inscribed *Brentwood School C.C.F.* In gilding-metal.

Bridlington School, Yorks

(1) On a shield three B's with, below, the inscription *Vitai lampada tradunt* and below this a scroll inscribed *Bridlington School O.T.C.* In gilding-metal (Fig. 2514).

(2) As above but with the school-title-scroll omitted. In bronzed-brass.

(3) As above but with a different shaped shield and with three-quarter-oval motto-scroll. In bronzed-relief gilding-metal.

Brighton College, Sussex

A shield charged with the arms of the College superimposed on crossed rifles. On either side of the shield sprays of oak and the shield surmounted by a flattened crown. Below, a scroll inscribed with a Greek motto. The whole superimposed on crossed rifles. In bronze (Fig. 2515).

Brighton Grammar School, Sussex

The Star of the Order of the Garter superimposed on the Roussillon plume. Below, a scroll inscribed *Brighton Grammar School.* In white-metal (Fig. 2516). Formerly in bronzed-brass.

2496 2497 2498 2499

2500 2501 2502 2503

2504 2505 2506 2507

2508 2509 2510 2511

2512 2513 2514 2515

Bristol Grammar School

(1) A cock's head, carrying a spray of leaves in its beak, on a torse. Below, the letters *B.G.S.O.T.C.* In white-metal (Fig. 2517). Also in gilding-metal.
(2) As above, but with the letters *B.G.S.J.T.C.* In gilding-metal.
(3) As above, but with the letters *B.G.S.C.C.F.* In gilding-metal.

Bromsgrove School, Worcs

On an eight-pointed star the Garter proper. In the centre the Lion of England. Below, a scroll inscribed *Bromsgrove School O.T.C.* In gilding-metal (Fig. 2518).

Bury Grammar School, Lancashire

On a torse a swan's head and neck issuing from a coronet and holding a key in its beak. Below, a scroll inscribed *Sanctas clavis fores aperit.* In bronze (Fig. 2519).

Cambridge and County School

Within a laurel-wreath on a solid ground a castle. Below the castle the inscription *Camb. & County O.T.C.* In gilding-metal (Fig. 2520).

Campbell College, Belfast

(1) An escutcheon bearing the arms of the college. Above, a boar's head on a torse. Below, a scroll inscribed *Campbell Coll. O.T.C.* In gilding-metal (Fig. 2521).
(2) A boar's head. Below, a scroll inscribed *Campbell College.* In chrome.

Canford School, Wimborne, Dorset

A strap inscribed *Canford School O.T.C.* In a voided-centre an oak-tree on a torse. Below, a scroll inscribed *Nisi Dominus Frustra.* In gilding-metal (Fig. 2522). Also in bronzed brass. Also in chrome worn by C.C.F.

Chard School, Somerset

Two shields side-by-side: the dexter charged with a chevron between three lions' heads erased; the sinister three escallops in pale. Below, a scroll inscribed *Uniti Vircamus.* In gilding-metal (Fig. 2523).

Charterhouse School, Godalming, Surrey

(1) The Paschal Lamb carrying a flag with swallow-tail on ground. Below, a scroll inscribed *Charterhouse O.T.C.* In bronze (Fig. 2524).
(2) Smaller badge. The Paschal Lamb on a torse, carrying a square-ended flag. Scroll inscribed as above. In bronze.

Cheltenham College

A bugle surmounted by an Imperial crown and with *O.T.C.* in the curl. Worn with a red-cloth backing. In blackened-brass (Fig. 2525).

Chigwell School, Essex

A Bishop's mitre in gilding-metal (Fig. 2526). Formerly in blackened-brass.

Christ's Hospital, Horsham

On an ornamental escutcheon the arms of the School. In gilding-metal (Fig. 2527). Also anodised, worn by C.C.F.

2516 2517 2518 2519

2520 2521 2522 2523

2524 2525 2526 2527

2528 2529 2530 2531

2532 2533 2534 2535

Churcher's College, Petersfield
Within a complete laurel-wreath and in a voided-centre a three-masted ship on a torse with the Hampshire Rose above and the letters *O.T.C.* below. Across the base of the wreath a scroll inscribed *Credita Coelo.* In gilding-metal (Fig. 2528).

Clifton College, Bristol
A shield charged with the arms of the College. Below, a scroll inscribed *Spiritus intus alit.* In gilding-metal (Fig. 2529).

Cork Grammar School
A roundel inscribed *Schol gramm corkag sigill commun deum timete regem honorificate* with, in the centre, the arms of the See and City of Cork. Below, the date *A.D. MDCCCLXXXII* and, below the roundel, a scroll inscribed *O.T.C.J.D.* In black-metal (Fig. 2530).

Cranbrook School
(1) A shield charged with three lions rampant. Above, the crest of a talbot on a torse. Below, a scroll inscribed *Cranbrook School O.T.C.* In blackened-brass (Fig. 2531). Also in bronze.
(2) As above, but scroll inscribed *Cranbrook School C.C.F.*

Cranleigh School, Surrey
(1) The Paschal Lamb carrying a flag with swallow-tail. Below, a scroll inscribed *Cranleigh O.T.C.* In bronze (Fig. 2532).
(2) Larger badge: the Paschal Lamb carrying a square-ended flag and on a torse. Scroll inscribed as above. In blackened-brass.
(3) As (2) same design but smaller. In blackened-brass.
(4) As (2) but scroll inscribed *Cranleigh C.C.F.* In blackened-brass.

Dartford Grammar School, Kent
A six-part scroll inscribed *Dartford Grammar School Combined Cadet Force* completely encircling a shield charged with a pall. In white-metal (Fig. 2533).

Dean Close School, Cheltenham
(1) A shield charged with the arms of the School. Below, a scroll inscribed *Virgum dei lucerna* and, below this, a further scroll inscribed *Dean Close School O.T.C.* In gilding-metal.
(2) As above, but bottom-scroll inscribed *Dean Close School C.C.F.* In gilding-metal (Fig. 2534).

Denstone College, Staffs
An escutcheon, charged with a cross potent between four crosses patée, surmounted by the Stafford Knot. Below, a scroll inscribed *Denstone.* In gilding-metal (Fig. 2535).

Derby School
(1) A circlet inscribed *Derby School C.C.F.* and surmounted by a Bishop's mitre. In the centre a shield charged with the arms of the School. In gilding-metal (Fig. 2536).
(2) As above but circlet inscribed *Derby School O.T.C.* In bronze. Worn previous to (1).
(3) As above but circlet inscribed *Derby School J.T.C.* In gilding-metal.

Dollar Academy, Clackmannanshire

(1) A shield bearing the school arms of an ancient ship, with a lamp top-left and an open book top-right. Superimposed on this the letters *D* and *A* on either side of the sail of the ship and *O.T.C.* on the waves below. Above the shield a scroll inscribed *Juventutis veno fortunas*. In white-metal (Fig. 2537).

(2) As above but with the letters *C.C.F.* in the waves.

Dorchester School

The arms of the School with helm crest and mantling: on an escutcheon a chevron charged with three lions' heads erased with two escallops in chief and one in base. The crest of a demi-dragon on a torse. Below, a scroll inscribed *Dorchester School O.T.C.* In gilding-metal (Fig. 2538). Also in white-metal. Previously worn in bronzed-brass.

Dover College

The seal of the College: St. Martin dividing his cloak with, above, a shield charged with the arms of the Cinque Ports all within a diamond-shaped scroll. Below, a scroll inscribed *Non reguso laborem*. In gilding-metal (Fig. 2539). Also in white-metal. Previously worn in bronzed-brass.

Downside School, Bath

(1) A shield charged with a cross moline. Below, a scroll inscribed *Downside School O.T.C.* In gilding-metal (Fig. 2540).

(2) On a cross moline two scrolls inscribed *Downside School* and surmounted by a crown. In black-metal (Fig. 2541).

(3) As (2) but half-size and in silver-and-enamel. Worn by officers.

Duke of York's Royal Military School, Dover

(1) The Royal Cypher of King George VI within a circlet inscribed *Royal Military School* surmounted by an Imperial crown. The cypher in white-metal, remainder in gilding-metal (Fig. 2542). Sealed 15th February 1937.

(2) As above but with the cypher of Queen Elizabeth II and with a St. Edward's crown (Fig. 2543). Sealed 24th February 1953.

Dulwich College, London, S.E.21

On an oval escutcheon a chevron between three cinquefoils. Above, the Crest: issuant from flames of fire a cubit arm, the hand grasping a heart, on a torse. Above the escutcheon to the left the date *A.D. 1619* and to the right *A.D. 1858*. Below the escutcheon the words *God's Gift*. All upon ornamental scroll-work. In bronze (Fig. 2544).

Eastbourne College

(1) On the Roussillon plume an eight-pointed star. On this a circle within which an escutcheon charged with the arms of the College. Below the star-and-plume a scroll inscribed *Eastbourne/Officers Training Corps/College*. In bronzed-brass (Fig. 2545).

(2) As above, but scroll inscribed *Eastbourne/Junior Training/Corps/College*. In bronze.

(3) As above, but scroll inscribed *Eastbourne/Combined Cadet Force/College*. In white-metal.

Edinburgh Academy

A continuous laurel-wreath on the rim of a disc. Within this the head of Homer surrounded by an inscription in Greek and within a laurel-wreath. Chromed (Fig. 2547). Several similar types in different sizes exist but not all are in the same format, mostly in white-metal, but one is chromed.

Elizabeth College, Guernsey

(1) A bugle, mouthpiece to the right, surmounted by three leaves on a torse. Below, a scroll inscribed *Guernsey O.T.C.* In gilding-metal (Fig. 2548).
(2) The Royal Arms of Queen Elizabeth I in gilding-metal (Fig. 2549). Also in white-metal.

Ellesmere College, Shropshire

A strung bugle-horn, the strings tied in three bows. Within the bend of the bugle and below the bows the letters *O.T.C.* voided above *Ellesmere* on a solid base. In white-metal (Fig. 2546).

Emanuel School, Wandsworth

(1) A shield charged with the school arms surmounted by a baron's coronet. Below, a scroll inscribed *Pour bien desirer* and below this a further scroll inscribed *Emanuel School O.T.C.* In gilding-metal (Fig. 2580). Also in bronzed-brass. Another pattern worn by officers is in gilt with silver motto and title-scrolls.
(2) As above, but without the title-scroll. In gilding-metal.

Epsom College

An eagle's head and wings on a torse. Below, a scroll inscribed *Epsom.* In gilding-metal (Fig. 2551).

Eton College

A strap inscribed *Floreat Etona* surmounted by an Imperial crown. In the centre, on an escutcheon, the College arms of three lilies with on a chief per pale a fleur-de-lys and a lion passant guardant. In white-metal (Fig. 2552).

Exeter School

(1) An eight-pointed star with the topmost-point displaced by an Imperial crown. On this a circlet inscribed *Exeter School O.T.C.* In a voided-centre the Castle of Exeter above the motto *Semper Fidelis.* In gilding-metal (Fig. 2553).
(2) As above, but inscribed *Exeter School J.T.C.*
(3) As above, but inscribed *Exeter School C.C.F.*

Felsted School, Essex

A shield charged with a chevron between three crosses botonny. Below, a scroll inscribed *Felsted.* In gilding-metal (Fig. 2554).

Fettes College, Edinburgh

The school arms, helm, crest and supporters. Below, a scroll inscribed *Industria.* In white-metal (Fig. 2555). Also in gilding-metal.

2536 2537 2538 2539

2540 2541 2542 2543

2544 2545 2546 2547

2548 2549 2550 2551

2552 2553 2554 2555

Forest School, Walthamstow, E.17

(1) An oval inscribed *In pectore robur*. In a voided-centre a sprig of oak with acorns. Below, a tri-part scroll inscribed *Forest School O.T.C.* The oak-leaves in white-metal, remainder in gilding-metal (Fig. 2556).

(2) An eight-pointed star and on this a circlet inscribed *In pectore robur 1883.* In the centre a sprig of oak with acorns. Below, a scroll inscribed *Forest School C.C.F.* The star in gilt, scrolls gold on blue-enamel with red-enamel backing to the centre (Fig. 2557). Another pattern has the enamel missing from the circlet.

Framlingham College, Norfolk

(1) A shield charged with a chevron between three antique crowns. Below, a scroll inscribed *F.C.O.T.C.* In gilding-metal (Fig. 2558). Worn previously in white-metal and also in blackened-brass.

(2) As above, but inscribed *F.C.J.T.C.*

George Heriot's School, Edinburgh

The school arms with helm, crest and mantling. Above the crest a scroll inscribed *I distribuet chierfully*. In gilding-metal (Fig. 2559).

George Watson's College, Edinburgh

(1) A circlet inscribed *George Watson's College A.D. 1870.* In the centre an escutcheon, helm and crest. Cornucopias either side of the escutcheon and, above the crest, a scroll inscribed *Ex corde charitas*. A thistle-wreath surrounds the circlet which is surmounted by an Imperial crown. The thistle-wreath and crown are joined by a scroll inscribed *Nemo me impune lacessit.* In white-metal (Fig. 2560).

(2) The same centre as above but superimposed on the Star of the Order of the Thistle. In white-metal (Fig. 2561).

Giggleswick School, York

The seal of the School. Below a scroll inscribed *Giggleswick School O.T.C.* In gilding-metal (Fig. 2562).

Glasgow High School

(1) A circlet inscribed *High School of Glasgow O.T.C.* In a voided-centre a shield charged with the arms of the City of Glasgow. In gilding-metal (Fig. 2563). Several types of this badge exist.

(2) The arms of the City of Glasgow. The Shield: on a mount an oak-tree proper, the stem at the base thereof surmounted by a salmon on its back also proper with a signet-ring in its mouth. On the top of the tree a robin-redbreast and in the sinister fess-point an ancient handbell both also proper. The Crest: issuing from a wreath the half-length figure of St. Kentigern affronte, mitred, his right hand raised in the act of benediction and having in his left hand a crozier. The Supporters: two salmon each holding in the mouth a signet-ring. Below the shield a scroll entwined with the compartment inscribed *Let Glasgow Flourish.* In gilding-metal (Fig. 2564).

Gordon Boys School, Old Woking, Surrey

A circular scroll inscribed on the lower portion *Semper Fidelis.* Across the centre, and overlapping on each side of the scroll, an ornamental band inscribed *Gordon.* Above this a knight's helm with the crest of an arm grasping a spear on an heraldic-wreath. In gilding-metal (Fig. 2565). Also anodised.

2556 2557 2558 2559

2560 2561 2562 2563

2564 2565 2566 2567

2568 2569 2570 2571

2572 2573 2574 2575

Gresham's School, Holt, Norfolk
The figure of Britannia holding a sprig of olive in her right hand, a trident in her left hand resting against her left shoulder; below her left arm an oval shield bearing the Great Union. The whole enclosed in a laurel-wreath. Below, a scroll inscribed *O.T.C. Gresham's School.* In bronze (Fig. 2566).

Grimsby School
An escutcheon charged with the arms of Grimsby. Above the escutcheon the Sphinx on a plain plinth. Below the escutcheon a scroll inscribed *Res non verba* and below this a further scroll inscribed *Grimsby O.T.C.* In gilding-metal (Fig. 2567). Also in bronze.

Haberdashers' Aske's School, Elstree and Hatcham
The arms of the Worshipful Company of Haberdashers of the City of London on a scroll inscribed *Serve and Obey.* In bronzed-brass (Fig. 2568). Also in gilding-metal. Also in gold and red- and blue-enamel.

Haileybury and Imperial Service College, Herts
(1) A Maltese cross superimposed on an eight-pointed star. On this the Garter proper. In the centre a hart crossing a ford. Below, a scroll inscribed *Haileybury O.T.C.* The scroll in gilding-metal, remainder in white-metal (Fig. 2569). Also in bronze.
(2) As above, but scroll inscribed *Haileybury & I.S.C.C.C.F.*
(3) On a disc with ornamental border a crossed sword and anchor with, superimposed thereon, a book inscribed *Fear God, Honour the King* on the cover, a mural crown to the left of the book and a naval crown to the right. The whole surmounted by a winged lion on a torse. In gilding-metal (Fig. 2570).

Harrow County School
A sword point uppermost. Above the hilt the letters *HCS.* Across the top of the blade a scroll inscribed *Virtus non stemma.* In gilding-metal (Fig. 2571).

Harrow School
On a laurel-wreath two crossed arrows, points-downwards, with a plain ribbon at the point of intersection. Across the top of the wreath a scroll inscribed *Dec^{r}*. 30 1859. In white-metal (Fig. 2572). Previously worn in blackened-brass. The date is that of the foundation of the Corps. The badge has been worn recently with a white-plastic-disc backing.

Hereford Cathedral School
A shield charged with five chevronels being the arms of the Dean and Chapter of Hereford. In gilding-metal (Fig. 2573). Also in white-metal.

Herne Bay School, Kent
An escutcheon charged with the arms of the School. Below, a scroll inscribed *Delectando pariterque monendo.* In bronze (Fig. 2574). Also in gilding-metal.

Hertford Grammar School
A shield charged with a chevron embattled and counter-embattled. Below, a scroll inscribed *Doctrine cum virtute.* In gilding-metal (Fig. 2575).

The Hulme Grammar School, Oldham

(1) A lion's head in white-metal (Fig. 2576). Also a smaller size in white-metal.
(2) A demi-lion with, above, two scrolls: the top inscribed *H.G.S.* and the lower one *Cadet Corps.* A scroll below inscribed *Fide sed cui vide.* In gilding-metal (Fig. 2577).

Hurstpierpoint College, Sussex

(1) An eagle with wings displayed and inverted on a torse. Below, a scroll inscribed *Hurstpierpoint College O.T.C.* In gilding-metal (Fig. 2578).
(2) As above, but scroll inscribed *Hurstpierpoint College C.C.F.*

Hymer's College, Hull

An eight-pointed star and on this a laurel-wreath enclosing the White Rose of York. The Rose in white-metal, remainder in gilding-metal (Fig. 2579). Also same design in a smaller size and another, smaller still, all with slider-fasteners.

Ipswich School, Suffolk

The Tudor Royal Arms with crown above with a greyhound and a dragon as supporters. Below, a scroll inscribed *Ipswich School O.T.C.* In gilding-metal (Fig. 2580).

Kelly College, Tavistock

The Prince of Wales's plumes and coronet with the motto replaced by the words *Kelly College.* In gilding-metal (Fig. 2581). First worn in blackened-brass.

Kelvinside Academy, Glasgow

(1) A mullet above a bugle stringed. Issuing from each end of the bugle and enclosing the mullet a spray of thistles joined at the head by the letters *KA.* In white-metal (Fig. 2582).
(2) A circlet inscribed *Kelvinside Academy O.T.C. 1893* with, in the centre, the bust of Minerva surmounted by a Greek motto. Laurel-sprays below the circlet. Minerva in gilt-relief, remainder in white-metal (Fig. 2583).

King Alfred's School, Wantage

(1) On an ornamental ground surmounted by an ancient crown a shield charged with a cross patonce between four martlets. Below the shield an ornamental scroll inscribed *Domine quis Habitabit.* Below this a further scroll inscribed *Wantage School O.T.C.* In gilding-metal (Fig. 2584).
(2) As above, but bottom-scroll inscribed *Wantage School C.C.F.*
(3) As above, but with the shield on a voided-centre and the scroll below inscribed *Alfredus Rex Fundator.* A scroll below extending half-way either side of the shield inscribed *King Alfred's School O.T.C. Wantage.* In gilding-metal (Fig. 2585).

King Charles I School, Kidderminster

The Royal Arms on an escutcheon surmounted by a crown with the letters *C* on the left and *R* on the right. Below, a scroll inscribed *Fortiter ex animo.* In white-metal (Fig. 2586).

King's College School, Wimbledon

Within the Garter a shield charged with the Royal Arms of George IV surmounted by the Royal Crest. Below the shield a scroll inscribed *Sancte et sapienter.* In blackened-brass (Fig. 2587). Also worn in gilt by officers.

King Edward's Five Ways School, Birmingham
A phoenix arising from flames with, below, a scroll inscribed *K. E. Five Ways School.* In chrome (Fig. 2588). Also in bronze.

King Edward VI Grammar School, Bury St. Edmunds
Two crossed arrows, points uppermost, on a torse with a Tudor Rose at the point of intersection; all superimposed on a horse-shoe-shaped scroll inscribed *Bury School.* The whole ensigned with an Imperial crown. In gilding-metal (Fig. 2589).

King Edward VI Grammar School, Lichfield
(1) A strap inscribed *Grammar School of King Edward VI Lichfield.* In a voided-centre an escutcheon charged with the arms of King Edward VI surmounted by a crown. In gilding-metal (Fig. 2590).
(2) Superimposed on the Stafford Knot a shield charged with the arms of the School, the differenced arms of Lichfield. Below a scroll inscribed *KES Lichfield CCF.* In chrome (Fig. 2591).

King Edward's School, Bath
Within the Garter proper the arms of King Edward VI surmounted by the Royal Crest. Below, a scroll inscribed *Edv VI Schol Regal Bathon.* In white-metal (Fig. 2592). Also voided in bronzed-brass.

King Edward's School, Birmingham
(1) An escutcheon charged with the arms of King Edward VI with, below, a scroll inscribed *K.E.S. Birmingham J.T.C.* In gilding-metal (Fig. 2593).
(2) As above, but scroll inscribed *K.E.S. Birmingham O.T.C.* in brass.
(3) As above, but scroll inscribed *K.E.S. Birmingham C.C.F.* In bronzed-brass, also in white-metal.

King Edward VII School, Sheffield
A strap inscribed *Req Edward VII schola scaf.* Across the top of the strap a mural crown and above this a crest on a torse. Within the strap an escutcheon charged with the arms of the school. On the left of the escutcheon twin scrolls inscribed *Fac recte* and on the right, twin-scrolls inscribed *Mil time.* In bronze (Fig. 2594).

King's School, Bruton
A Dolphin. Below, a scroll inscribed *King's School Bruton O.T.C.* In gilding-metal (Fig. 2595).

King's School, Canterbury
(1) Within a circlet inscribed *King's School Canterbury C.C.F.* the arms of the Dean and Chapter of Canterbury. In gilding-metal (Fig. 2596).
(2) As above, but circlet inscribed *King's School Canterbury O.T.C.* Worn previous to (1).

King's School, Ely
On an eight-pointed star a circlet inscribed *Ex humili potens* with, in the centre, three keys. On the star, and below the circlet, a scroll inscribed *The King's School, Ely.* The scroll in gilding-metal, remainder in white-metal (Fig. 2597).

2576 2577 2578 2579

2580 2581 2582 2583

2584 2585 2586 2587

2588 2589 2590 2591

2592 2593 2594 2595

King's School, Grantham
The Sphinx resting on a plain plinth. A scroll below inscribed *Grantham School O.T.C.* The scroll in gilding-metal, remainder in white-metal (Fig. 2598).

King's School, Peterborough
A shield charged with two swords in saltire between four crosses fitchy. Below, a scroll inscribed *Schol Reg Petriburg.* In gilding-metal (Fig. 2599).

King's School, Rochester
(1) An escutcheon charged with the arms of the See of Rochester and surmounted by the Bishop's mitre. Below, a scroll inscribed *King's School Rochester O.T.C.* In gilding-metal (Fig. 2600).
(2) A slightly smaller version with scroll inscribed *King's School Rochester C.C.F.* Anodised.

King's School, Worcester
On an eight-pointed star the Garter proper and within this the Lion of England. Below, a scroll inscribed *King's School O.T.C.* In blackened-brass (Fig. 2601). Also in bronze.

King William's College, Isle of Man
(1) A shield charged with the arms of the College and surmounted by a bishop's mitre. Below, a scroll inscribed *Assiduitate non desidia.* In gilding-metal (Fig. 2602). Also in bronzed-brass.
(2) The College-seal in gilding-metal (Fig. 2603).

Kirkcaldy High School
An oval inscribed *High School Kirkcaldy: Usque Conabor.* In a voided-centre a castle with spires on three turrets. In gilding-metal (Fig. 2604).

Lancing College, Sussex
(1) A lion rampant grasping a fleur-de-lys in its raised paw. Below, a scroll inscribed *Lancing/O.T.C./College.* In gilding-metal (Fig. 2605).
(2) A lion rampant on a shaped tablet inscribed *Lancing College O.T.C.* In bronze. Worn by officers.
(3) As (1), but scroll inscribed *Lancing/C.C.F./College.*

Leeds Grammar School
A fleece in white-metal (Fig. 2606). Also in gilding-metal.

Leys School, Cambridge
(1) A solid disc inscribed on the rim *In fide fiducia* with, in the centre, the school arms, helm, crest and mantling. Below, a scroll inscribed *Leys.* In gilding-metal (Fig. 2607). Also chromed.
(2) The arms, crest and mantling only, omitting the motto and title. Chromed.

Liverpool College
(1) An eight-pointed star, the topmost-point displaced by a bishop's mitre. On the star a circlet inscribed *Liverpool College O.T.C.* In the centre the College arms. In gilding-metal (Fig. 2608). Also in bronze.
(2) As above, but circlet inscribed *Liverpool College C.C.F.*

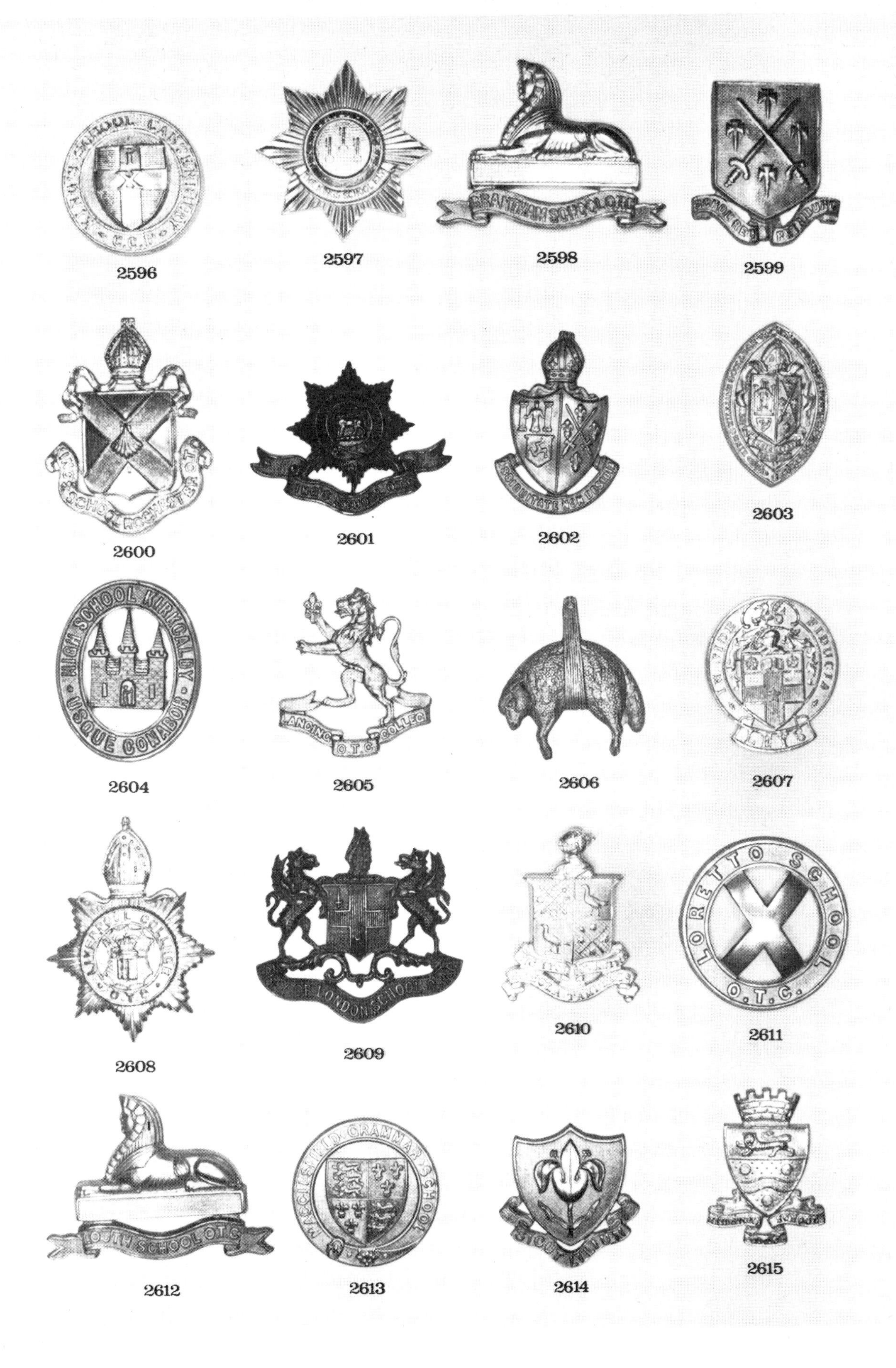

2596 2597 2598 2599

2600 2601 2602 2603

2604 2605 2606 2607

2608 2609 2610 2611

2612 2613 2614 2615

City of London School
The arms, crest and supporters of the City of London. Below, a scroll inscribed *City of London School O.T.C.* In blackened-brass (Fig. 2609). Also in white-metal.

Lord William's School, Thame
A shield charged with the school arms and surmounted by a knight's helm. Below, a scroll inscribed *Sic itur ad astra* and below this a further scroll inscribed *Schola tamensis*. In white-metal (Fig. 2610).

Loretto School, near Edinburgh
(1) A circlet inscribed *Loretto School O.T.C.* In a voided-centre St. Andrew's Cross. In white-metal (Fig. 2611). Previously worn in brass.
(2) As above, but *O.T.C.* replaced by small star-device. In chrome. Worn by C.C.F.

Louth School, Lincolnshire
A Sphinx resting on a blank plinth. Below, a scroll inscribed *Louth School O.T.C.* The Sphinx and plinth in white-metal, the scroll in gilding-metal (Fig. 2612).

Macclesfield Grammar School
A strap inscribed *Macclesfield Grammar School*. In the centre a shield charged with the arms of King Edward VI. In white-metal (Fig. 2613). Also in brass.

Magdalen College School, Oxford
On a shield a lily (from the arms of Magdalen College). Below, a scroll inscribed *Sicut lilium*. In gilding-metal (Fig. 2614).

Maidstone Grammar School
(1) A shield charged with the arms of Maidstone. Above the shield a mural crown. Below, a scroll inscribed *Maidstone School O.T.C.* In gilding-metal (Fig. 2615). Also in bronze.
(2) As above, but with the scroll inscribed *Olim meminisse juvabit* following the line of the base of the shield. In brass.
(3) As (1), but scroll inscribed *Maidstone School J.T.C.*

Malvern College, Worcestershire
A shield charged with five torteaux between two chevronels all between three heraldic-fountains. Below, a scroll inscribed *Sapiens qui prospicit*. In gilding-metal (Fig. 2616).

Manchester Grammar School
A circlet inscribed *Manchester Grammar School*. Within the circlet, and extending outside at the head, an owl on a twig with three leaves at the end. In gilding-metal (Fig. 2617). Also in white-metal.

Marlborough College, Wilts
(1) A circlet inscribed *Marlborough College O.T.C. Corps*. In a voided-centre a bishop's mitre. In black-metal (Fig. 2618).
(2) A shield charged with the arms of the college and surmounted by a mitre. Below, a scroll inscribed *Marlborough*. In gilding-metal (Fig. 2619). Previously worn in blackened-brass.

Mercers School
The charge from the arms of the Mercers' Livery Company: a demi-virgin couped below the shoulders issuing from clouds and crowned with an Eastern crown. Below, a scroll inscribed *Honor Deo*. In gilding-metal (Fig. 2620). There is an officers' pattern in gilt with motto-scroll in silver.

Merchant Taylors School
The arms, supporters and motto of the Merchant Taylors' Company: a pavilion imperial between two mantles; on a chief a lion passant guardant. Supporters: on either side a camel. Motto: *Concordia parvae res crescunt*. In gilding-metal (Fig. 2621). Also in blackened-brass, and in white-metal.

Merchiston Castle School, Edinburgh
An oval strap inscribed *Ready Aye Ready*. In a voided-centre an escutcheon charged with the school arms with, above, the crest of a dexter hand grasping a crescent. Silver-plated white-metal (Fig. 2622). Also in white-metal non-voided.

Millfield School
A shield charged with the sails of a windmill and four crosses botonny. Below, a scroll inscribed *Molire Molendo*. In white-metal (Fig. 2623).

Mill Hill School
On an ornamental plaque a shield charged with the arms of the school. Below, a scroll inscribed *Et virtutem et musae*. In gilding-metal (Fig. 2624). Previously worn in blackened-brass.

Monmouth School
(1) An oval inscribed on the base *Serve and Obey*. In a voided-centre a lion rampant. In black-metal with red-cloth backing (Fig. 2625).
(2) The Welsh Dragon on ground. In gilding-metal (Fig. 2626). Also worn in gilt-finish anodised.

Monkton Combe School, Bath
(1) A double-headed eagle with a shield on its breast inscribed with the monogram *MC*. Above the heads of the eagle and between the tips of the wings the letters *O.T.C.* In gilding metal (Fig. 2627).
(2) A circular scroll inscribed *Monkton Combe School* in the centre of which a sword, point upwards, with an Eastern crown at the join with the scroll. In the centre, on the sword, the letters *O.T.C.* In white-metal (Fig. 2628). Also in blackened-brass and in gilding-metal.

Morgan Academy
A stag's head erased, with collar and chain, in a voided-centre surrounded by a wreath of leaves and berries with in the top centre the monogram *C.C.F.* Below the wreath a scroll inscribed *Morgan Academy*. In chrome (Fig. 2629).

Morrison's Academy, Edinburgh

(1) On a seeded ground the monogram *MAC* within a thistle-wreath. In white-metal (Fig. 2630).

(2) The arms, helm, crest and mantling of the School. Below, a scroll inscribed *Ad summa tendendum.* In white-metal (Fig. 2631).

Moseley Grammar School

A shield charged with a bendlet between six cross crosslets fitchy all within a bordure of ermine. Below, a scroll inscribed *Timor Domini Principium Sapientia.* In bronze (Fig. 2632). Also in white-metal.

Mount St. Mary's College, Spinkhill, Derbyshire

On a torse a lily with a wing on either side. Below, a scroll inscribed *Sine Macula.* The lily in white-metal, remainder in gilding-metal (Fig. 2633).

Newcastle High School, Staffs

(1) The Stafford Knot surmounted by the Prince of Wales's plumes, coronet and motto. Below, a scroll inscribed *Newcastle O.T.C.* The Knot and coronet in gilding-metal, remainder in white-metal (Fig. 2634).

(2) As above, but the Imperial crown replacing the Prince of Wales's plume.

Nottingham High School

A Maltese cross surmounted by an Imperial crown. In the centre of the cross a wreath of oak and within the wreath a stag lodged. On the left arm of the cross and across the left branch of the wreath a half-scroll inscribed *Nottingham.* On the right arm of the cross and across the right branch of the wreath a half-scroll inscribed *School.* Below the cross a scroll inscribed *Officers Training Corps.* All in white-metal except the bottom scroll which is in gilding-metal (Fig. 2635). Also in bronze.

Northampton Grammar School

A shield bearing the arms of the County Borough of Northampton. Below, a scroll inscribed *Northampton School.* In gilding-metal (Fig. 2636).

Oakham School, Rutland

The Royal Tiger on ground with a scroll above charged with a laurel-wreath. Below, a scroll inscribed *Oakham School O.T.C.* In bronze (Fig. 2637).

The Oratory School, Woodcote, Reading

(1) A cardinal's hat with the letters *O.T.C.* between the tassels. In black-metal.

(2) As above, but with the letters *J.T.C.* between the tassels (Fig. 2638). In black-metal, also in gilding-metal.

(3) As above, but with the letters *C.C.F.* between the tassels. In gilding-metal.

Oundle School, Peterborough, Northants

(1) The arms, helm, crest and supporters of the Grocers' Company, founders of the School. Below, a scroll inscribed *Oundle O.T.C.* In gilding-metal (Fig. 2639). Also in bronze.

(2) As above, but scroll inscribed *Oundle School* only.

2616 2617 2618 2619

2620 2621 2622 2623

2624 2625 2626 2627

2628 2629 2630 2631

2632 2633 2634 2635

The Paston School
A shield charged with six fleurs-de-lys and a chief dancetty. Below, a scroll inscribed *De mieux en mieux pour tout.* In gilding-metal (Fig. 2640).

Perse School, Cambridge
(1) A Pelican in its piety on a torse. Below, a scroll inscribed *Perse School O.T.C.* In gilding-metal (Fig. 2641). First worn in blackened-brass.
(2) As above, but scroll inscribed *Perse School C.C.F.* In brass.

Portsmouth Grammar School
The arms of Dr. William Smith, the founder of the School, with helm, crest and mantling. On either side of the shield a spray of laurels. In gilding-metal (Fig. 2642).

Portsmouth Northern Grammar School
A shield charged with the arms of the School. Above the shield an eagle with crossed swords superimposed and, overall, a fouled anchor. The whole enclosed in a scroll inscribed *Northern Grammar School Portsmouth.* In gilding-metal (Fig. 2643).

Portsmouth Southern Grammar School
A shield charged with the arms of the School. Above the shield, the crest of a phoenix arising from flames. Below the shield a scroll inscribed *Valdus corpore animoque* with a cross at each end of the scroll. In gilding-metal (Fig. 2644). Also in white-metal.

Price's School, Fareham
A lion rampant reguardant on a wreath with, below on a solid ground, the dates *1721–1908.* In white-metal (Fig. 2645).

Queen Mary's School, Basingstoke
A Tudor Rose in gilding-metal (Fig. 2646). Also in smaller-size fitted with slider.

Queen Victoria School, Dunblane
(1) The Royal Crest for Scotland with Imperial crown, the whole within a wreath of thistles and oak. On the lower part of the wreath a scroll inscribed *Queen Victoria School.* In white-metal. Sealed 7th September 1947. (Fig. 2647).
(2) As above, but with St. Edward's crown. In silver-anodised. Sealed 7th December 1964.

Radley College, Abingdon
The arms of the School and, below, a scroll inscribed *Sicut colombae.* In gilding-metal (Fig. 2648). Also in bronze.

Reading School
(1) The arms of Reading with helm and mantling. Below the shield a scroll inscribed *Reading School O.T.C.* In gilding-metal (Fig. 2649).
(2) As above, but scroll inscribed *Reading School* only.
(3) As above, but scroll inscribed *Reading School C.C.F.*

2636 2637 2638 2639

2640 2641 2642 2643

2644 2645 2646 2647

2648 2649 2650 2651

2652 2653 2654 2655

Reigate Grammar School
The Paschal Lamb carrying a swallow-tailed flag. Below, a scroll inscribed *Reigate School O.T.C.* In blackened-brass (Fig. 2650).

Repton School, Derby
(1) On an escutcheon the arms of the founder, Sir John Port: a fesse engrailed ermine between three pigeons. Below, a scroll inscribed *Repton O.T.C.* In gilding-metal (Fig. 2651).
(2) As above, but scroll inscribed *Repton J.T.C.*
(3) As above, but scroll inscribed *Repton C.C.F.*

Rossall School, Fleetwood, Lancs
(1) The Rose of Lancaster surmounted by the Royal Crest. Below, a scroll inscribed *Rossall School O.T.C.* The Royal Crest in white-metal, remainder in gilding-metal (Fig. 2652).
(2) As above, but scroll inscribed *Rossall School J.T.C.*
(3) As above, but scroll inscribed *Rossall School C.C.F.*

Royal Belfast Academical Institution
The letters *R.B.A.I.* on a voided-ground with, above, the Royal Arms and, below, a shamrock on ornamental ground. In bronze (Fig. 2653).

Royal Grammar School, Guildford
The Paschal Lamb carrying a swallow-tailed flag. Below, a scroll inscribed *Guildford School O.T.C.* The scroll in white-metal, remainder in gilding-metal (Fig. 2654).

Royal Grammar School, Lancaster
(1) The Rose of Lancaster surmounted by an Imperial crown within a laurel-wreath and resting on a scroll inscribed *Lancaster.* Below this a further scroll inscribed *Royal Grammar School.* Between the two scrolls the letters *O.T.C.* In gilding-metal (Fig. 2655). Also in bronzed-brass.
(2) As above, but omitting the letters *O.T.C.* In bronzed-brass. Worn by C.C.F.

Royal Grammar School, Newcastle-upon-Tyne
(1) A horse's head with *O.T.C.* below and, below this, scroll inscribed *Newcastle-on-Tyne R. G. School.* In bronze (Fig. 2656).
(2) As above, but *O.T.C.* replaced by *C.C.F.*

Royal Grammar School, Worcester
(1) A complete laurel-wreath with, in a voided-centre, the letters *W.R.G.S.* In gilding-metal (Fig. 2657).
(2) The castle and inescutcheon from the arms of Worcester surmounted by an ancient crown. On the ground below the castle the letters *O.T.C.* All on an ornamental oval with the rim inscribed *Worcester Royal Grammar School.* In blackened-brass (Fig. 2658). Later worn in brass.
(3) On an eight-pointed star the Garter proper with, in the centre, the Lion from the Royal Crest. Below the Garter a scroll inscribed *Firm.* Below the star a scroll inscribed *W.R.G.S.O.T.C.* In gilding-metal (Fig. 2659).

Royal Liberty School
A sword and anchor in saltire with three seaxes below all superimposed with a cross flory, surmounted by an ancient crown and surrounded by a wreath. Below, a scroll inscribed *Semper procedens.* In white-metal (Fig. 2660).

Royal Wanstead School
A stork, with a scroll below inscribed *Abeunt studia in mores.* In white-metal (Fig. 2700).

Royal Wantage School
A design representing a bird with wings outstretched. In the centre a picture of swans on water within a circlet inscribed *Semper Fidelis.* Above the top row of feathers a scroll inscribed *R. W. S. Wanstead.* In gilding-metal (Fig. 2661).

Rugby School, Warwickshire
The crest of the School: a lion's paw holding a bunch of dates. Below, a scroll inscribed *Rugby.* In gilding-metal (Fig. 2662). First worn in blackened-brass.

Rutlish School
A shield fretty charged with five eagles displayed. Below, a scroll inscribed *Modeste strenus sancto.* In gilding-metal (Fig. 2663).

St. Bee's School, Cumberland
(1) A shield charged with the arms of the School. Above, a scroll inscribed *Expecta Dominum.* Below, a scroll inscribed *St. Bees School O.T.C.* In gilding-metal (Fig. 2664).
(2) As above, but bottom scroll inscribed *St. Bees School C.C.F.*

St. Brendan's College
An ancient ship with sail and six oars. Below, a scroll inscribed *St. Brendan's College C.C.F.* with a further scroll below that inscribed *Fidelitas Veritas.* Separating the ends of the two scrolls a five-pointed star on the left and a shamrock-leaf on the right. In gilding-metal (Fig. 2665).

St. Benedict's School, Ealing, W.5
A shield charged with a cross potent within two sprays of laurel joined at the base with the Stafford Knot. Below, a scroll inscribed *St. Benedict's School.* In white-metal (Fig. 2666).

St. Columba's College
A circlet inscribed *Saint Columba's College O.T.C.* surmounted by an Imperial crown. In the centre the college arms. In bronze (Fig. 2667). Also a smaller version approximately two-thirds the above size.

St. Dunstan's College, Catford, S.E.6
(1) A shield charged with a canton in the first quarter all within a scroll inscribed *Albam/O.T.C./Exorna* with, above, a scroll inscribed *St. Dunstan's College.* In gilding-metal (Fig. 2668). First worn in blackened-brass.
(2) As above, but *O.T.C.* replaced by a blank space in the scroll.

St. Edmund's School, Canterbury

An escutcheon charged with the arms of St. Edmund: three blazing suns. Behind it are crossed a pastoral staff and provincial cross and the whole is surmounted by a mitre. Below, a scroll inscribed *St. Edmund's School O.T.C.* In gilding-metal (Fig. 2669). Also in bronze.

St. Edmund's School, Ware

(1) A shield charged with the arms of St. Edmund within a laurel-wreath. Across the base of the wreath and below the shield a scroll inscribed *Avita profide* and, below this, a further scroll inscribed *O.T.C.* In white-metal (Fig. 2670). Also in blackened-brass and, later, chromed.
(2) As above, but *O.T.C.* replaced by *C.C.F.* Chromed.

St. Edward's School, Oxford

A seven-pointed star surmounted by a coronet. On this an escutcheon charged with the School arms. In gilding-metal (Fig. 2671).

St. Ignatius College

(1) On a shield in the first and fourth quarters three bendlets and in the second and third a cauldron suspended by a chain supported by two wolves. Below, a scroll inscribed *Ad majorem Dei gloriam.* The first and fourth quarters in green- and red-enamel, the second and third quarters in bronze. The scroll in blue-enamel (Fig. 2672). This pattern was worn by the Junior Training Corps.
(2) The school arms with helm, crest and mantling. On the shield: three bendlets with in chief a cauldron suspended by a chain supported by two wolves. Above the helm the crest on a torse. Below the shield a scroll inscribed *Ad majorem Dei gloriam.* The badge in white-metal with green-, yellow-, and light-blue-enamel, viz. Shield: green and yellow. Scroll: yellow. Mantling: green. Helm: light-blue (Fig. 2673). This type was worn by the Combined Cadet Force and had to be sewn on the cap.

St. John's School, Leatherhead

(1) An eagle rising, wings displayed and inverted on a torse. Below, a scroll inscribed *St. John's School Leatherhead O.T.C.* In gilding-metal (Fig. 2674).
(2) A shield charged with the school arms surmounted by an eagle rising, wings displayed and inverted, on a torse. Below, a scroll inscribed *Rather deathe than false of faythe.* In gilding-metal (Fig. 2675). An earlier type was in bronze and omitted the crescent and star from the shield.

St. Lawrence College, Ramsgate

Two serpents entwined and tied together on a torse. Below a scroll inscribed *In bono vince.* In gilding-metal (Fig. 2676). Also in bronze.

St. Peter's School, York

(1) The crossed keys of St. Peter surmounted by an Imperial crown. Below, a scroll inscribed *St. Peter's/O.T.C./School.* In gilding-metal (Fig. 2677).
(2) As above, but without the crown.
(3) As (1) but with *C.C.F*: in the scroll.

2656 2657 2658 2659

2660 2661 2662 2663

2664 2665 2666 2667

2668 2669 2670 2671

2672 2673 2674 2675

St. Paul's School, London, W.14

A shield charged with the arms of Dean Colet, the founder of the School. Above, an Imperial crown. Below, a scroll inscribed *Fide et literis*. In gilding-metal (Fig. 2678). Also in white-metal.

Sedbergh School, Yorks

(1) An escutcheon charged with the school arms within a laurel-wreath. Joining the heads of the wreath a scroll inscribed *O.T.C.* Below the wreath a tri-part scroll inscribed *Dura virum nutrix* and, below this, a further scroll inscribed *Sedbergh*. In gilding-metal (Fig. 2679). Also in bronzed-brass and in bronze.

(2) As above but *O.T.C.* replaced by *J.T.C.* In bronzed-brass, also in gilding-metal.

(3) As above, but small scroll at head of wreath left blank.

Sevenoaks School, Kent

A shield charged with seven acorns and two Greek characters. Below, a scroll inscribed *Sevenoaks*. In white-metal (Fig. 2680).

Shaftesbury School, Dorset

The school arms with helm, crest and mantling. Below the shield a scroll inscribed *Shaftesbury*. In gilding-metal (Fig. 2681).

Shrewsbury School

A shield charged with the Royal Arms of King Edward VI surmounted by a crown. Below, a scroll inscribed *Shrewsbury O.T.C.* In gilding-metal (Fig. 2682). First worn in blackened-brass, later bronze.

Sir Roger Manwood's School

On a shield with two pallets a crescent at the honour-point. On a chief a demi-lion. In gilding-metal (Fig. 2683).

Skinners School

The arms, helm, crest and supporters of the Skinners' Company. Below, the motto *To God only be All Glory* and below this a scroll inscribed *Skinners School O.T.C.* In gilding-metal (Fig. 2684).

Solihull Grammar School, Warwickshire

(1) A solid disc inscribed on the rim *Solihull Grammar School Perseverantia*. In the centre, on an ornamental ground, a shield charged with the school arms. In gilding-metal (Fig. 2685).

(2) Within a laurel-wreath a shield charged with the school arms. Below, a scroll inscribed *Solihull School O.T.C.* In gilding-metal (Fig. 2686).

(3) As (2) but scroll inscribed *Solihull School C.C.F.* In gun-metal.

Stamford School, Lincs

A swan with wings displayed sitting on a nest. Below, a scroll inscribed ✠ *me spede*. In gilding-metal (Fig. 2687).

2676 2677 2678 2679

2680 2681 2682 2683

2684 2685 2686 2687

2688 2689 2690 2691

2692 2693 2694 2695

Stonyhurst College, Blackburn
An eagle displayed resting on a scroll inscribed *Quant je puis*. In gilding-metal (Fig. 2688). Also in blackened-brass, and chromed.

Stowe School, Bucks
Within a circlet inscribed *Persto et Praesto* a shield charged with the school arms. In bronze (Fig. 2689).
Also worn in dark-brown plastic two-thirds the above size and non-voided. Worn in silver-anodised by the Combined Cadet Force. Officers wore the first pattern with a gilt shield, remainder in silver.

Sutton Valence School, Maidstone
A lamb. Below, a scroll inscribed *Sutton Valence School*. In gilding-metal (Fig. 2690).

Taunton School, Somerset
(1) A shield charged with the arms of the School. Below, a scroll inscribed *Taunton School C.C.F.* In gilding-metal (Fig. 2691).
(2) As above, but scroll inscribed *Taunton School O.T.C.* Worn previous to (1).

Tonbridge School, Kent
(1) The arms of the School with helm, crest and mantling. Below, a scroll inscribed *Tonbridge School O.T.C.* In gilding-metal (Fig. 2692). Also in anodised-aluminium.
(2) The arms of the School with crest and mantling. Below, a scroll inscribed *Tonbridge School*. In black-plastic on a yellow-plastic disc.

Trent College, Long Eaton, Derbyshire
A Maltese cross surmounted by an Imperial crown. In the centre of the cross a wreath of oak and within the wreath a shield charged with an open book and seven stars. On the left arm of the cross and across the left branch of the wreath a half-scroll inscribed *Trent*. On the right arm of the cross and across the right branch of the wreath a half-scroll inscribed *College*. Below the cross a scroll inscribed *Officers Training Corps*. In blackened-brass (Fig. 2693).

Trinity College, Glenalmond
A double-headed spread eagle on which an ornamental shield charged with the Paschal Lamb. Below, a scroll inscribed *Pro Rege Lege et Grege*. In white-metal (Fig. 2694).

University College School, London
Within a laurel-wreath an oval inscribed *XXth Middlesex Artists Rifle Volunteers*. In the centre a representation of Mars and Minerva with, on the left, an inscription worded *Cum Marte Minerva*. A scroll above the oval inscribed *Cadet Corps* and surmounted by an Imperial crown. A scroll below the wreath inscribed *University College School London*. In black-metal (Fig. 2695).

Uppingham School, Rutland
(1) The seal of the School. Below, a scroll inscribed *Quasi Cursores*. In gilding-metal (Fig. 2696).

(2) The Royal Tiger with scroll above bearing a laurel-wreath. Below, a scroll inscribed *Uppingham*. In bronze (Fig. 2697).
(3) The Royal Tiger in gilding-metal with a scroll below inscribed *Uppingham* in white-metal (Fig. 2698). Also in bronzed-brass.

Victoria College, Jersey
An escutcheon charged with the three lions-leopardé of Jersey surmounted by a crown. In gilding-metal (Fig. 2699).

Warwick School
(1) A portcullis and chains on a torse surmounted by the Bear and Ragged Staff. Below, a scroll inscribed *Altiora Peto*. In gilding-metal (Fig. 2701).
(2) A portcullis and chains surmounted by a crown. Below, a scroll inscribed *Altiora Peto*. In gilding-metal (Fig. 2702). Also found with non-voided crown.

Welbeck College, Worksop, Notts
Within a circlet inscribed *Welbeck College* a cross moline all superimposed upon crossed swords hilts-downwards. The cross and sword-blades in white-metal, remainder in gilding-metal. Sealed 28th May, 1953 (Fig. 2703).

Wellingborough School, Northants
(1) The Castle and Key of Gibraltar within a laurel-wreath. Above the castle a scroll inscribed *O.T.C.* and below the castle a blank scroll. On the lower part of the stems of the wreath a scroll inscribed *Wellingborough School*. In white-metal (Fig. 2704). Also in bronzed-brass.
(2) As above, but top scroll inscribed *J.T.C.* In bronzed-brass.
(3) As above, but top scroll blank. In bronzed-brass, also in gilding-metal.

Wellington College, Berks
The crest of the Duke of Wellington: out of a ducal coronet a demi-lion rampant, holding a forked pennon flowing to the sinister, one-third per pale from the staff, charged with the cross of St. George. Below, a scroll inscribed *Wellington College*. In gilding-metal (Fig. 2705). Formerly worn in bronzed-brass.

Wellington College, Salop
Name changed to Wrekin College in 1921
(1) A lion rampant. In gilding-metal (Fig. 2706).
(2) A lion rampant. Below, a scroll inscribed *Wellington College Salop*. In gilding-metal (Fig. 2707).

Wellington School, Somerset
The crest of the Duke of Wellington. Below, a scroll inscribed *Wellington Somerset*. In gilding-metal (Fig. 2708).

Westminster City School
(1) A shield charged with the arms of the City of Westminster. Below, a scroll inscribed *Westminster School C.C.F.* In gilding-metal (Fig. 2709).
(2) As above, but scroll inscribed *Westminster School O.T.C.* In bronze-finish, also in black-finish; both worn previously to (1).

Weymouth College
A medieval ship with five oars, sail set and flags flying fore-and-aft all within a circular scroll inscribed *Weymouth College O.T.C.* In gilding-metal (Fig. 2710).

Whitgift School, Croydon
A shield charged with the arms of Archbishop Whitgift, the founder, and surmounted by a mitre. Below, a scroll inscribed *Vincit qui patitur.* In gilding-metal (Fig. 2711).

Wilson's Grammar School
(1) A shield charged with the arms of the School. Below, a scroll inscribed *Wilson's O.T.C.* In blackened-brass (Fig. 2712).
(2) As above but without the scroll. In gilding-metal (Fig. 2713).

Winchester College
The Hampshire Rose within a laurel-wreath. Below, a scroll inscribed *Winchester.* In gilding-metal (Fig. 2714). Also in bronzed-brass.

Windsor Grammar School
A shield charged with a stag beneath a tree. In bronze (Fig. 2715). Worn by the C.C.F.

Wolverhampton Grammar School
A shield charged with the arms of the founder, Sir Stephen Jenyns, superimposed on the Stafford Knot and surmounted by a crest. Below, a scroll inscribed *Wolverhampton O.T.C.* In gilding-metal (Fig. 2716).

Woodbridge School
A shield charged with the arms of the School. Below, a scroll inscribed *Pro Deo Rege Patria.* In gilding-metal (Fig. 2717).

Worksop College, Notts
A Maltese cross surmounted by an Imperial crown. In the centre of the cross a wreath of oak and within the wreath a stag lodged. On the left arm of the cross and across the left branch of the wreath a half-scroll inscribed *Sherwood.* On the right arm of the cross and across the right branch of the wreath a half-scroll inscribed *Foresters.* Below the cross a scroll inscribed *Worksop College O.T.C.* All in white-metal except the bottom scroll which is in gilding-metal (Fig. 2718). Also in blackened-finished.

Wrekin College, Wellington, Salop
A lion rampant on a scroll inscribed *Wrekin College Shropshire.* In gilding-metal (Fig. 2719).

2696 2697 2698 2699

2700 2701 2702 2703

2704 2705 2706 2707

2708 2709 2710 2711

2712 2713 2714 2715

2716 2717 2718 2719

CHAPTER 20

Further Notes for Collectors

In the first volume of this work we dealt with the basics of the hobby: fields of interest, methods of presentation, cleaning and repairs, preservation. Here, we are adding a few notes on the main societies which can be of help to the collector and a selected list of books for further reading.

THE SOCIETIES

The Society for Army Historical Research
c/o The National Army Museum,
Royal Hospital Road,
Chelsea, London, S.W.3.
Annual subscription, 1979: £7 (U.S.A. $14). Journal: published quarterly; coloured and b/w plates; military history, uniforms and badges. Write to the Honorary Secretary at the above address.

The Military Historical Society
Turks Row,
The Duke of York's Headquarters,
Chelsea, London, S.W.3.
Annual subscription, 1979: £3 (U.S.A. $8). Journal: four issues per annum; b/w illustrations; military history, uniforms and badges. Regular meetings held at The Duke of York's Headquarters. Write to the Honorary Secretary, J. W. F. Gaylor, at 7 East Woodside, Bexley, Kent, DA5 3PG.

Crown Imperial
5 Warwick Crescent,
Harrogate, Yorkshire.
Annual subscription, 1978/9: £3 (U.S.A. $6). Journal: published quarterly; b/w illustrations; military history, uniforms and badges. Regular meetings at Strensall, Yorkshire. Write to the Honorary Secretary, Major C. B. Cowie, O.B.E., at the above address.

The Scottish Military Collectors Society
17/14 St. Andrew's Crescent,
Glasgow, Scotland.
Annual subscription, 1979: £5. Journal: the *Dispatch*, issued quarterly; b/w illustrations;

military history, uniforms and badges, especially those of Scottish origin. Regular meetings in Glasgow. Write to the Honorary Secretary, James B. McKay, at the above address.

The foregoing represent the senior societies of this country. In addition there are numerous local groups, some of them branches of the senior societies, and even overseas groups dedicated to the collection of badges of the British Army.

Once you join a senior society you will find the officers are pleased to help newcomers and normally will supply additional information on request. However, when you make a written request, do remember to include a stamped and self-addressed envelope: honorary secretaries will go to considerable lengths to help you but you cannot expect them to pay for the privilege of doing so!

ADDITIONAL READING

General

Regimental Badges, 6th revised edition by the late Major T. J. Edwards, M.B.E., F.R.Hist.S., revised by Arthur L. Kipling. Charles Knight & Co. Ltd., London, 1974.
A basic text-book for all who include modern badges in their field-of-interest. There have been six editions so far, each covering the badges in wear at the time of preparing the edition. All are worth acquiring if you wish to follow the changes since the Second World War.

Glengarry badges of the British Line Regiments to 1881 by W. Y. Carman, F.S.A., F.R.Hist.S. Arms and Armour Press, London, 1973.
Black-and-white illustrations on every page covering almost all known patterns. Of particular interest are the notes on actual dimensions and the placement of the loop-fittings at the back of the badge.

Dress Regulations for the Officers of the Army (including the Militia), 1900. A reprint of a War Office publication with special introduction by W. Y. Carman, F.S.A., F.R.Hist.S. Arms and Armour Press, London, 1969.
The first Dress Regulations to include full details and photographic illustrations of head-dress badges.

The Lineage Book of the British Army, Mounted Corps and Infantry, 1660–1968 by J. B. M. Frederick. Hope Farm Press, Cornwallville, New York, U.S.A., 1969.
For the advanced collector this is a 'must'. It includes a detailed history of every unit, with all volunteer and militia battalions, and all changes in organisation and designation. Regimental titles have varied from period to period and this publication helps to match the badge to the title.

Regimental and regional

Military Insignia of Cornwall and Supplement by D. Endean Ivall and Charles Thomas. Penwith Books, Institute of Cornish Studies, Trevenson House, Poole, Redruth, Cornwall, 1974. Supplement, 1976.
A model of how a Regiment's badges should be presented. Meticulously accurate illustrations by Mr. Ivall accompanied by exact descriptions from Professor Thomas, right down to overall measurements.

The Highland Light Infantry: the uniforms of the Regiment, 1881–1914 by James B. McKay and Douglas N. Anderson. James B. McKay, 14/17 St. Andrew's Crescent, Glasgow, Scotland, 1977.
Nicely detailed history of uniforms and badges with superb lively line-illustrations by Mr. Anderson.

Historical Record of The London Regiment by Colonel A. R. Martin, O.B.E., T.D. Published privately. No date. Indispensable for those who wish to weave their way through the maze of amalgamations and changes from the Second World War onwards. Thumb-nail line-drawings of the main patterns of badges worn by each battalion/regiment.

Scottish Regimental Badges: 1793–1971 by W. H. and K. D. Bloomer. Arms and Armour Press, London, 1973.
Black-and-white illustrations on every page and indispensable for the Scottish buff.

The Uniform of the London Scottish, 1859–1959 by J. O. Robson. The London Scottish Regiment/Ogilby Trust, London, 1960.
Coloured and black-and-white photographs in abundance showing all aspects of dress and badges.

The Uniforms of the Royal Armoured Corps by Malcolm Dawson. Almark Publishing Co. Ltd., London, 1974.
Very useful details of the dress and badges of all the cavalry regiments which comprise the modern Royal Armoured Corps.

The Staffords, 1881–1978 by G. Rosignoli and Captain C. J. Whitehouse. Rosignoli, 18 High Park Road, Farnham, Surrey, 1978.
Well-produced booklet setting out the history, uniforms and badges of the two Staffordshire infantry regiments, their volunteer and militia battalions, Home Guard and Officers Training Corps. Excellent line-drawings of badges and the uniforms on which they are worn.

West York Rifle Volunteers, 1859–1887 by K. Dixon Pickup. K. D. Pickup, 21 Bankart Avenue, Oadby, Leicester, 1978.
An essential work for any collector interested in the badges of Yorkshire and of considerable interest to anyone who specialises in the volunteers generally. Many photographic illustrations of uniforms, head-dress and badges.

RESTRIKES

No serious work on badges of the British Army can avoid comment of one kind or another on the phenomenon of restrikes.

The earliest known examples of any consequence go back to the beginning of this century when a Southsea firm, Fox and Company, produced a series of restrikes of pre-Territorial Glengarry-badges from original dies. They were listed and offered to collectors at reasonable prices and, because originals were comparatively scarce, some collectors accepted them as substitutes until such time as they could obtain an original. Today, they are still accepted – as substitutes – but there are dealers and collectors, either unscrupulous or ignorant of their subject, who persist in offering them as originals to unsuspecting beginners, and at prices one would expect to pay for the authentic item.

Reproductions from the Middle- and Far-East have become commonplace and very cheap. Inevitably cast and crudely finished, with weak lugs or sliders, they are not likely to fool any but the most inexperienced. However, some collectors had no objection to filling difficult gaps with these and it is not unusual to find in older collections, for instance, a cast specimen of the elephant/double-scroll pattern of the 19th Hussars (KK790): collectors in those days *knew* that their chance of obtaining an original of such a badge was well-nigh negligible.

Into a somewhat different category fall the commercial strikes made available through military-accessories shops during the 1930s, 1940s and 1950s. Usually these were of patterns currently in use by regiments and most were purchased as replacements or mementos by serving soldiers. To the collector they offered a useful source of supply at a few coppers a time with the additional bonus that, occasionally, he might even find an obsolete pattern, if he was lucky!

Little happened during the 1960s except that the news of the formation of the large Brigades, and the break-up of the old regimental system, kindled a new and lively interest in the old badges which, we were told, would vanish forever. There was the occasional restriking being practised but most of the material produced was of poor quality and only of passing interest to beginners. Strangely enough, one curiosity of those days has survived until the present in the shape of a white-metal version of King Edward's Horse with Imperial crown (KK1507)! This never was produced for, or worn by, that regiment in white-metal and yet it appears quite frequently in sales lists and in auctions. Even experienced collectors will proudly display a specimen of that badge with the claim: 'It must be original, I've had it for ten years.' Sad to say, it is *not* original, and ten years does *not* cloak it with any respectability: the writer also has possessed one for ten years and that was purchased from a restrike-manufacturer for a few shillings!

During the early 1970s, a well-known badge-manufacturer issued a series of restrikes of obsolete badges. They were offered through the trade as new stock at very reasonable prices and there is no doubt that the original intention, in this case, was simply to meet a new, known demand. There could be no question of an attempt to pass off these badges as originals: the prices asked were so low that no-one could really believe them to be authentic. In fact, in time, unscrupulous parties did artificially age this type of restrike and offer them at high prices as authentic original badges.

However innocent may have been the 1970s restrikes, their acceptance opened up new fields of possibility. In the years that had passed since the Fox restrikes, the hobby had expanded and grown beyond recognition. What had been an obscure hobby practised by a small and select group of collectors had become a highly popular craze and, unfortunately, there were nowhere near enough stocks available to meet the new level of demand. Indeed, by the close of the 1960s most stock-carrying dealers' lists looked very thin and the contemporary situation, as expressed by one dealer, was: 'like sitting in a gold mine without a pick and shovel!'

Human nature being what it is, such a set of circumstances could lead to one conclusion only: inevitably some bright entrepreneur was going to produce the supply to meet the demand, and someone did! Today, the manufacture of restrikes and reproductions is a sizeable industry with firms producing anything from cap-badges to shako-plates. Supporting it is a network of large and small dealers who hawk this material as original and at very fancy prices. There is the sad story of one victim who had acquired at considerable expense what he believed to be an original specimen of a very rare badge. He began to suspect its authenticity and took it to a so-called badge-dealer who, without hesitation, confirmed his worst fears and offered him another which, he alleged, was the 'real thing'. In fact, the new offering was simply a better class of restrike and the only conclusion one can draw from that story is that either the dealer was patently dishonest or that he did not know his trade. In either case he is not the type that is wanted in our hobby.

The situation that arose might have been contained from the very beginning if the main body of the hobby, backed by its Societies, had made a firm stand against the people behind restrikes – and nobody can claim seriously that the culprits were not known – but that was not to be.

In 1973, a delegation from the York and District Branch of the Military Historical Society made a special trip to London to lay before the national annual general meeting the fears and concern of their branch in relation to restrikes. The chilly reception they received so incensed them that the delegation left the meeting and broke away from the Society to form a small group of their own dedicated to the anti-restrike cause.

Under the able leadership of Major Charles B. Cowie, O.B.E., that small group has grown into *Crown Imperial*, a Society in its own right, and already it has assisted in securing the conviction of a counterfeit-medal manufacturer. It demands a high standard of conduct between its members and between member and dealer and it deserves the fullest support of all fair-minded collectors. Above all it has proved that, contrary to what has been said in other quarters, it is possible to take action if the intention and determination are there!

In detailing the general history of restrikes the intention has been to give the reader an insight into cause and effect: a background to the problems that beset the hobby. What it does not do is to help him in identifying the offending items. Unfortunately, the sheer number of badges restruck to date is so substantial that a completely separate detailed work would be necessary to fulfil such a need and it could not be encompassed within the limits of this volume.

The only advice that can be offered here is largely commonsense and, in all probability, it applies to most hobbies:

1. Join a society and make contact with other collectors.
2. Enquire about dealers, try to find one who is trustworthy and let him help you.
3. Do not rush into buying badges. Study as many lists as you can obtain, see how prices compare and, above all, beware of the dealer who consistently offers a large number of scarce and rare badges. If stocks of more common badges were running-out back in 1970, ask yourself how there come to be so many rarer badges available now!
4. If a dealer sells to you, or to someone you know, a badge that proves to be a restrike, drop him like the proverbial hot brick. These people can survive only so long as you, the collector, support them.

IDENTIFICATION OF BADGES

Since the publication of the first volume of this work the authors have been asked frequently to identify badges. This they are pleased to do and if you have such a request the following is the best procedure to follow:

1. Send a rubbing or sketch of the badge with full details of the metals used and the type of fitting. If you use a sketch, indicate overall measurements.
2. Enclose a stamped and addressed envelope for the reply.

3. Some people prefer to send the actual badge and, of course, this does make for easier identification. But, if you decide on this course, do remember that the authors cannot accept any responsibility for items sent to them. If you think the badge may be of value, register the packet and include sufficient postage to enable it to be returned by the same means.

CHAPTER 21

Glossary of Terms Used

We have tried to be consistent in the description of badges given in this work and the following terms have been employed:

Circlet	The circular band, with unbroken edges, containing the title or motto.
Strap	Where the circle carrying the inscription has a buckle.
Garter	Only used when carrying the Garter motto of *Honi soit qui mal y pense.*

No two illustrations throughout the two volumes bear the same reference number and collectors may find it an advantage when writing to other collectors to use these numbers as a code and thereby avoid long written descriptions. For example: reference 'KK725' would avoid the necessity of describing in detail this particular lance-cap plate of the 21st Lancers, or KK2673, the intricate shield of St. Ignatius College O.T.C.

Some terms commonly used by collectors are:

Crowns

Q.V.C.	The crown used during Queen Victoria's reign, 1837 to 1901. It varies, slightly, usually rounded but sometimes square-ended.
K.C.	The crown used on badges struck between 1902 and 1954. Referred to sometimes as 'King's' or 'Tudor' crown and in this work as the 'Imperial' crown.
QC-EIIR	The St. Edward's crown of H.M. Queen Elizabeth II used from 1954 to date.
Flat-topped	A crown with a slightly-sloping curved-shape from the cross and orb. As an example see Palace of Westminster Home Guard (Fig. 2433).
Looped	The Indian crown in which loops of pearls are a feature. As an example see 7th Hussars: 1898 to 1901 (Fig. 759).
Scottish	The crown as used on the badge of the Scottish Horse (Fig. 1387).

Description of Badges

Die-struck	Struck with considerable force using a steel die to effect the design. Fully die-struck badges are recognisable by the fact that the design can be seen clearly in reverse on the back of the badge.
H/P	Helmet-plate.
H.P.C.	Helmet-plate centre.
O.S.D.	Badges, invariably of bronze finish, used on officers' service-dress.
P/T	Pre-Territorial badges worn prior to 1881 when all Infantry of the Line were known by their regimental numbers.

Prong	Sometimes called a slider. A single tongue on the reverse of the badge. Used to a greater degree after 1914 to serve the same purpose as shanks. Puggaree-badges often had stouter, and longer, prongs.
Semi-solid	When manufactured only part of the design can be seen on the reverse of the badge, other parts being solid usually to strengthen the design. Mostly found on officers' badges.
Shanks	The copper loops used to fasten the badge to the head-dress and through which is passed the split-wire pin to hold it firmly in position.
Solid	When referred to the frontal design of a badge it means 'non-voided', that is, the outline of the badge only being cut out. When referred to manufacture it implies that the reverse of the badge is made from heavy-gauge metal and appears smooth and devoid of features.
Voided	Describes the process whereby the format of the badge is enhanced by the removal of metal to give depth or to emphasise a design.

Metals

Anod	Anodised aluminium. Used in the manufacture of recent badges.
Bi/M.	Where two metals are used on a single badge, i.e. white-metal and gilding-metal. Where bronzed-brass is used the abbreviation would be Bze and W/M.
Blk.	Blackened-brass. Usually found on rifle regiments' badges.
Brass	Yellow-brass: used for badge-making chiefly before 1883 although there are a few instances since that date. Not to be confused with gilding-metal.
Bze.	Bronze. Usually copper or gilding-metal finished in a dull service-dress brown. More often found on officers' service-dress badges but occasionally on other-ranks' badges.
Enam.	Enamelling. Either as part of the badge, and mounted thereon, or the badge itself.
Gilt	A plating of gold. (Requires gentle treatment for preservation.)
G/M.	Gilding-metal. A brass-metal containing a higher content of copper than the yellow-brass mentioned above.
G/S/Enam.	A badge composed of gilt, silver and enamelling.
H.M.Sil.	Hall-marked silver. The marks give the identity of the Assay Office and the date of manufacture.
Sil.	Silver-plated.
W/M.	White-metal.

CHAPTER 22

Regimental Titles

The change of regimental titles between the end of the Great war and the present day is shown below: where regiments have been amalgamated or formed 'large' regiments the new title is given for each.

Title at the end of the Great War	*Present day*
The 1st Life Guards	The Life Guards
The 2nd Life Guards	The Life Guards
Royal Horse Guards (The Blues)	The Blues and Royals (Royal Horse Guards and 1st Dragoons)
1st (King's) Dragoon Guards	1st The Queen's Dragoon Guards
2nd Dragoon Guards (Queen's Bays)	1st The Queen's Dragoon Guards
3rd (Prince of Wales's) Dragoon Guards	The Royal Scots Dragoon Guards (Carabiniers and Greys)
The 4th Royal Irish Dragoon Guards	4th/7th Royal Dragoon Guards
The 5th (Princess Charlotte of Wales's) Dragoon Guards	5th Royal Inniskilling Dragoon Guards
The 6th Dragoon Guards (Carabiniers)	The Royal Scots Dragoon Guards (Carabiniers and Greys)
7th (the Princess Royal's) Dragoon Guards	4th/7th Royal Dragoon Guards
1st (Royal) Dragoons	The Blues and Royals (Royal Horse Guards and 1st Dragoons)
2nd Dragoons (Royal Scots Greys)	The Royal Scots Dragoon Guards (Carabiniers and Greys)
The 3rd (King's Own) Hussars	The Queen's Own Hussars
The 4th (Queen's Own) Hussars	The Queen's Royal Irish Hussars
The 5th (Royal Irish) Lancers	16th/5th The Queen's Royal Lancers
6th Inniskilling Dragoons	5th Royal Inniskilling Dragoon Guards
7th (The Queen's Own) Hussars	The Queen's Own Hussars
8th (King's Royal Irish) Hussars	The Queen's Royal Irish Hussars
9th (Queen's Royal) Lancers	9th/12th Royal Lancers (Prince of Wales's)
10th (The Prince of Wales's Own Royal Regiment) Hussars	The Royal Hussars (Prince of Wales's Own)

The 11th (Prince Albert's Own) Hussars	The Royal Hussars (Prince of Wales's Own)
The 12th (Prince of Wales's Royal) Lancers	9th/12th Royal Lancers (Prince of Wales's)
13th Hussars	13th/18th Royal Hussars (Queen Mary's Own)
14th (King's) Hussars	14th/20th King's Hussars
15th (The King's) Hussars	15th/19th The King's Royal Hussars
16th (The Queen's) Lancers	16th/5th The Queen's Royal Lancers
The 17th (Duke of Cambridge's Own) Lancers	17th/21st Lancers
The 18th (Queen Mary's Own) Royal Hussars	13th/18th Royal Hussars (Queen Mary's Own)
19th (Queen Alexandra's Own Royal) Hussars	15th/19th The King's Royal Hussars
20th Hussars	14th/20th King's Hussars
21st (Empress of India's) Lancers	17th/21st Lancers
The Royal Scots (Lothian Regiment)	The Royal Scots (The Royal Regiment)
The Queen's (Royal West Surrey Regiment)	The Queen's Regiment
The Buffs (East Kent Regiment)	The Queen's Regiment
The King's Own (Royal Lancaster Regiment)	The King's Own Royal Border Regiment
The Northumberland Fusiliers	The Royal Regiment of Fusiliers
The Royal Warwickshire Regiment	The Royal Regiment of Fusiliers
The Royal Fusiliers (City of London Regiment)	The Royal Regiment of Fusiliers
The King's (Liverpool Regiment)	The King's Regiment
The Norfolk Regiment	The Royal Anglian Regiment
The Lincolnshire Regiment	The Royal Anglian Regiment
The Devonshire Regiment	The Devonshire and Dorset Regiment
The Suffolk Regiment	The Royal Anglian Regiment
Prince Albert's Somerset Light Infantry	The Light Infantry
The Prince of Wales's Own (West Yorkshire Regiment)	The Prince of Wales's Own Regiment of Yorkshire
The East Yorkshire Regiment	The Prince of Wales's Own Regiment of Yorkshire
The Bedfordshire Regiment	The Royal Anglian Regiment
The Leicestershire Regiment	The Royal Anglian Regiment
The Royal Irish Regiment	Disbanded in 1922
Alexandra, Princess of Wales's Own (Yorkshire Regiment)	The Green Howards (Alexandra, Princess of Wales's Own Yorkshire Regiment)
The Lancashire Fusiliers	The Royal Regiment of Fusiliers
The Royal Scots Fusiliers	The Royal Highland Fusiliers (Princess Margaret's Own Glasgow and Ayrshire Regiment)
The Cheshire Regiment	The Cheshire Regiment
The Royal Welsh Fusiliers	The Royal Welch Fusiliers

The South Wales Borderers	The Royal Regiment of Wales (24th/41st Foot)
The King's Own Scottish Borderers	The King's Own Scottish Borderers
The Cameronians (Scottish Rifles)	Disbanded in 1968
The Royal Inniskilling Fusiliers	The Royal Irish Rangers (27th (Inniskilling), 83rd and 87th)
The Gloucestershire Regiment	The Gloucestershire Regiment
The Worcestershire Regiment	The Worcestershire and Sherwood Foresters Regiment (29th/45th)
The East Lancashire Regiment	The Queen's Lancashire Regiment
The East Surrey Regiment	The Queen's Regiment
The Duke of Cornwall's Light Infantry	The Light Infantry
The Duke of Wellington's (West Riding Regiment)	The Duke of Wellington's Regiment (West Riding)
The Border Regiment	The King's Own Royal Border Regiment
The Royal Sussex Regiment	The Queen's Regiment
The Hampshire Regiment	The Royal Hampshire Regiment
The South Staffordshire Regiment	The Staffordshire Regiment (The Prince of Wales's)
The Dorsetshire Regiment	The Devonshire and Dorset Regiment
The Prince of Wales's Volunteers (South Lancashire Regiment)	The Queen's Lancashire Regiment
The Welsh Regiment	The Royal Regiment of Wales (24th/41st Foot)
The Black Watch (Royal Highlanders)	The Black Watch (Royal Highland Regiment)
The Oxfordshire and Buckinghamshire light Infantry	The Royal Green Jackets
The Essex Regiment	The Royal Anglian Regiment
The Sherwood Foresters (Nottinghamshire and Derbyshire Regiment)	The Worcestershire and Sherwood Foresters Regiment (29th/45th)
The Loyal North Lancashire Regiment	The Queen's Lancashire Regiment
The Northamptonshire Regiment	The Royal Anglian Regiment
Princess Charlotte of Wales's (Royal Berkshire Regiment)	The Duke of Edinburgh's Royal Regiment (Berkshire and Wiltshire)
The Queen's Own (Royal West Kent Regiment)	The Queen's Regiment
The King's Own Yorkshire Light Infantry	The Light Infantry
The King's (Shropshire Light Infantry)	The Light Infantry
The Duke of Cambridge's Own (Middlesex Regiment)	The Queen's Regiment
The King's Royal Rifle Corps	The Royal Green Jackets
The Duke of Edinburgh's (Wiltshire Regiment)	The Duke of Edinburgh's Royal Regiment (Berkshire and Wiltshire)
The Manchester Regiment	The King's Regiment
The Prince of Wales's (North Staffordshire Regiment)	The Staffordshire Regiment (The Prince of Wales's)
The York and Lancaster Regiment	Disbanded in 1968

The Durham Light Infantry	The Light Infantry
The Highland Light Infantry	The Royal Highland Fusiliers (Princess Margaret's Own Glasgow and Ayrshire Regiment)
Seaforth Highlanders (Ross-shire Buffs, The Duke of Albany's)	Queen's Own Highlanders (Seaforth and Cameron)
The Gordon Highlanders	The Gordon Highlanders
The Queen's Own Cameron Highlanders	Queen's Own Highlanders (Seaforth and Cameron)
The Royal Irish Rifles	The Royal Irish Rangers (27th (Inniskilling), 83rd and 87th)
Princess Victoria's (Royal Irish Fusiliers)	The Royal Irish Rangers (27th (Inniskilling), 83rd and 87th)
The Connaught Rangers	Disbanded in 1922
Princess Louise's (Argyll and Sutherland Highlanders)	The Argyll and Sutherland Highlanders (Princess Louise's)
The Prince of Wales's Leinster Regiment (Royal Canadians)	Disbanded in 1922
Royal Munster Fusiliers	Disbanded in 1922
Royal Dublin Fusiliers	Disbanded in 1922
The Rifle Brigade (The Prince Consort's Own)	The Royal Green Jackets

Index

Text references in roman type
Figure references in bold face type
Abbreviated titles are used in the index

CAVALRY AND ROYAL ARMOURED CORPS

Blues and Royals: 2, 3, 4, **1879**
Carabiniers, The: 6, **747**
Carabiniers, 3rd: 8, 18, **1888**
Dragoon Guards, 1st King's: 6, **735, 1885**
Dragoon Guards, 1st Queen's: 6, **1887**
Dragoon Guards, 3rd: 6, **739**
Dragoon Guards, 4th: 8, **740**
Dragoon Guards, 4th/7th: 8, 18, **742**
Dragoon Guards, 5th: 8, **744**
Dragoon Guards, 5th Royal Inniskilling: 8, 18, **745, 1891**
Dragoon Guards, 7th: 8, **749**
Dragoon Guards, Royal Scots: 8, **1890**
Dragoons, Royal: 10, **751, 1892, 1893**
Dragoons, 22nd: 14, **1912**
Dragoons, 25th: 14, **1915**
Household Cavalry: 2, **1880, 1881, 1882, 1883, 1884**
Hussars, 3rd: 10, **753, 1894**
Hussars, 4th: 10, **756, 1897**
Hussars, 7th: 10, **760, 1895**
Hussars, 8th: 10, 18, **762, 1927, 1928**
Hussars, 10th: 12, 18, **765, 1929**
Hussars, 11th: 12, **766**
Hussars, 13th: 12, **771**
Hussars, 13th/18th: 12, **1904, 1905, 1906**
Hussars, 14th: 13, **774**
Hussars, 14th/20th: 13, 18, **775, 1907, 1908**
Hussars, 15th: 13, **777**
Hussars, 15th/19th: 13, **778, 1909**
Hussars, 18th: 12, **788**
Hussars, 19th: 13, **791**
Hussars, 20th: 13, **793**
Hussars, 23rd: 14, **1913**
Hussars, 26th, 14, **1916**
Hussars, Queen's Own: 10, 18, **1896**
Hussars, Queen's Royal Irish: 10, **1898, 1899**
Hussars, Royal: 12, **1903**
Inniskillings, The: 8, **758**
Lancers, 5th: 13, **757**
Lancers, 9th: 10, **764, 1900**
Lancers, 9th/12th: 12, **1902**
Lancers, 12th: 12, **768, 1901**
Lancers, 16th: 13, **781**
Lancers, 16th/5th: 14, 18, **1910, 1911**
Lancers, 17th: 14, **782**
Lancers, 17th/21st: 14, 18, **782**
Lancers, 21st: 14, **797**
Lancers, 24th: 14, **1914**
Lancers, 27th: 16, **1917**
Life Guards, 1st: 1, **727**
Life Guards, 2nd: 1, **728**
Life Guards, The: 1, 2, 3, 4, **706, 707, 729, 730, 1874, 1875, 1876**
Queen's Bays: 6, **737, 1886**
Reconnaissance Corps: 16, 18, 108, **1925, 1926, 1930, 2201**
Royal Armoured Corps: 16, 107, **1918, 1919, 1920, 2199**
Royal Horse Guards: 2, 3, **731, 1877, 1878**
Royal Scots Greys: 8, **752, 1889**
Royal Tank Regiment: 16, 107, **1156, 1921, 1922, 1923, 1924, 2200**

ROYAL ARTILLERY

General patterns: 20, 108, **808, 1935, 1936, 1937, 1938, 2202, 2203**
Royal Horse Artillery: 20, **1931, 1932, 1933, 1934**

ROYAL ENGINEERS

General patterns: 20, 22, 108, **853, 1939, 1940, 1941, 1942, 2204**
Royal Engineer Services: 22, **1943**
Royal Engineers Militia: 22, **1944**
Royal Monmouthshire R.E.(M): 22, **1945, 1946**

ROYAL CORPS OF SIGNALS

General patterns: 22, 108, **888, 1947, 1948, 2205**

FOOT GUARDS

Grenadier Guards: 23, 108, **891, 893, 894, 896, 1949, 1950, 1951, 1952, 1953, 1954, 2206**
Coldstream Guards: 24, 108, **897, 898, 899, 901, 902, 903, 904**

Scots Guards: 24, 108, **905, 906, 907, 908, 910, 911, 2207**
Irish Guards: 26, **912, 913, 914, 915, 916, 917, 918, 919**
Welsh Guards: 26, **920, 921**
Guards Parachute Coy.: 26

INFANTRY OF THE LINE
Regular, Territorial and T.A.V.R.

Argyll & Sutherland Highlanders: 42, 46, 64, 116, **698, 2261**
Bedfordshire Regt.: 164, **2383**
Bedfs. & Herts. Regt.: 31, 52, 110, 165, **610, 611, 2220, 2385**
Black Watch: 37, 45, 59, 112, 154, **656, 657, 1736, 2002, 2003, 2004, 2241, 2361**
Border Regt.: 36, 58, 112, 152, **645, 1725, 1726, 1996, 2234**
Buckinghamshire Bn.: 117, 155, 165, **1736, 2267, 2391**
Buffs: 29, 50, 108, **591, 2210**
Cambridgeshire Regt.: 117, 160, 162, **1816, 1817, 2266**
Cameron Highlanders: 42, 64, 116, 158, **688, 2258, 2364**
Cameronians: 34, 56, 150, **631, 1719, 1989**
Cheshire Regt.: 32, 44, 54, 111, **1960, 1987, 2224**
Devonshire Regt.: 30, 52, 110, 149, **602, 1709, 1979, 2216**
Devonshire & Dorset Regt.: 44, 68, **2043**
Devonshire Territorials: 162, **2378**
Dorset Regt.: 37, 59, 112, 154, **651, 1734, 2000, 2238**
Dorset Territorials: 165, **2389**
Duke of Cornwall's Lt. Infty.: 35, 58, 111, **641, 2232**
Duke of Edinburgh's Royal Regt.: 45, 70, **2051**
Duke of Wellington's Regt.: 35, 45, 58, 111, **642, 2233**
Durham Light Infantry: 41, 64, 116, 156, 166, **681, 1747, 1748, 2015, 2016, 2256, 2396, 2397**
East Anglian Bde.: 67, **2029**
East Lancashire Regt.: 35, 56, 111, 152, **638, 1722, 1992, 2230**
East Surrey Regt.: 35, 58, 111, 152, **640, 1723, 1724, 1993, 1994, 1995, 2231**
East Yorkshire Regt.: 31, 52, 110, **609, 2219**
Essex Regt.: 38, 60, 112, 155, **660, 1738, 2242**
Forester Bde.: 67, **2028**
Fusilier Bde.: 67, **2027**
Gloucestershire Regt.: 34, 45, 56, 111, 152, **634, 635, 1720, 2228, 2229**
Gordon Highlanders: 42, 45, 64, **687**
Green Howards, 32, 44, 54, 110, **616, 617, 1984, 1985, 2222**
Green Jackets Bde.: 68, **2037**
Hampshire & I.O.W. Territorials: 165, **2387**
Herefordshire Regt.: 160, **1793**
Herefordshire Lt. Infty.: 166, **2394**
Hertfordshire Regt.: 160, 164, **1805, 1806, 2384**
Highland Lt. Infty.: 41, 64, 116, 156, 166, **684, 1750, 1751, 2017, 2257, 2363, 2398, 2399, 2400**
Highland Bde.: 68, **2036**
Highland Regt.: 66, 117, **2023, 2265**
Home Counties Bde.: 67, **2025**
Hon. Artillery Coy.: 158, 161, **1761, 1762, 1763, 1764, 1765, 2365, 2367, 2368, 2369, 2370, 2371, 2372, 2373, 2374, 2375**
King's Own Royal Border Regt.: 43, 68, **2039**
King's Own Royal Regt.: 39, 51, 108, **592, 1971, 2211**
King's Own Scottish Borderers: 34, 44, 56, **629, 1988**
King's Own Yorkshire Lt. Infty.: 39, 62, 114, **670, 2009, 2248**
King's Regt.: 29, 43, 51, 68, 110, 148, 149, 162, **598, 1701, 1702, 1703, 1706, 1974, 1975, 2041, 2214, 2357, 2358, 2359, 2377**
King's Royal Rifle Corps: 40, 62, 114, **1965, 2011, 2012, 2251**
King's Shropshire Lt. Infty.: 39, 62, 114, **671, 2010, 2249**
Lancashire Fusiliers: 32, 54, 111, 150, **618, 1716, 2223**
Lancastrian Bde.: 67, **2026**
Light Infantry: 44, 68, **2031**
Light Infantry Bde.: 67, **2031**
London Regiments
1st to 4th (Royal Fusiliers): 170, **1818, 2404**
5th (London Rifle Bde.): 170, **1819, 1820, 1821, 2405**
6th (City of London Rifles): 170, **1824**
7th (Post Office Rifles): 171, **1826, 2406**
9th (Queen Victoria's Rifles): 171, **1828, 2407, 2408, 2409, 2410, 2411**
10th (Hackney): 171, **1832, 1833**
11th (Finsbury Rifles): 171, **1834, 2412**
12th (Rangers): 171, **1838, 2413, 2414, 2415, 2416, 2417, 2418**
13th (P.L. Kensington Regt.): 172, **1839**
14th (London Scottish): 172, **1840, 1841**

16th (Queen's Westminsters): 172, **1846, 2419**
Queen's Royal Rifles: 174, **2420**
17th (Poplar & Stepney Rifles): 174, **1847**
17th (Tower Hamlets Rifles): 174, **2421, 2422**
18th (London Irish Rifles): 174, **1848, 2423, 2424**
19th (St. Pancras): 174, **1851**
20th (The Queen's Own): 176, **1852**
21st (First Surrey Rifles): 176, **1853**
22nd (The Queen's): 176, **1854**
23rd: 176, **1855, 2425**
24th (The Queen's): 176, **1854**
28th (Artist's Rifles): 176, **1855, 2426**
London Yeomanry & Territorials: 166, **2401**
Lowland Bde.: 66, **2024**
Lowland Regt.: 66, **2022**
Loyal Regt.: 38, 60, 114, **664, 665, 2007, 2244**
Manchester Regt.: 40, 62, 116, 156, **1746, 2014, 2253**
Mercian Bde.: 67, **2033**
Middlesex Regt.: 40, 62, 114, 156, **672, 1743, 2250**
Monmouthshire Regt.: 160, **1769, 1770, 1777, 1783, 2366**
Northamptonshire Regt.: 38, 60, 114, 155, **1741, 1742, 2008, 2245**
North Irish Bde.: 67, **2035**
North Staffordshire Regt.: 41, 62, 116, **678, 2254**
Oxf. & Bucks. Lt. Infty.: 38, 60, **658, 2005**
Oxfordshire Territorials: 165, **2390**
P.W.O. Regt. of Yorkshire: 44, 68, 164, **2044**
Queen's Lancashire Regt.: 45, 70, **2049**
Queen's Own Highlanders: 45, 70, **1968, 2052**
Queen's Regt.: 43, 68, **2038**
Queen's Royal Regt.: 28, 50, 108, **590, 1969, 1970, 2209**
Queen's Royal Surrey Regt.: 162, **2376**
Rifle Brigade: 43, 66, 116, **705, 2019, 2020, 2262**
Royal Anglian Regt.: 43, 68, **2042**
Royal Berkshire Regt.: 39, 60, **667, 1962, 1963, 1964**
Royal Berkshire Territorials: 166, **2393**
Royal Fusiliers: 29, 51, 110, **597, 1973, 2213**
Royal Green Jackets: 46, 70, **2053**
Royal Hampshire Regt.: 36, 45, 58, 66, 112, 154, 165, **642, 1729, 1730, 1731, 1732, 1733, 1961, 1966, 1967, 1997, 1998, 2021, 2236, 2386**
Royal Highland Fusiliers: 44, 68, **2045**
Royal Inniskilling Fusiliers: 34, 56, 111, **632, 1990, 2227**
Royal Irish Fusiliers: 42, 64, 116, **694, 2260**
Royal Irish Rangers: 44, 70, **2047**
Royal Leicestershire Regt.: 31, 52, 110, 150, **612, 1714, 1982, 1983, 2221**
Royal Lincolnshire Regt.: 30, 52, 110, 149, **600, 1708, 1957, 1958, 1978, 2215**
Royal Norfolk Regt.: 30, 51, **599, 1976, 1977**
Royal Northumberland Fusiliers: 29, 51, 110, **593, 1972, 2212**
Royal Regt. of Fusiliers: 43, 68, **2027**
Royal Regt. of Wales, 44, 68, **2046**
Royal Scots: 28, 43, 50, 108, 148, **589, 1697, 1955, 2208**
Royal Scots Fusiliers: 32, 54, **620, 1959, 1986**
Royal Sussex Regt.: 36, 58, 112, 152, **646, 1728, 2235**
Royal Ulster Rifles: 42, 64, 116, **691, 2018, 2259**
Royal Warwickshire Fusiliers: 29, 51, **594**
Royal Welch Fusiliers: 32, 44, 54, 111, **623, 2225**
Royal Wiltshire Territorials: 166, **2395**
Seaforth Highlanders: 41, 64, 158, **685, 1754, 1755, 1756, 1757, 1758**
Sherwood Foresters: 38, 60, 114, 155, 165, **662, 1740, 2006, 2243, 2362, 2392**
Somerset Lt. Infty.: 31, 52, 149, **607, 1711, 1981**
Somerset Yeo. & Lt. Infty.: 162
South Lancashire Regt.: 37, 59, 112, 154, **652, 1735, 2001, 2239**
South Staffordshire Regt.: 36, 59, 112, **649, 1999, 2237**
South Wales Borderers: 34, 54, 111, 150, **625, 1717, 1718, 2226**
Staffordshire Regt.: 45, 70, 165, **2050, 2388**
Suffolk Regt.: 30, 52, 110, 149, **605, 1710, 2217**
Suffolk & Cambridgeshire Regt.: 166, **2379**
Ulster Defence Regt.: 168, **2403**
Welch Regt.: 37, 59, 112, **654, 2240**
Welsh Bde.: 67, **2034**
Wessex Bde.: 67, **2030**
Wessex Regt.: 168, **2402**
West Kent Regt. Q.O. Royal: 39, 60, 114, **668, 2247**
West Yorkshire Regt.: 31, 52, 110, 149, **608, 1712, 2218, 2360, 2380, 2381, 2382**
Wiltshire Regt.: 40, 62, 114, 158, **676, 1745, 2013, 2252**
Worcestershire Regt.: 34, 56, **636, 1991**
Worcestershire & Sherwood Foresters Regt.: 45, 70, **2048**
York & Lancaster Regt.: 41, 62, 116, **679, 2255**
Yorkshire Bde.: 67, **2032**

AIRBORNE FORCES

Army Air Corps: 72, 117, **2054, 2055, 2056, 2264**

Glider Pilot Regt.: 72, **2057, 2058**
Parachute Regt.: 72, 117, **2059, 2060, 2263**
Special Air Service Regt.: 72, **2061, 2062, 2063**

SPECIAL SERVICE FORCES
2nd World War
No. 2 Commando: 74, **2064, 2065**
Nos. 50, 51 & 52 Commandos: 74, **2066**
No. 1 Demolition Squadron: 74, **2068, 2069, 2070**
Long Range Desert Group: 74, **2067**
Raiding Support Regt.: 74, **2071**
'V' Force: 74, **2072**

Brigade of Ghurkhas
Boys Coy.: 82, **2095**
Gurkha Indep. Para. Coy.: 82
Gurkha Military Police: 80, **2092, 2093**
Gurkha Rifles, 2nd: 75, **2073, 2074**
Gurkha Rifles, 6th: 76, **2075, 2076, 2077, 2078**
Gurkha Rifles, 7th: 76, **2079, 2080, 2081, 2082**
Gurkha Rifles, 10th: 78, **2083, 2084, 2085, 2086**
Gurkha Transport Regt.: 80, **2090, 2091**
Queen's Gurkha Engineers: 79, **2087, 2088**
Queen's Gurkha Signals: 79, **2089**
Staff Band: 82, **2094**

The Royal Marines
General patterns: 83, 114, **1099, 1100, 2096, 2097, 2098, 2099, 2100, 2101, 2246**
R.M. Band, Chatham: 84, **1118, 2108**
R.M. Band, Plymouth: 84, **1117, 2107**
R.M. Band, Portsmouth: 84, **1113, 2103, 2104, 2105, 2106**
R.M. Police: 83, **2102**
R.M. School of Music: 86, **2109, 2110**

Department & Corps
Army Catering Corps: 94, 118, **2156, 2157, 2158, 2159, 2277**
Army Legal Services: 96, **2167**
Army Physical Training Corps: 94, 118, **1060, 2154, 2155, 2276**
Army Scripture Readers: 88, **2114**
Corps of Royal Military Police: 91, 118, **1031, 2130, 2131, 2132, 2272**
General Service Corps: 96, 118, **1084, 2164, 2165, 2166, 2278**
Intelligence Corps: 94, 118, **2152, 2153, 2275**
Military Provost Staff Corps: 92, **2142, 2143**
Mobile Defence Corps: 94, **2160**
Non-Combatant Corps: 94, **2163**
Royal Army Chaplains Dept.: 88, **973, 974, 976, 2110, 2111, 2112, 2113**
Royal Army Dental Corps: 92, **1057, 2147, 2148**
Royal Army Educational Corps: 92, 118, **1056, 2144, 2145, 2146, 2273**
Royal Army Medical Corps: 90, 117, **1006, 2122, 2123, 2269**
Royal Army Ordnance Corps: 90, 117, **1025, 2124, 2125, 2126, 2270**
Royal Army Pay Corps: 91, **1036, 2133, 2134, 2135, 2136, 2137, 2138**
Royal Army Service Corps: 88, 117, **992, 2115, 2116, 2117, 2118, 2268**
R.A.S.C. Fleet: 90, **2120, 2121**
Royal Army Veterinary Corps: 91, **1044, 2139**
Royal Corps of Transport: 90, **2119**
Royal Defence Corps: 94, **1063, 2162, 2163**
Royal Electrical & Mechanical Engineers: 90, 117, **2127, 2128, 2129, 2271**
Royal Pioneer Corps: 92, 118, **2149, 2150, 2151, 2274**
Small Arms School Corps: 91, **2140, 2141**

Schools & Miscellaneous
Allied Control Commission for Austria: 102
Army Apprentices Schools: 101, **2176, 2177**
Army Dept., Fire Service: 102, **2181**
Army Depot Police Cyprus: 102, **2180**
Control Commission, Germany: 102, **2184**
Control Commission, Germany, Police: 102, **2185**
Crown Film Unit, 102, **2182**
Extra-Regimentally Employed List: 101, **1083**
General List: 101, **1084**
Ministry of Defence Police: 102, **2179**
Mons Officer Cadet School: 100, **2172**
Royal Hospital, Chelsea: 100, **2174, 2175**
Royal Military Academy: 98, **1068**
Royal Military Academy Sandhurst: 98, **2170, 2171**
Royal Military College: 98, **1075, 1076, 2168, 2169**
Royal Military School of Music: 100, **1077, 2173**
War Correspondents: 101
War Dept. Constabulary: 101, **2178**
War Office Messengers: 102, **2183**

Women's Services
Anglo-French Ambulance Corps, 106, **2194**
American Ambulance, Great Britain: 106, **2193**
Auxiliary Territorial Service: 104, 118, **2188, 2279**

Entertainments National Service Association: 106, **2196**
First Aid Nursing Yeomanry: 104, **1064**
Mechanised Transport Training Corps: 106, **2192**
Navy, Army & Air Force Institutes: 106, **2197, 2198**
Q.A. Royal Army Nursing Corps: 104, **2186, 2187**
Women's Royal Army Corps: 104, **2189, 2190**
Women's Transport Service: 106, **2191**
Women's Volunteer Reserve: 106, **2195**

Yeomanry
Ayrshire Yeomanry: 126, **1416, 2297, 2298, 2299**
Bedfordshire Yeomanry: 136, **1488**
Berkshire & Westminster Dragoons: 121, **2280**
Berkshire Yeomanry: 121, **1449, 2281**
Cheshire Yeomanry: 126, **2300, 2301**
City of London Yeomanry: 134, **1484, 2320, 2321, 2322**
County of London Yeomanry, 3rd: 124, **1486, 1487, 2289, 2290, 2291**
Denbighshire Yeomanry: 144, **1433, 2350, 2351**
Derbyshire Yeomanry: 141, **1443, 2343**
Dorset & West Somerset Yeomanry: 142, **2348**
Dorset Yeomanry: 142, **1446, 2349**
Duke of Lancaster's Own Yeomanry: 130, **1428, 2310**
East Riding Yeomanry: 126, **1496**
Essex Yeomanry: 137, **1491, 1493, 2331, 2332, 2333**
Fife & Forfar Yeomanry: 133, **1474, 2316**
Glamorgan Yeomanry: 137, **2330**
Glasgow Yeomanry: 132, **1469, 1470, 2314**
Hampshire Carabiniers: 141, **1440, 2305**
Hertfordshire & Bedfordshire Yeomanry: 136, **1324**
Hertfordshire Yeomanry: 136, **1458, 2325**
Highland Yeomanry: 133, **2315**
Inns of Court & City Yeomanry: 133, **2317**
Inns of Court Regt.: 133, **2318, 2319**
Kent & County of London Yeomanry: 122, **2288**
Lanarkshire Yeomanry: 132, **1430, 2312**
Lancashire Hussars: 138, **1472**
Leicestershire & Derbyshire Yeomanry: 140, **2341**
Leicestershire Yeomanry: 140, **1424**
Lothians & Border Horse: 132, **1467**
Lovat Scouts: 138, **1500, 2336**
Lowland Yeomanry: 132, **2311**
Loyal Suffolk Hussars: 136, **1455, 2327**
Mercian Yeomanry: 129, **2305**
Middlesex Yeomanry: 138, **1451, 2334, 2335**
Montgomeryshire Yeomanry: 144, **1465**
Norfolk Yeomanry: 137, **1417, 2328, 2329**
North Irish Horse: 125, **1503, 2292**
North Somerset Yeomanry: 145, **1426, 2354, 2355**
Northamptonshire Yeomanry: 141, **1494, 2344**
Northumberland Hussars: 125, **1431, 2294**
Oxfordshire Hussars: 145, **1461, 1462, 1463**
Pembroke Yeomanry: 145, **1437, 2352, 2353**
Queen's Own Yeomanry: 125, **2293**
Royal Bucks Hussars: 142, **1441, 2346, 2347**
Royal Devon Yeomanry: 128, **1454, 2302, 2303, 2304**
Royal East Kent Yeomanry: 124, **1438**
Royal Gloucestershire Hussars: 128, **1447**
Royal Wiltshire Yeomanry: 122, **1407, 2283, 2284**
Royal Yeomanry Regt.: 121
Scottish Horse: 133, **1501, 1502**
Sherwood Rangers Yeomanry: 122, **1410, 2285, 2286, 2287**
Shropshire Yeomanry: 130, **1415, 2308, 2309**
South Nottinghamshire Hussars: 145, **1432**
Staffordshire Yeomanry: 130, **1413, 1414, 2307**
Suffolk & Norfolk Yeomanry: 136, **2326**
Surrey Yeomanry: 140, **1473, 2337, 2338, 2339, 2340**
Sussex Yeomanry: 134, **1480, 2323**
Warwickshire & Worcestershire Hussars: 129, **2306**
Warwickshire Yeomanry: 129, **1408**
Wessex Yeomanry: 128
West Kent Yeomanry: 134, **1459**
Westminster Dragoons: 121, **2282**
Westmorland & Cumberland Yeomanry: 145, **1435, 2356**
West Somerset Yeomanry: 144, **1460**
Worcestershire Hussars: 129, **1458**
Yorkshire Dragoons: 126, **1420, 2296**
Yorkshire Hussars: 126, **1409**
Yorkshire Yeomanry: 125, **2295**

The Home Guard
Caithness & Sutherland: 178, **1754, 1755, 1756, 1757, 1758**
1st American Squadron, 178, **2434**
Huntingdonshire: 177, **1870**
Isle of Man: 177, **2428, 2429**
Palace of Westminster: 178, **2433**
Radnor: 178, **2434, 2435**

Rutland: 177, **2431**
Ulster: 177, **2427**
Upper Thames Patrol: 177, **2430**
Windsor Castle Coy.: 178

Officers Training Corps
Senior & Junior Divisions
Aberdeen University: 180, **2436, 2437**
Abingdon School: 188, **2496**
Adams Grammar School: 189, **2497**
Aldenham School: 189, **2498**
Alleyn's School: 189, **2499**
All Hallows School: 189, **2500**
Ampleforth College: 189, **2501**
Ardingly College: 189, **2502**
Army School: 189, **2503**
Bancroft's School: 189, **2504**
Barnard Castle School: 189, **2505**
Batley Grammar School: 189, **2506**
Beaumont College: 190, **2507**
Belfast (Queen's University): 181, **2438, 2439**
Birkenhead School: 190, **2508**
Birmingham University: 181, **2440, 2441, 2442**
Bloxham School: 190, **2509**
Blundell's School: 190, **2510**
Bournemouth School: 190, **2511**
Bradfield College: 190, **2512**
Brentwood School: 190, **2513**
Bridlington School: 190, **2514**
Brighton College: 190, **2515**
Brighton Grammar School: 190, **2516**
Bristol Grammar School: 192, **2517**
Bristol University: 181, **2443, 2444**
Bromsgrove School: 192, **2518**
Bury Grammar School: 192, **2519**
Cambridge & County School: 192, **2520**
Cambridge University: 181, **2445, 2446, 2447**
Campbell College: 192, **2521**
Canford School: 192, **2522**
Cardiff University: 181, **2046**
Chard School: 192, **2523**
Charterhouse School: 192, **2524**
Cheltenham College: 192, **2525**
Chigwell School: 192, **2526**
Christ's Hospital: 192, **2527**
Churcher's College: 194, **2528**
Clifton College: 194, **2529**
Cork Grammar School: 194, **2530**
Cranbrook School: 194, **2531**
Cranleigh School: 194, **2532**
Dartford Grammar School: 194, **2533**
Dean Close School: 194, **2534**
Denstone College: 194, **2535**
Derby School: 194, **2536**
Dollar Academy: 195, **2537**
Dorchester School: 195, **2538**
Dover College: 195, **2539**
Downside School: 195, **2540, 2541**
Dublin University: 181, **2448, 2449, 2450**
Duke of York's R.M. School: 195, **2542, 2543**
Dulwich College: 195, **2544**
Durham University: 182, **2451**
Eastbourne College: 195, **2545**
East Midlands Universities: 184
Edinburgh Academy: 196, **2547**
Edinburgh and Heriot-Watts Universities: 182, **2452, 2453, 2454, 2455**
Elizabeth College: 196, **2548, 2549**
Ellesmere College: 196, **2546**
Emanuel School: 196, **2550**
Epsom College: 196, **2551**
Eton College: 196, **2552**
Exeter School: 196, **2553**
Exeter University: 182, **2456**
Felsted School: 196, **2554**
Fettes College: 196, **2555**
Forest School: 198, **2556, 2557**
Framlingham College: 198, **2558**
George Heriot School: 198, **2559**
George Watson's College: 198, **2560, 2561**
Giggleswick School: 198, **2562**
Glasgow High School: 198, **2563, 2564**
Glasgow and Strathclyde Universities: 182, **2457, 2458, 2459, 2460**
Gordon Boys School: 198, **2565**
Gresham's School: 200, **2566**
Grimsby School: 200, **2567**
Haberdashers' Aske's School: 200, **2568**
Haileybury & Imperial Service College: 200, **2569, 2570**
Harrow County School: 200, **2571**
Harrow School: 200, **2572**
Hereford Cathedral School: 200, **2573**
Herne Bay School: 200, **2574**
Hertford Grammar School: 200, **2575**
Hulme Grammar School: 201, **2576, 2577**
Hurstpierpoint College: 201, **2578**
Hymer's College: 201, **2579**
Ipswich School: 201, **2580**
Kelly College: 201, **2581**
Kelvinside Academy: 201, **2582, 2583**
King Alfred's School: 201, **2584, 2585**
King Charles I School: 201, **2586**
King's College School: 201, **2587**

King Edward's Five Ways School: 202, **2588**
King Edward VI Grammar School, Bury St. Edmunds: 202, **2589**
King Edward VI Grammar School, Lichfield: 202, **2590, 2591**
King Edward's School, Bath: 202, **2592**
King Edward's School, Birmingham: 202, **2593**
King Edward VII School: 202, **2594**
King's School, Bruton: 202, **2595**
King's School, Canterbury: 202, **2596**
King's School, Ely: 202, **2597**
King's School, Grantham: 204, **2598**
King's School, Peterborough: 204, **2599**
King's School, Rochester: 204, **2600**
King's School, Worcester: 204, **2601**
King William's College: 204, **2602, 2603**
Kirkcaldy High School: 204, **2604**
Lancing College: 204, **2605**
Leeds Grammar School: 204, **2606**
Leeds University: 182, **2462, 2463**
Leys School: 204, **2607**
Liverpool College: 204, **2608**
Liverpool University: 184, **2464**
London, City of: 206, **2609**
Lord William's School: 206, **2610**
Loretto School: 206, **2611**
Louth School: 206, **2612**
Macclesfield Grammar School: 206, **2613**
Magdalen College School: 206, **2614**
Maidstone Grammar School: 206, **2615**
Malvern College: 206, **2616**
Manchester Grammar School: 206, **2617**
Manchester and Salford Universities: 184, **2467**
Marlborough College: 206, **2618, 2619**
Mercers School: 207, **2620**
Merchant Taylors School: 207, **2621**
Merchiston Castle School: 207, **2622**
Millfield School: 207, **2623**
Mill Hill School: 207, **2624**
Monkton Combe School: 207, **2627, 2628**
Monmouth School: 207, **2625, 2626**
Morgan Academy: 207, **2629**
Morrison's Academy: 208, **2630, 2631**
Moseley Grammar School: 208, **2632**
Mount St. Mary's College: 208, **2633**
Newcastle High School: 208, **2634**
Nottingham High School: 208, **2635**
Nottingham University: 184, **2468, 2469, 2470**
Northampton Grammar School: 208, **2636**
Northumbrian Universities: 182, **2451**
Oakham School: 208, **2637**
Oratory School: 208, **2638**
Oundle School: 208, **2639**
Oxford University: 184, **2471, 2472, 2473, 2474, 2475, 2476, 2477, 2478, 2479**
Paston School: 210, **2640**
Perse School: 210, **2641**
Portsmouth Grammar School: 210, **2642**
Portsmouth Northern Grammar School: 210, **2643**
Portsmouth Southern Grammar School: 210, **2644**
Price's School: 210, **2645**
Queen Mary's School: 210, **2646**
Queen Victoria School: 210, **2647**
Radley College: 210, **2648**
Reading School: 210, **2649**
Reading University: 186, **2480, 2481**
Reigate Grammar School: 212, **2650**
Repton School: 212, **2651**
Rossall School: 212, **2652**
Royal Agricultural College: 186, **2482**
Royal Belfast Academical Institution: 212, **2653**
Royal College of Surgeons (Ireland): 186, **2483**
Royal Dick Veterinary College: 186, **2484**
Royal Grammar School, Guildford: 212, **2654**
Royal Grammar School, Lancaster: 212, **2655**
Royal Grammar School, Newcastle-upon-Tyne: 212, **2656**
Royal Grammar School, Worcester: 212, **2657, 2658, 2659**
Royal Liberty School: 213, **2660**
Royal Veterinary College of Ireland: 186, **2485**
Royal Wanstead School: 213, **2700**
Royal Wantage School: 213, **2661**
Rugby School: 213, **2662**
Rutlish School: 213, **2663**
St. Andrew's University: 186, **2486, 2487, 2488**
St. Bee's School: 213, **2664**
St. Brendan's College: 213, **2665**
St. Benedict's School: 213, **2666**
St. Columba's College: 213, **2667**
St. Dunstan's College: 213, **2668**
St. Edmund's School, Canterbury: 214, **2669**
St. Edmund's School, Ware: 214, **2670**
St. Edward's School: 214, **2671**
St. Ignatius College: 214, **2672, 2673**
St. John's School: 214, **2674, 2675**
St. Lawrence College: 214, **2676**
St. Paul's School: 216, **2678**
St. Peter's School: 214, **2677**
Sedbergh School: 216, **2679**
Sevenoaks School: 216, **2680**
Shaftesbury School: 216, **2681**

Sheffield University: 188, **2489, 2490**
Shrewsbury School: 216, **2682**
Sir Roger Manwood's School: 216, **2683**
Skinner's School: 216, **2684**
Solihull Grammar School: 216, **2685, 2686**
Southampton University: 188, **2491, 2492**
Stamford School: 216, **2687**
Stonyhurst College: 218, **2688**
Stowe School: 218, **2689**
Sutton Valence School: 218, **2690**
Taunton School: 218, **2691**
Tayforth Universities: 188, **2493**
Tonbridge School: 218, **2692**
Trent College: 218, **2693**
Trinity College: 218, **2694**
University College School: 218, **2695**
University of London: 184, **2465, 2466**
University of Wales: 188, **2494, 2495**
Uppingham School: 218, **2696, 2697, 2698**
Victoria College: 219, **2699**
Warwick School: 219, **2701, 2702**
Welbeck College: 219, **2703**
Wellingborough School: 219, **2704**
Wellington College, Berks: 219, **2705**
Wellington College, Salop: 219, **2706, 2707**
Wellington School: 219, **2708**
Westminster City School: 219, **2709**
Weymouth College: 220, **2710**
Whitgift School: 220, 2711
Wilson's Grammar School: 220, **2712, 2713**
Winchester College: 220, **2714**
Windsor Grammar School: 220, **2715**
Wolverhampton Grammar School: 220, **2716**
Woodbridge School: 220, **2717**
Worksop College: 220, **2718**
Wrekin College: 220, **2719**